M000267770

The Archaeology of Removal in North America

UNIVERSITY PRESS OF FLORIDA

Florida A&M University, Tallahassee
Florida Atlantic University, Boca Raton
Florida Gulf Coast University, Ft. Myers
Florida International University, Miami
Florida State University, Tallahassee
New College of Florida, Sarasota
University of Central Florida, Orlando
University of Florida, Gainesville
University of North Florida, Jacksonville
University of South Florida, Tampa
University of West Florida, Pensacola

THE ARCHAEOLOGY OF REMOVAL IN NORTH AMERICA

EDITED BY
Terrance Weik

University Press of Florida
Gainesville · Tallahassee · Tampa · Boca Raton
Pensacola · Orlando · Miami · Jacksonville · Ft. Myers · Sarasota

Copyright 2019 by Terrance Weik
All rights reserved
Published in the United States of America.

This book may be available in an electronic edition.

24 23 22 21 20 19   6 5 4 3 2 1

Library of Congress Cataloging-in-Publication Data
Names: Weik, Terrance M., editor.
Title: The archaeology of removal in North America / edited by Terrance Weik.
Description: Gainesville : University Press of Florida, 2019. | Includes
  bibliographical references and index.
Identifiers: LCCN 2018047770 | ISBN 9780813056395 (cloth : alk. paper)
Subjects: LCSH: Forced migration—North America—History. | Indians of North
  America—Relocation—North America—History. | African
  Americans—Relocation—North America—History. |
  Prisoners—Relocation—North America—History. | Human
  beings—Relocation—North America—History.
Classification: LCC HB1951 .A73 2019 | DDC 362.87097—dc23
LC record available at https://lccn.loc.gov/2018047770

The University Press of Florida is the scholarly publishing agency for the State University System of Florida, comprising Florida A&M University, Florida Atlantic University, Florida Gulf Coast University, Florida International University, Florida State University, New College of Florida, University of Central Florida, University of Florida, University of North Florida, University of South Florida, and University of West Florida.

University Press of Florida
2046 NE Waldo Road
Suite 2100
Gainesville, FL 32609
http://upress.ufl.edu

Contents

List of Figures   vii

List of Tables   ix

Acknowledgments   xi

1. Introduction: Anthropological, Theoretical, and Historical Contexts
   of Removal   1
   Terrance Weik

2. "We Can Fly No Farther": Colonialism and Displacement among the
   Piscataway of Southern Maryland   19
   Alex J. Flick and Julia A. King

3. Mapping Chickasaw Removal   45
   Terrance Weik

4. Whitewashing an African American Landscape: The Impact of
   Industrial Capitalism on the Removal of Rural People   73
   Stefan Woehlke and Matthew Reeves

5. Worth(Less): Value and Destruction in a Nineteenth- and
   Twentieth-Century Quarry Town   103
   Adam Fracchia

6. Removal and Remembering: Archaeology and the Legacies of
   Displacement in Southern Appalachia   127
   Audrey Horning

7. Creating a Community in Confinement: The Development of
   Neighborhoods in Amache, a World War II Japanese American
   Internment Camp   157
   April Kamp-Whittaker and Bonnie J. Clark

8. Topographies of Removal: Rethinking the Archaeology
   of Prisons   189
   Maria Theresia Starzmann

9. The Janus Face of Removal   216
   Charles E. Orser

   List of Contributors   227
   Index   229

Figures

2.1. Piscataway and Piscataway-related archaeological sites discussed in this chapter 28

3.1. Levi Colbert Prairie Settlement 53

3.2. Surface finds and archivally identified nineteenth-century architecture at LCP 54

3.3. Locally made cup excavated from Novotny 57

3.4. Novotny site in Section 7 of General Land Office plat map excerpt 58

3.5. US plat map attached to letter from Benjamin Reynolds to Lewis Cass, August 28, 1835 60

3.6. Scouting party map of potential Oklahoma removal route 66

4.1. Map showing the location of Orange County in the Piedmont region of Virginia 76

4.2. Photograph of the Gilmore cabin 91

5.1. John Landragan House 104

5.2. Location of the town of Texas in Baltimore County, Maryland 108

5.3. Workers in a Texas quarry and adjacent limekilns in 1892 108

5.4. Distribution of the provinces and counties in Ireland listed on headstones in the St. Joseph's Church cemetery in Texas 111

5.5. Detail of an 1877 map showing the village of Texas 113

5.6. Poe-Burns duplex 114

5.7. Thomas Fortune house 115

5.8. Buttons recovered from the residence of a laborer and his family 117

6.1. Map of Shenandoah National Park study location 129

6.2. Cellulose card calendar found in Corbin Hollow 130

6.3. Toy truck recovered from Corbin Hollow 150

7.1. Map of all ten War Relocation Authority camps 160

7.2. Layout of a typical residential block 162

7.3. Map showing the location of six blocks at Amache overlaid on the historic schematic map of the camp 166

7.4. Changes in neighborhood composition from 1943 to 1945 170

7.5. View of the same block at Amache when internees first arrived and after internee landscaping efforts 178

7.6. Page from a former internee's scrapbook 181

7.7. Oval garden bed in 9L as exposed during excavations 182

8.1. Cameron Rowland, *Attica Series Desk*, 2016 196

8.2. Satellite view of Guantánamo Bay Detention Center 201

8.3. Traffic sign on the shoulder of I-84/NY-52 reading "Correctional Facility Area—No Stopping" 204

8.4. Results from the view-shed analysis carried out in Google Earth Pro 205

8.5. Google Street View from Matteawan Road in Beacon, New York 207

8.6. Unknown road, Carltonville, Johannesburg, South Africa, 2012 210

Tables

2.1. Decrease in the proportion of Native-made ceramics and tobacco pipes over time   31

7.1. Composition of residential blocks included in this study   169

7.2. Counts of artifacts recovered in each residential block during pedestrian survey   176

7.3. Number of landscaping features identified during pedestrian survey in each residential block   179

Acknowledgments

I would like to thank Meredith Morris-Babb for encouraging me to pursue this edited volume. Although removal profoundly shaped the sources of evidence and events concerning the Africans, Seminoles, and antislavery actors that I wrote about early in my career, it was always in the background. Thus, the *The Archaeology of Removal in North America* is a nice opportunity to explore a new but familiar topic that has been latent in my scholarship. I am also grateful to the enslaved and free Africans and to the past and present members of the Chickasaw Nation whose courage, vulnerabilities, and efforts inform my contributions to this book. I am also indebted to the contributors whose chapters embody this book and their willingness to accompany me on this journey through the rigors of publication. Special thanks is also due to various other scholars whose willingness to share ideas during conversations and conference symposia has helped me understand the multifaceted nature of human displacement.

I would like to also express my appreciation for the many forms of support various people and institutions provided. The logistical aid Brad Lieb, Brady Davis, Joseph Smith, and the cultural resource staff of the Chickasaw Nation provided was a crucial component in the completion of my field, lab, and archival research on the Chickasaws. Kirk Perry, Michelle Cooke, Josh Hinson, and other members of the Chickasaw Nation provided me with valuable insights on the history and culture of their ancestors. John Lieb, Michael Malski, and Martha Cheney are among the many people who greatly aided my fieldwork. The Wenner Gren Foundation and the University of South Carolina Provost and Aspire Grant programs provided generous financial support at different stages of my Chickasaw research. I'd like to thank the countless volunteers and members of the public whose interest and labor enriched this project.

I would like to thank various people for their help with the final stages of this book project. I am grateful for the comments of the scholars whose reviews greatly improved this manuscript. I wish to thank the University Press of Florida, specifically Marthe Walters and Lilly Dunaj, for their editorial assistance. Finally, many thanks to anyone who has helped me but I have failed to mention.

1

Introduction

Anthropological, Theoretical, and Historical Contexts of Removal

TERRANCE WEIK

This edited volume brings together people who seek to understand what happens when human beings are forced out of their homes and away from their usual places of work, play, worship, and well-being. It illustrates how archaeologists are situated among the anthropologists and other scholars who are investigating the catalysts, dynamics, and meanings of removal. Historical and anthropological research suggests that humans have been forced to move in response to a diverse range of factors such as wars, overpopulation, tenant evictions, factory closings, state expansions, diseases, natural disasters, eminent domain policies, nuclear bomb testing, censorship, and economic hardship (Campbell et al. 2007; Colson 2003; Kirsch 2001; Orser 2005). Early Americanist anthropology was greatly influenced by studies of Native Americans, who faced not only the coerced relocations of what chroniclers' called "Indian Removal" but also various other forms of subjugation such as colonial ideologies, racist government policies, Eurocentric legislation, trauma, and genocide. In more recent years, anthropologists have discussed "anthropologies of removal" that are concerned with other groups, such as Somalis and Muslims deported from Canada and the United States (Peutz 2006). Oddly, Native American or First Nation experiences and studies were not part of this conversation. Nonetheless, the explicit attention to the dispossessed contrasts with the earlier neglect that anthropologists exhibited toward systematic, violent nineteenth- and twentieth-century displacements of indigenous people to reservations in the United States and to other locations in Africa and around the world (Colson 2003, 4). Many parallel contexts (e.g., children forced out of their homes into assimilative school programs) and theoretical concerns beg for a broader perspective that brings American Indian, First Nation, or Native American removal experiences into wider discourses on displacement and dispossession around the world (see Glenn 2015, 54–74; Merlan 2005).

In order to explore the idea of removal and related discourses about dispossession, *The Archaeology of Removal in North America* examines colonial and postcolonial human dislocation, emphasizing seventeenth- to twenty-first-century places and material culture. Although most of the contributors to this book focus on North America, a concern for global connections can be found in various chapters. A primary goal of this edited volume is to advance anthropological discourses by providing case studies and conceptual essays that help scholars, students, and popular audiences understand archaeologists' contributions to knowledge of the materialities, causes, and consequences of human removal. Much of the current archaeological writings on displacement have focused on landscapes "on the move" (notions of place people carry) or of "clearance" (Bender 2001; Branigan and Bumsted 2005; Howard 2012; Smith and Gazin-Schwartz 2008). Lively discussions on topics such as the relocation of cemeteries continue to emerge on media such as the Historical Archaeology listserv (HISTARCH@asu.edu). *The Archaeology of Removal in North America* will build on landscape concerns while exploring other interpretive and explanatory directions.

Removal and Kindred Concepts of Dispossession

Removal is part of a growing metadiscourse that implicates a number of cognate concepts or research categories that all point to the nexus of power, violence, and place: involuntary migration, clearance, dislocation, forced resettlement, displacement, exile, uprooting, deportation, and expulsion (Cernea and Guggenheim 1993; Lieber 1977; Loizos 1999; Malkki 1995b; Oliver-Smith 2010; Peutz 2006). It is difficult to completely separate or untangle the ideas from different schools of thought and disciplines that investigate dispossession from the scholarship on removal. Anthropologists and archaeologists have contributed to various tributaries that feed the metadiscourse on human displacement and removal (Colson 2003; Malkki 1995b).

Ethnographers who have examined forced migrants and refugees over the twentieth century have created one primary intellectual stream feeding this metadiscourse (Colson 2003). This field of refugee and coerced migrant studies has emerged from earlier studies of immigrant communities, migrant labor, and transnational economics. These studies employed theories on networks, international law, functionalist social systems, conflict mechanisms, reciprocity, rites of passage, community boundary maintenance, and validation myths. Much academic and institutional attention in the West has been given to the millions of people who were relocated in Europe just after World War II and to the influential role of military administration in those relocations. Since the mid-twentieth century, the field has expanded to include a greater diversity of interests such as refugee camp relations, critiques of humanitarianism, remedies for the dehistoricization of uprooted people, globalized flows, power dynamics, diasporan politics, identity labeling, activist scholarship, host societies, and emotional responses to resettlement.

Another major part of the dispossession metadiscourse involves displacement. The terms "displaced person" and "displacement" have been used problematically. Historically, studies of displacement have largely been undertaken by commentators on international law to describe refugees and stateless persons. However, the term displacement remains undertheorized in many studies (Malkki 1995b). Similarly, the use of the term refugee as a label is not just a subject of academic discussion, as it has important manifestations elsewhere. For instance, in the context of Hurricane Katrina, poor African Americans were stigmatized by media and public commentary that ascribed racial stereotypes of criminality and individual irresponsibility to refugees, thus naturalizing inequalities they faced (Masquelier 2006, 737).

Another theoretical stream that more directly informed removal studies of the mid-twentieth-century involved "salvage anthropologies"; an example is the "urgent anthropology" projects that the Smithsonian Institution has sponsored. These programs were largely institutional responses to government or military relocation programs. Salvage archaeologies and anthropologies involved rapid data collection, they accepted development as an inevitable paradigm, and they involved extinctionist notions of social groups (especially Native Americans), structuralist principles of society, and trait-based, bounded notions of community (e.g., Hester 1968).

The concept of exile constitutes another major discursive flow that has informed thinking on dispossession. Historically, exile was largely the conceptual legacy of theology, poetry, novels, and art (Malkki 1995b). The tropes of exile as heroic isolation or valorized estrangement emerged within these traditions of thought and aesthetics. This contrasts with more ancient ideas such as banishment that involved socially sanctioned ostracism and stigma. Academics have appropriated the idea of exile as a laudable representation of their daily work and the occupational demands of social remoteness that help them find the exotic and develop objective insights. Said, who explores the tension between idealized exiles and actual refugees, notes how the idealized exiles of literature and theology can obscure and objectify our understandings of modern refugee experiences (Said 1994). Said also notes the contributions that poets and scholars in exile have made to illuminating the multidimensionality of sorrow caused by refugees' uncertainty about the future (e.g., finding a new home or returning home), their anguish at the human and material losses along their path of flight, and the weight of the shame they bear from having an unsettled status.

Material culture studies are making their own unique contributions to the study of human displacement. For example, Parkin articulates the role of material culture in human displacement in a richly layered statement:

> Dramatic and less metaphysical expressions of human-object movement occur in the increasingly documented cases of human displacement, including those of refugees, in which peoples carry not only what they need for subsistence and exchange purposes but also, if they can, articles of sentimental value which both inscribe and are inscribed by their own memories of self and personhood. While art, artefacts and ritual objects are conventionally located in predictable contexts of use, items taken under pressure and in crisis set up contexts less of use and more of selective remembering, forgetting and envisioning. (Parkin 1999, 304)

Parkin shows the shared interests and insights of archaeologists and ethnographers on various dimensions of human removal. The implications of this point are important for understanding the discussion that follows and the perspectives of contributors to *The Archaeology of Removal in*

North America. Because of the shared concerns of anthropological sub-fields and dispossession discourses, it is unproductive to suggest that "removal" studies need be confined to a limited set of contexts, analytical focal points, or theoretical principles. It is more productive for archaeologists to draw on insights from various fields interested in human displacement, as they converge and resonate with removal scholarship in ways that transcend specializations concentrated on particular social identities, regions, time periods, programmatic objectives, data collection methods, or intellectual cohorts.

Defining Removal and Other Terms of Dispossession

Removal often involves the suffering of communities grappling with the disintegration of social ties, the transformation and imposition of identities (e.g. group labels), disorientations of personhood, uncertainties about resettlement, doubts about the intentions of agencies or host societies, ambiguities of repatriation, and grief over losses (e.g., homes) (Colson 2003, 10; King and Eoin 2014, 206). While unique factors affect any given case, there are also fruitful comparisons such as the state of liminality refugees describe who have languished in camps in places such as Hungary or Palestine. A holistic vantage point for understanding the consequences of Native American removal in the nineteenth century is evident in the experiences of the Choctaw:

> Furthermore, the land onto which they were forced was present-day Oklahoma, which the Choctaws considered a dangerous place where spirits of the dead traveled low to the ground or lived permanently. As a result of their forced relocation, the Choctaws suffered disease, starvation, suicides, murder, and a general anomie that dislocated them for generations. (Akers 1999, 63)

The Chickasaws, the Choctaws' neighbors, experienced trauma and corruption at the hands of their U.S. government stewards, but they also had more control over the timing, direction, and resources in their removal (Paige, Bumpers, and Littlefield 2010). Similarly, members of any given society experience removal differently, as in cases where it shifts gender dynamics and balances of power (Indra 1999).

Conquests, nation building, imperial expansion, and colonialism are primary causes of removal. Settlers and states have forcibly dislocated people for many centuries. Archaeologists have studied Spanish colonial policies of *reduccione*, the relocation of indigenous people to increase control over their labor and politics in South America and elsewhere (Jamieson 2005, 358). The ethno-racial dispossessions Anglo-American militaristic invasions have caused were rationalized using the ideology of "empty lands," which settlers used to justify their claims on Native American lands in what became the United States (Zimmerman and Makes Strong Move 2008, 190). The dispossessed of different continents have responded variously to military, political, economic, and cultural forms of coercion. Depending on factors such as the size of the populations of locals and invaders, the terrain, and the relative strength of the opposing forces, people were swept away or locked in short- or long-term battles. Some of the dispossessed have attempted to maneuver in the face of divide-and-conquer colonizing strategies, broken treaties, and confusion over the ethical inability of settlers and states to honor basic human rights (Perdue and Green 1995, 19, 26). Others have shifted in their level of commitment to either protecting collective indigenous land claims or pursing individual residence rights.

Armed conflict, one of the leading causes of dispossession in the twentieth and twenty-first centuries, had displaced 43.7 million people worldwide as of 2010 (Jacques 2012, 1–2). Governments, scholars, activists, and various publics around the world have noticed the social dysfunctions, health problems, legal disputes, and demographic scope of these inter- and intranational disruptions. However, war-based removals involve more than just the study of refugees or victims of (neo)conquests. Removal also involves cultural losses, intellectual displacements, and dislocated consciousness, all of which complicate our understandings of social theory and history (Robinson 2013). Minds are colonized, bodies are reduced to captive labor, organic and institutional intellectuals are forced into exile, place-based heritage is disrupted (e.g., shrines are destroyed).

Conversely, removal also inspires innovation, nostalgia, resistance, and reworkings of memory (Colson 2003; Oliver-Smith 1991). In many times and places, the dispossessed (or their proponents) have quickly emerged to criticize, lament, or challenge the agents and conditions of removal. For example, although much has been written about Cherokee removal, a growing number of scholars are discussing those who avoided removal. An archaeological case in point is Welch town, where a white and Cherokee slaveholding couple gave refuge to hundreds of Cherokees who remained in their homeland after their peers were removed (Greene 2011, 55–59, 64–65; Malkki 1995a, 515). Similarly, excavations of illicit nineteenth-century Scottish whiskey stills and documentation of families who reinhabited damaged houses after being driven out of their destroyed highland habitations by agents of "improvement" speak to the resilience of people in the face of removal (Given 2004). Collective responses to group exile sometimes take the form of reconstitutive projects such as ethnic identity making, political consciousness raising, revival of ancestral languages, and the creation of national libraries (Said 1994, 146). The perspective of displaced persons is a crucial part of analyses, as we cannot understand people without reference to the world views and identities that move with them, regardless of how far they are pushed from their homes. The emergence and persistence of indigenous, African diasporan, and African-centered movements and writings are examples of displaced persons' hopes for restoration, revitalization, cultural survival, and vindication (Skinner 1999). Thus, displacement is not just the suffering of those who experience violence in dispersion; it also presents opportunities to discover solidarity or safety in numbers (see Sartorius and Seigel 2010; Flick and King, this volume).

Public discourses and remembrance programs are worth some consideration, whether they are enacted by dispossessed persons or their descendants or scholars involved in public engagement. For instance, exhibits and cartographic representations of removal on the Internet such as the Holocaust map created by French historians and Nazi hunters suggest a way that the experience of children removed to concentration camps during the 1940s can be remembered.[1]

The perspectives of post-humanist thought and anthropologies of materiality help expand this conversation by drawing attention to ways that the agents, victims, and targets of removal are not always human, even if people are involved. From this view, it is possible to see material things, machines, and landscapes as casualties of processes and events such as the "tram massacres" of Sydney, Australia (ca. 1955–1961). This involved the removal of trams, tracks, stations, and related infrastructure, objects, and architecture. People's responses and roles varied from support to opposition or involved indirect causal agency, such as their increasing reliance on automobiles and buses, the biggest transportation competitors (Howard 2012, 93–97). Another example involves "mountaintop removal," which has enriched the coal-mining companies that removed the mountain peaks, provided jobs, polluted waterways, moved activists to protect natural resources, and caused residents to fear for the loss of their heritage and cemeteries (Cook 2001, 15). Alternately, sometimes the earth removes people. Cases in point occurred almost 2,000 years ago at Pompeii and Herculaneum, well-known archaeological sites more famous for the people who failed to escape deadly volcanic eruptions. Archaeology in Mesoamerica has identified various human experiences with volcanism: relocation processes spanning centuries, rapid reinhabitation of abandoned sites and vulnerabilities emerging in nation-states. Volcanism also created counterintuitive effects, such as the ash from eruptions fertilizing the soil and generating crop surpluses (Sheets 2001).

The agents and victims of removal and catastrophe are being addressed in various ways. For example, tram landscapes have been memorialized via methods such as plaques or the preservation of trams, work sheds, or tracks (Howard 2012, 95). Institutions such as UNESCO and governments around the world have been investing hundreds of millions of dollars in conservation, research, and tourism related to Pompeii and Herculaneum (Hammer 2015). Alternative paths have been chosen for landscape features deemed symbolic of violence, hate, and exploitation. For instance, campus opinion polls and vandalism convinced officials to remove a statue of Cecil Rhodes, the colonial-era mining magnate, from the campus of the University of Cape Town in 2015. That same year, the murder of African Americans in Charleston, South Carolina, by a man who wielded flags of apartheid-era South Africa, colonial Rhodesia, and the U.S. Confederacy, convinced politicians to remove the Confederate flag from the South Carolina statehouse grounds. However, in both cases, a number of politicians and other supporters protested the removal of the icons. Politics, social critics, and economics sway opinions for and against these removal and commemoration projects.

Situating Removal in Theory and Archaeological Practice

Removals have been central to the history of anthropology's practices and precursors, whether they be colonial projects, nationalistic settler invasions, or imperial conquests (Trouillot 1995). In lands occupied by indigenous people in what became the United States, archaeology's "practice of scientific colonialism" has played a role in both human removals and "intellectual landscapes of clearance" (Zimmerman and Makes Strong Move 2008, 190–191). This problem is the product of the way the taxonomies of indigenous groups are constructed, how people articulate concepts of abandonment and displacement, how assumptions about discontinuities in social identities over space and time are promulgated, and how epistemologies of cultural affiliation are addressed. Some of the earliest archaeologists and more recent laypersons have erased Native Americans from antiquity by promoting mound-building myths (Zimmerman and Makes Strong Move 2008, 205). Similarly, "the removal of American Indians from the entire history of 'modern' America . . . served to perpetuate racist stereotypes of Indians" (Greene 2011, 7).

A complicated case of removal is the mid-twentieth-century role of Louis Leakey, the icon of paleoanthropology and human evolution. While Leakey advocated for indigenous African land rights and contributions to human origins, he also worked for the colonial police and vocally criticized prominent activists for Kenyan independence such as Jomo Kenyatta. Like others who were branded too militant, Kenyatta was forcibly removed to a penal reservation after his home was destroyed as part of British colonists' native relocation program.

Whatever recorded or oral history may say about the antiquity of removals, Leakey expressed skepticism about twentieth-century evolutionary perspectives that suggested that conflict—and by extension violent displacement—were natural or frequent historical occurrences (Leakey and Ardrey 1971). One case in point, which Leakey criticized, was the "killer ape" theory, the idea that ancient hominins and primates were innately and cooperatively violent. In Leakey's thinking, plentiful resource spaces and daily challenges to survival precluded extensive early hominin conquests or intergroup aggression. Violence quickly comes to mind for some scholars and filmmakers who are trying to understand the nature of modern human and Neandertal encounters. Archaeologists and bioarchaeologists have worked to challenge outdated theories and faulty evidence of cannibalistic violence, but some see interpersonal violence as significant and ancient. To date, there is little evidence of frequent or large-scale violence prior to the development of sedentary, agricultural societies; such evidence includes an isolated case of stone points embedded in human bones that date to circa 13000 BP (Dawson and Farber 2012; Fry 2007; Horgan 2012; Wrangham and Peterson 1996). It remains to be seen if archaeologists and paleontologists will shift back the time depth on our understanding of the origins of coercive human displacements and violence.

The removals dam building has prompted brought archaeologists (and other anthropologists) into contact with dislocations through twentieth-century cultural resource salvage projects in places such as the China's Yellow River, the Tennessee River Valley, and the Aswan region of Egypt (Hester 1968). In the twenty-first century, archaeologists moved dam studies beyond simplistic salvage objectives in order to more fully grapple with a range of complex issues, such as the anguish caused by landscape losses, compensatory disputes (e.g., over land value), conflicting conceptualizations of heritage, diverse stakeholder interests, growing demands for energy, and contested development policies (Brandt 2004; Hafsaas-Tsakos 2011; King and Eoin 2014).

The social violence of economic exploitation, a primary cause of many dislocations, has long been a concern of Marxist and political economic perspectives, which have made valuable contributions to our understanding of forms of alienation (e.g., from means of production). Proponents of these perspectives have given special attention to primitive accumulation theory and factors such as privatization (e.g., of land) (Chakrabarti and Dhar 2010). Sociologists note how immigration and economics create displacement, as when corporations close unionized plants and reopen them as nonunion factories worked by lower-paid laborers (Waters, Kasinitz, and Asad 2014, 380). The work on post-peasant internal displacement, which examines industrialization and the rural exodus of former farmers (e.g., in Algeria), has put forward various theories such as Bourdieu's "hysteresis" model, a conceptualization of displacement as dissonances between capital and fields of practice. Critiques of dispossession and indigeneity have examined how activists, subalterns, NGOs, governments, and colonial agents have taken various, sometimes unexpected positions regarding land alienability, communalism, commodification, and enclosure (Li 2010, 386). Archaeological research on the Great Dismal Swamp in North Carolina has drawn on the Marxist models of rural, colonial, capitalistic modes of production that alienated enslaved and self-liberated African canal workers (Sayers 2014).

Cultural displacement is another aspect of relocation that, along with concepts of diaspora, have invigorated social theory, complicating conceptualizations of power, identity constructivism, cultural translation, and transformation (Bhabha 1994, 172). We find these themes embedded in some archaeological works. For instance, Weik's (2009) exploration of African Seminole ethnogenesis at Pilaklikaha in Sumter County, Florida, examines identity transformations embedded in a multiphase fallback trajectory of maroon resettlement, transitory residence, and village abandonment in the face of the US military's attacks. Another archaeological example involves the ways that Christianization removed and marginalized pagan landscapes (e.g., by leveling funeral mounds) in the medieval Netherlands (Roymans et al. 2009). Some pagan relics and sacred places became demonized spaces, repurposed as locales of public execution that Christians and authorities viewed as wastelands. This research raises interpretive possibilities that are relevant to discourses inspired by postcolonial writers such as Cesaire and Fanon, who criticized assimilationist European colonialism and examined the psychological and social consequences of conversion, identity loss, and the criminalization of heritage, people, and places.

The anthropological turn toward spatial relationships and deterritorialized social analyses can be seen in the ethnographic work of Peutz (2006), who proposes a globalized, embodied, chronotopical model of Somali deportation. Archaeologies of removals of the Potawatomi and other indigenous groups in the northern United States have similarly realized the benefits of multisited, multiscalar strategies for examining how people resituated homelands, modified cultural practices (e.g. headstones and other types of burial marker), negotiated power struggles, and adapted to shifting resettlement conditions and identities (Cipolla 2013; Schurr 2010).

Over the twentieth century, the United Nations Commission on Human Rights has shaped writings and policies on social justice, calling for displaced persons to have protection for their graves and their families, to participate in resettlement plans, to have access to resources (such as possession of property they have left behind), and to have aid (e.g., government medicine or sanitation) (Deng and United Nations 2004, 9–11). Important distinctions emerge in this discussion of human rights, such as the varying circumstances of internally displaced persons versus international refugees. The UN is on the ground in places such as Colombia, marshaling monetary and other assistance to some of the nearly six million people displaced by drug wars, land grabbing, and state-supported violence (Grajales 2013). Colombia ranks second only to Syria as the nation with the highest number of internally displaced persons since 1998 (Bilak et al. 2016).

Some critics have articulated the role of institutions in removal. Historical and present-day governments rely heavily on professional militaries, paramilitary groups, and mobs to do the violent work of destroying people, the will of locals to resist, and resources (e.g., subsistence crops or homes), thus setting the stage for human dislocation (Grajales 2013). Politicians and officials develop the rationale for removal (e.g., civilizing missions or property rights), while engineers and surveyors encode Eurocentric ideals on maps (Weik, this volume). The result is the establishment of new economic and spatial orders and the erasure, confinement, and resettlement of indigenous populations. For example, in discussing a 2008 World Bank report, Li (2010, 396) suggests that it

> recommends that farmers unable to compete in the world of commercial agriculture should stop trying to farm and migrate to cities or look for wage work. It offers no discussion of the social movements that have formed to resist eviction or reclaim land for the landless, hence it fails to recognize the strength and vigor of these movements as a reflection of the important role that land still plays in providing a modicum of security in a drastically uncertain world.

Like other anthropologists, archaeologists have been critical of "development" and legal or political modes of dislocation that destroy or dislocate cultural resources and people, suggesting the need for more proactive advocacy approaches (McDavid 2011; Hafsaas-Tsakos 2011; Schmidt 2000). Archaeologists have proposed a number of forms of activist research, such as including locals in research designs, training residents to conduct research, giving communities input into "development" objectives, including ecological and human rights standards in heritage research, and creating context-specific ethical codes (see Meskell 2009).

Chapter Overview

The chapters of this volume are organized chronologically. The primary theoretical issues that resonate in various chapters and provide coherence for the volume include forced migration, memory and forgetting, landscapes, racialization, capitalistic exploitation, violence, government intervention, identity (trans)formation, and confinement. More specific topics also link chapters, such as the role of rhetoric discussed in Horning's analysis of national parks in Appalachia and Weik's examination of Chickasaw removal in the Lower Mississippi River Valley. Orser's chapter serves as a commentary on the most salient themes within this book. It frames the contributors' ideas within a transatlantic perspective, derived in part from his research on colonial eviction in nineteenth-century Ireland.

The early chapters of the book examine Native American and colonial situations. Flick and King's chapter explores the intersection of memory, dispossession, and place in the context of seventeenth-century Piscataway in what became Maryland. They show how behavioral remnants, documents, artifacts, and oral histories illustrate place making and ties to the land that materialized during a period of removal. Flick and King frame Native American removal within a global comparative perspective on (dis)emplacement. They also show the utility of balancing attention to destructive colonial forces with Native American countermeasures of communal reformulation and reclamation. Flick and King's chapter helps readers understand the diverse experiences and responses to removal within a single cultural group.

Weik's chapter explores representations of land such as maps and surveyors' notes and the roles they played in facilitating the institutionalized removal of Mississippi Chickasaws in the nineteenth century. This chapter discusses the epistemology of maps and property claims and the social implications of land division and commoditization. It also follows the multidirectional tactics of displacement and nascent articulations of the land rights of modern indigenous people. Weik illustrates how archaeologists can play a role in tracking Native American experiences before, during, and after removal.

Another chapter set in the nineteenth century is Reeves and Woehlke's analysis of the political economy and racialization of agricultural transformations in Virginia and in African American "self-deportation." They illustrate the diverse communities and individuals, including a U.S. president, that contributed to Orange County's dispossessive processes of land use and (re)settlement. Demographic data play an important role in their analysis. This case study provides a model for analyzing regional settlement while giving attention to the globalizing dimensions of removal.

The rest of the book focuses on twentieth- and twenty-first-century cases of displacement. Fracchia's chapter on the twentieth-century development and destruction of a quarry town takes a Marxist approach to class and race relations. He examines ideas about value that are at work in the logic of ineffective preservation for this industrial community in order to explain the ongoing and drastic decline of cultural resources in the area. Fracchia invites us to ask what role archaeology and capitalism play in the removal and commemoration of historic homes, labor history, and town remnants. What is valuable and how does this relate to what will be maintained or erased from the landscape?

Horning's study examines how government policy, the building of national parks, and popularized representations of hill people displaced residents and changed how land was used in Appalachia in the 1920s and 1930s. This chapter explores how racialized conservation, poverty, development, and social engineering created removal. Her analysis of artifacts, former residents' writings, and other archival evidence illustrate how uprooted people's views and lifestyles challenged popular, academic, and institutional narratives about the dispossessed. This chapter nicely captures the multiscalar nuances of intimate individual experiences and social interests and the insights of a comparative perspective.

Kamp-Whittaker and Clark develop the concept of neighborhood and apply it to a 1940s Japanese American internment camp at Amache, Colorado. They investigate how relocated people were able to marshal networks, cultural behavior, possessions, and geographical ties in order to cultivate distinct neighborhood identities. Kamp-Whittaker and Clark also illustrate how people cope with removal processes set in motion by a government that addressed national security by managing race and ethnicity during a world war.

Starzmann's chapter draws on various theories to uncover the politics of institutionalized removal in late-twentieth-century New York prisons. Her examination of material culture and carceral landscapes incorporates concepts of exile and political death in ways that foster comparisons to global issues such as UN definitions of internally displaced persons. Starzmann shows how archaeologists can use spatial and landscape approaches to restore public discourses about those made invisible while shedding light on processes that remove a class of people from people's daily view.

Note

1. "Map Shows Every French Child Deported during the Holocaust," *Tablet*, February 20, 2014, http://www.tabletmag.com/scroll/163429/map-shows-every-french-child
-deported-during-the-holocaust.

References Cited

Akers, D. L. 1999. Removing the Heart of the Choctaw People: Indian Removal from a Native Perspective. *American Indian Culture and Research Journal* 23:63–76.

Bender, Barbara. 2001. Landscapes On-the-Move. *Journal of Social Archaeology* 1:75–89.

Bhabha, Homi K. 1994. *The Location of Culture*. London; New York: Routledge.

Bilak, Alexandra, Gabriel Cardona-Fox, Justin Ginnetti, Elizabeth Rushing, Isabelle Sherer, Marita Swain, Nadine Walicki, Michelle Yonetani, and Jeremy Lennard. 2016. Global Report on Internal Displacement. Geneva: Internal Displacement Monitoring Centre.

Brandt, Steven A. 2004. *Damming the Past*. Lanham, MD: Rowman & Littlefield.

Branigan, Keith, and J. M. Bumsted. 2005. *From Clan to Clearance : History and Archaeology on the Isle of Barra, ca. 850–1850 AD*. Oxford: Oxbow Books.

Campbell, John R., Michael Goldsmith, Kanyathu Koshy, and Asia Pacific Network for Global Change Research. 2007. *Community Relocation as an Option for Adaptation to the Effects of Climate Change and Climate Variability in Pacific Island Countries (PICs)*. Kobe, Japan: Asia-Pacific Network for Global Change Research.

Cernea, Michael M., and Scott E. Guggenheim. 1993. *Anthropological Approaches to Resettlement: Policy, Practice, and Theory*. Boulder, CO: Westview Press.

Chakrabarti, Anjan, and Anup Kumar Dhar. 2010. *Dislocation and Resettlement in Development: From Third World to the World of the Third*. London: Routledge.

Cipolla, Craig N. 2013. Resituating Homeland: Motion, Movement, and Ethnogenesis at Brothertown." In *Archaeologies of Mobility and Movement*, edited by M. C. Beaudry and T. G. Parno, 117–132. New York: Springer Press.

Colson, Elizabeth. 2003. Forced Migration and the Anthropological Response. *Journal of Refugee Studies* 16(1):1–18.

Cook, Samuel. 2001. A Vested Interest: Activist Anthropology in the Mountaintop Removal Debate. *Practicing Anthropology* 23(2):15–18.

Dawson, Grant, and Sonia Farber. 2012. *Forcible Displacement throughout the Ages towards an International Convention for the Prevention and Punishment of the Crime of Forcible Displacement*. The Hague: Martinus Nijhoff.

Deng, Francis Mading, and UN Office for the Coordination of Humanitarian Affairs. 2004. *Guiding Principles on Internal Displacement*. Geneva: UN Office for the Coordination of Humanitarian Affairs .

Fry, Douglas P. 2007. *Beyond War: The Human Potential for Peace*. Oxford: Oxford University Press.

Given, Michael. 2004. *The Archaeology of the Colonized*. New York: Routledge.

Glenn, Evelyn Nakano. 2015. Settler Colonialism as Structure: A Framework for Comparative Studies of U.S. Race and Gender Formation. *Sociology of Race and Ethnicity Sociology of Race and Ethnicity* 1(1):52–72.

Grajales, Jacobo. 2013. State Involvement, Land Grabbing and Counter-Insurgency in Colombia. In *Governing Global Land Deals: The Role of the State in the Rush for Land*, edited by Wendy Wolfrod, Saturnino Borras, and Ruth Hall, 23–44. Hoboken: Wiley Blackwell.

Greene, Lance. 2011. Identity in a Post-Removal Cherokee Household, 1838–1850. In *American Indians and the Market Economy, 1775–1850*, edited by Timothy K. Perttula, Mark R. Plane, and Lance Green, 55–65. Tuscaloosa: University of Alabama Press.

Hafsaas-Tsakos, Henriette. 2011. Ethical Implications of Salvage Archaeology and Dam Building: The Clash between Archaeologists and Local People in Dar Al-Manasir, Sudan. *Journal of Social Archaeology* 11(February):49–76.

Hammer, Joshua. 2015. The Fall and Rise and Fall of Pompeii. *Smithsonian* 46(4):24–37.

Hester, James J. 1968. Pioneer Methods in Salvage Anthropology. *Anthropological Quarterly* 41:132–146.

Horgan, John. 2012. *The End of War.* San Francisco: McSweeneys Books.

Howard, P. 2012. A "Tram Massacre": Institutionalised Destruction in Sydney, 1955–1961. *Archaeology in Oceania* 47(July):91–98.

Indra, Doreen Marie. 1999. *Engendering Forced Migration: Theory and Practice.* New York: Berghahn Books.

Jacques, Mélanie. 2012. *Armed Conflict and Displacement: The Protection of Refugees and Displaced Persons under International Humanitarian Law.* Cambridge: Cambridge University Press.

Jamieson, Ross W. 2005. Colonialism, Social Archaeology and Lo Andino: Historical Archaeology in the Andes. *World Archaeology* 37(3):352–372.

King, Rachel, and Luíseach Nic Eoin. 2014. Before the Flood: Loss of Place, Mnemonics, and "Resources" Ahead of the Metolong Dam, Lesotho. *Journal of Social Archaeology* 14(June):196–223.

Kirsch, Stuart. 2001. Lost Worlds: Environmental Disaster, "Culture Loss," and the Law. *Current Anthropology* 42(2):167–98.

Leakey, L. S. B., and Robert Ardrey. 1971. *Aggression and Violence in Man: A Dialogue between Dr. Louis Leakey and Mr. Robert Ardrey.* Pasadena, Ca.: Munger Africana Library.

Li, Tania. 2010. Indigeneity, Capitalism, and the Management of Dispossession. *Current Anthropology* 51(3):385–414.

Lieber, Michael D. 1977. *Exiles and Migrants in Oceania.* Honolulu: University Press of Hawaii.

Loizos, Peter. 1999. Ottoman Half-Lives: Long-Term Perspectives on Particular Forced Migrations. *Journal of Refugee Studies* 12(3):237–263.

Malkki, Liisa H. 1995a. Refugees and Exile: From "Refugee Studies" to the National Order of Things. *Annual Review of Anthropology* 24:495–523.

———. 1995b. *Purity and Exile: Violence, Memory, and National Cosmology among Hutu Refugees in Tanzania.* Chicago: University of Chicago Press.

Masquelier, Adeline. 2006. Why Katrina's Victims Aren't Refugees: Musings on a "Dirty" Word. *American Anthropologist* 108(4):735–743.

McDavid, Carol. 2011. When Is "Gone" Gone? Archaeology, Gentrification, and Competing Narratives about Freedmen's Town, Houston. *Historical Archaeology* 45:74–88.

Merlan, Francesca. 2005. Indigenous Movements in Australia. *Annual Review of Anthropology* 34:473–494.

Meskell, Lynn. 2009. *Cosmopolitan Archaeologies*. Durham, NC: Duke University Press.

Oliver-Smith, Anthony. 1991. Involuntary Resettlement, Resistance and Political Empowerment. *Journal of Refugee Studies* 4(2): 132–149.

———. 2010. *Defying Displacement: Grassroots Resistance and the Critique of Development*. Austin: University of Texas.

Orser, Charles E. 2005. An Archaeology of a Famine-Era Eviction. *New Hibernia Review/ Iris Éireannach Nua* 9(1):45–58.

Paige, Amanda L., Fuller L. Bumpers, and Daniel F. Littlefield. 2010. *Chickasaw Removal*. Ada, OK: Chickasaw Press.

Parkin, David. 1999. Mementoes as Transitional Objects in Human Displacement. *Journal of Material Culture Journal of Material Culture* 4(3):303–320.

Perdue, Theda, and Michael D. Green. 1995. *The Cherokee Removal: A Brief History with Documents*. Boston: Bedford Books.

Peutz, Nathalie. 2006. Embarking on an Anthropology of Removal. *Current Anthropology* 47(2):217–41.

Robinson, Douglas. 2013. *Displacement and the Somatics of Postcolonial Culture*. Columbus: Ohio State University Press.

Roymans, Nico, Fokke Gerritsen, Cor Van der Heijden, Koos Bosma, and Jan Kolen. 2009. Landscape Biography as Research Strategy: The Case of the South Netherlands Project. *Landscape Research* 34(3):337–59.

Said, Edward. 1994. Reflections on Exile. In *Altogether Elsewhere: Writers on Exile*, by Marc Robinson, 137–149. San Diego: Harcourt Brace.

Sartorius, David, and Micol Seigel. 2010. *Dislocations across the Americas*. Durham, NC: Duke University Press.

Sayers, Daniel O. 2014. The Most Wretched of Beings in the Cage of Capitalism. *International Journal of Historical Archaeology* 18(3):529–554.

Schmidt, Peter. 2000. Human Rights, Culture, and Dams: A New Global Perspective. In *Dams and Cultural Heritage Management*, edited by Steven and Fekri Hassan Brandt, 13–14. Cape Town: World Commission on Dams Secretariat.

Schurr, Mark R. 2010. Archaeological Indices of Resistance: Diversity in the Removal Period Potawatomi of the Western Great Lakes. *American Antiquity* 75(1):44–60.

Sheets, Payson. 2001. The Effects of Explosive Volcanism on Simple to Complex Societies in Ancient Middle America. In *The Angry Earth: Disaster in Anthropological Perspective*, edited by Susanna Hoffman and Anthony Oliver-Smith, 36–58. New York: Routledge.

Skinner, Elliott P. 1999. The Restoration of African Identity for a New Millennium. *African Diaspora: African Origins and New World Identities*, 28–45. Bloomington: Indiana University Press.

Smith, Angèle, and Amy Gazin-Schwartz, eds. 2008. *Landscapes of Clearance: Archaeological and Anthropological Perspectives*. Walnut Creek, CA: Left Coast Press.

Trouillot, Michel-Rolph. 1995. *Silencing the Past: Power and the Production of History*. Boston, MA: Beacon Press.

Waters, Mary C., Philip Kasinitz, and Asad L. Asad. 2014. Immigrants and African Americans. *Annual Review of Sociology* 40(1):369–390.

Weik, Terrance M. 2009. The Role of Ethnogenesis and Organization in the Development of African-Native American Settlements: An African Seminole Model. *International Journal of Historical Archaeology* 13(2):206–238.

Wrangham, Richard W., and Dale Peterson. 1996. *Demonic Males: Apes and the Origins of Human Violence*. Boston: Houghton Mifflin.

Zimmerman, Larry, and Dawn Makes Strong Move. 2008. Archaeological Taxonomy, Native Americans, and Scientific Landscapes of Clearance: A Case Study from Northeastern Iowa. In *Landscapes of Clearance: Archaeological and Anthropological Perspectives*, edited by Angèle Smith and Amy Gazin-Schwartz, 190–212. Walnut Creek, CA: Left Coast Press.

2

"We Can Fly No Farther"

Colonialism and Displacement among the Piscataway of Southern Maryland

ALEX J. FLICK AND JULIA A. KING

In 1882, Dr. Elmer R. Reynolds, a co-founder of the Anthropological Society of Washington, DC, visited Indian Hill, a place he described as an "old Indian town . . . situated on the head waters of the Wicomico River, twenty-five miles from its junction with the Potomac" River (Reynolds [1883] 1968, 310–311). Reynolds, who was interested in documenting the region's precontact archaeological sites, also described Bead Hill, a nearby location "where glass beads . . . had been plowed" out of the ground. Although Reynolds's descriptions are vague, archaeologists are fairly certain that he was at Zekiah Fort, a circa 1680–1692 fortified Piscataway settlement located south of modern-day Waldorf, Maryland.

A self-identified Indian man named Swann took Reynolds to the old town. As far as Reynolds could tell, he was of the "original, unmixed Wicomico [Piscataway] blood" based on his appearance and his habits (Reynolds [1883] 1968, 313–314; Reynolds 1889, 259). Swann appears to have lived about eighteen miles away from Indian Hill, suggesting that his memory of the old town was based not on working the land and finding artifacts himself but on a broader awareness of an earlier landscape that, to western eyes, looked unremarkable and remained invisible. For Swann, however, Indian Hill and Bead Hill were clearly remembered places and carried some meaning; to him, these places were not invisible.

In 1934, over fifty years after Swann showed Reynolds the two hill sites, antiquarian William B. Marye (1935) set off in search of Zekiah Fort as part of the state's 300th anniversary celebration. Unlike Reynolds, Marye does not appear to have had any local informants, Native American or otherwise, who could take him to Zekiah Fort, and the fort's location appears to have vanished from local memory. It is possible that Marye failed to ask members of the local Native American population; more likely, knowledge that had survived from 1692 to 1882 had been lost sometime between 1882 and 1934. It is probably not a coincidence that this forgetting occurred during a period when the policy of the United States was to require indigenous people not only to assimilate and to become US citizens but also to leave their languages and practices behind (Tayac 1999).

This chapter explores the relationship between memory, place, and the dispossession of indigenous lands. The disappearance (or removal) of Zekiah Fort from local memory despite the continued presence of indigenous and mixed people in southern Maryland suggests the regrettable success of governmental assimilation programs that persisted well into the twentieth century. This erasure began well before the late nineteenth century and almost immediately after the first colonists arrived in Maryland. Although the archaeological record suggests that territorial displacements were not uncommon in the region in late prehistory (Potter 1993; Slattery and Woodward 1992), this chapter focuses on the post-contact period, revealing how the colonial dispossession of indigenous lands on Maryland's western shore and the displacement of Native American people proceeded hand in hand with the removal (or the appropriation) of the material signs of the indigenous past. These signs were important markers of memory and their disappearance is critical for understanding how the landscape transformed from a wholly indigenous one to an Anglicized one. These findings suggest the insidious ways colonialism often worked. They also suggest the practices displaced individuals use in their homeland and in the diaspora to resist the total erasure of indigenous existence.

Memory, Place, and Displacement: Marking Indigenous Territory

Archaeologists have begun to explore the relationship of Native Americans to social experience and their processes of place making in the eastern woodlands. Some of this work has focused on how habitation sites and practices relate to cosmology and status (Gallivan 2007, 2016) and emplacement and territorialization (Birch and Williamson 2015; Creese 2013). Other studies have examined the role of monumental features in the encoding and contestation of social memory in the landscape (Gallivan 2012; Handsman 2008). Watershed-based studies have been used to define indigenous cultural landscapes, offering deep histories of Native American place making over large areas (Strickland, Busby, and King 2015; Strickland et al. 2016; Sullivan, Chambers, and Barbery 2013). Another approach to human engagement with the landscape follows Ingold (1993), who focuses on everyday "acts of dwelling" and how they are enacted and reproduced over time and space. Practices such as manufacturing stone tools or ceramics are social acts. When these acts are routinized temporally and spatially, they are important acts of place making.

Social memory played a vital role in many practices of Native American place making. Intergenerational transmission of knowledge related to craft production, hunting, ritual, and other activities involved sharing both technical skills and spatial information. Revisiting the same places in the landscape to gather food or raw materials, hunt, feast, or mourn the dead enacted social memory and created and re-created places through time.

Experiences and memories aggregated through dwelling in an area over time contributes to a sense of place or feeling of home. But just as memory is subject to contestation, politicization, intentional or unintentional forgetting, and other alteration through time (Bradley 2003; Mills 2008), so too are places subject to perceptual and physical volatility. Physical alteration of the landscape and conflict-induced displacements, migrations, and removals can interrupt personal and social attachments to place. As Feld and Basso (1996, 11) note, though, "displacement is no less the source of powerful attachments than are experiences of profound rootedness."

The displacements of American Indian people in the Middle Atlantic and elsewhere may share important similarities with the conflict-induced forced migrations of, for example, Yugoslavia, the Balkans, or Sudan in the twentieth and twenty-first centuries. The images of these displacements are profoundly disturbing but are rarely considered in comparison to the colonization of British North America. And yet the issues these modern-day events raise are the same issues archaeologists—and many Piscataway—seek to understand: How did the uprooting and movement of Native American communities impact group cohesion, structure, and notions of identity? How did Piscataway people define and experience the losses brought about through displacement? How did the Piscataway use memory or notions of the past to reconstitute identity or to reestablish or redefine social control? This chapter aims to address these questions by exploring the material and documentary evidence of colonial-induced displacement of the Piscataway.

The anthropology of displacement (sometimes called forced migration studies) emerged at the end of World War II. Much of this work focuses on contemporary migrations propelled by conflict, development, or disaster. Sandra Dudley (2010), an anthropologist who has combined interests as varied as museums and forced migration, is especially concerned with the material culture of displacement, which she notes has received short shrift in forced migration studies. Her work with Karenni refugees in Burma has revealed the power of objects, including landscape, for coping with and responding to the loss brought about through displacement. Dudley is especially concerned with the "embodied interactions" people have with material culture and how these interactions play a critical role in experiencing and mitigating loss in part through remembrance. A closer reading of the archaeological and documentary evidence informed by Dudley's model may provide a bridge for what regional scholars have seen as an "evidentiary gap" in Piscataway history that led researchers as recently as 2004 to suggest that the Piscataway died, lost their cultural identity, or just moved away (in any case disappearing) (Miller 2004).

Dudley suggests that displaced people typically occupy an "in-between social world," yearning for a sense of emplacement and connections between "now" and "then," between "here" and "there." "Home" and place are critical components for understanding the varied responses to displacement. Dudley (2010, 9) argues that efforts to "feel at home" are a "fundamental aspect of coping with forced displacement." Strategies for "feeling at home" no doubt vary, she acknowledges, and defining what "home" means in the first place draws on a variety of aesthetics, sensibilities, and emotions. Dudley (2010, 9) regards "home" as both a spatial and a temporal concept. She suggests it is best encompassed (at least materially) by place and the embodied experiences of place, including, in her study of the Karenni, food, houses, and dress (especially women's dress). She also notes that notions of "home" are forged by spatial relationships of the comings and goings of everyday life, what might best be called everyday mobility. It is these relationships, she argues, that refugees aim to remake in their displaced condition as they struggle to reconstitute "home."

We have only the rarest glimpses into the meaning of "home" for the seventeenth-century Piscataway or, for that matter, any Native American group on Maryland's western shore. In some cases, it appears to be place based, as the *tayac* (leader) suggested when the Piscataway youth abandoned the group, which was in self-imposed exile in the period 1697–1699, to return to southern Maryland. Even so, familiar physical spaces without former social relationships constitute a form of political displacement. A Susquehannock Indian voiced this sensibility when he told a Choptico Indian "that his Nation was Ruin'd by the English assisted by Piscattoways, & tht now they were no People, that he had still tears in his Eyes when he thought of it" (Browne 1903, 187). These rare but revealing records can be coupled with an extraordinary and growing material culture record that provides insight into embodied practices and from there, possibly, the meaning of "home."

Historical Background

When the English arrived in the Potomac River in 1608, an estimated 2,000 to 7,000 Native American people occupied what would become Maryland's western shore (Cissna 1986, 49–53). This population was organized into a number of towns and hamlets, each controlled by local leaders subject to the Piscataway *tayac*, whose territorial influence extended over most of the villages between the fall line and the Chesapeake Bay.[1] However, Rev. Hugh Jones of Calvert County estimated that by 1699, the Native American population of the entire Maryland colony was no more than 500 fighting men, most of whom lived on the sparsely populated eastern shore. He attributed "the cause of their diminishing" to both internal conflict and smallpox (Kammen 1963, 372). Jones's report indicated the dramatic changes Maryland's indigenous people experienced during the seventeenth century, but like other contemporary English recorders, he failed to mention the role land-hungry colonists played in the territorial displacement of Native American people.

The English who settled Maryland in 1634 established a permanent settlement at St. Mary's City, purposely located downriver from the Piscataway capital on Piscataway Creek. As the colony's population grew, settlement rapidly expanded up the coast and along navigable waterways, where well-drained agricultural soils that were favorable for tobacco cultivation could be found (Kelly 1979; Smolek 1984). As they had done at St. Mary's City, the colonists often settled in extant or recently abandoned Indian habitations because of their agricultural productivity and because doing so saved the labor of clearing the land (Potter and Waselkov 1994). The expansion of English settlement resulted in increased interactions between colonists and Maryland Native Americans, which fomented conflict, trade, and working relations. Throughout the century, Indians accused colonists of throwing down fences, destroying Native American corn, and letting English livestock graze in Indian fields and gardens. Conversely, colonists frequently complained that Indians killed their roaming livestock (Browne 1884, 15; Browne 1885, 489, 534; Pleasants 1932, 139).

The colonial government experimented with land allotments for Native American people. In 1651, the Maryland proprietor set aside eight to ten thousand acres at the head of the Wicomico River that became Calverton (or Choptico) Manor (Browne 1883, 329–330). Thinking such a grant of land would encourage efforts "to bring [the Native American people] to Civility [and] also to Christianity" and to further submit to the Maryland government, Lord Baltimore, the colony's proprietor, directed the surveyor general to create the colony's first Indian reservation. Leaders of six local tribal groups would be allotted 200 acres each and individual Indians would be allotted 50 acres each. At least some Indians, including the Choptico, settled on Calverton Manor and remained there into the early eighteenth century (King, Trussell, and Strickland 2014).

In 1663, the queen of Portobac reported that her people had vacated their village along Port Tobacco River because of English encroachment (Browne 1885, 489). The Maryland government responded by designating a three-mile buffer around Indian towns where no colonists were to settle, but the buffer was routinely ignored and the complaints continued. Lord Baltimore patented the property containing the fort in the mid-1660s. In 1666, the Maryland government attempted to formalize its relationship with the several indigenous nations on the western shore and regulate interactions between English colonists and Native Americans via treaty. At the treaty conference, Mattagund, a Native American representative, insisted that English colonists continued to settle too close to Indian towns, forcing Native Americans to abandon their lands. He stated, "We can fly no farther let us know where to live [and] how to be secured for the future from the Hogs [and] Cattle." Another speaker, Choatick, asked colonial officials to officially recognize Indian hunting, fishing, and crabbing rights (Browne 1884, 14–15), subsistence activities that required mobility and access to traditional grounds that English settlement practices threatened (Harmon 2001).

Twelve groups signed the 1666 Articles of Peace and Amity, effectively subordinating the Native Americans of Maryland's western shore to colonial authorities (Cissna 1986, 159–163). The agreement attempted to control indigenous mobility, clearly a source of anxiety for the English (King, Mansius, and Strickland 2016). The treaty stipulated that the colonial government would survey the bounds of each Indian town and that no "foreign" Indians were to be hosted in these towns without permission from colonial authorities. The inhabitants of each town were to fence their fields to protect them from free-roaming English livestock. In return, the English promised the Indians that they would not remove them from the surveyed tracts (Browne 1884, 26). Native American individuals approaching English plantations could not wear paint and were required to call aloud when they came within 300 paces of an English settlement. Should a Native American meet an Englishman in the woods, the former was required to immediately throw down any weapons (Browne 1884, 25).

The agreement also contained a provision allowing the proprietor, Lord Baltimore, to appoint a place of refuge for the signatory nations in the event of hostilities with enemy tribal nations. In 1680, unrest in Maryland triggered this clause, but Native Americans were suspicious of Baltimore's efforts to relocate them. When Lord Baltimore initially recommended that Indians vacate their ancestral lands and take refuge among the Nanticoke across Chesapeake Bay, the Mattawoman predicted that if they complied, "they should be dispossessed of their Lands" (Browne 1896, 300). They refused to vacate their fort on Mattawoman Creek.

The Piscataway, driven by Susquehannock assaults on their town, eventually relented and relocated to Zekiah Swamp some thirteen miles inland. The move to Zekiah, which the Piscataway hastily made in late June 1680, required them to abandon their corn fields at Piscataway Creek and move an estimated 90 to 300 individuals. The fortified settlement was located in the Piscataway homeland in territory that had been used mostly for winter hunting. Although Susquehannock raids had abated by 1682, the Piscataway stayed at Zekiah for another decade, until Baltimore's proprietary government was overthrown and replaced in 1692 with a royal government less sympathetic to Indian affairs (Flick et al. 2012). The Mattawomans' reluctance to vacate their lands proved well-founded, as the Piscataway, who attempted to return to their ancestral lands on Piscataway Creek in the mid-1690s, found their homeland settled by English colonists. Francis Nicholson, the new governor, saw the potential for Indian lands to produce more tobacco to boost colonial revenue, and in 1695, he proposed "that some way be found out that may occasion the seating [of] a certain Indian Tract of Land, Scituated betwixt Pomunky & Mattawoman extending at least twenty Miles upon the River of Potomock" (Browne 1900, 282).

The Piscataway briefly attempted to coexist with the English who had "bought their lands over their heads," as one Piscataway described it. However, the colonists constantly harassed them, destroying their fences and corn fields and blaming them for killing English livestock. Eventually, in 1697, the Piscataway fled Maryland for the Virginia Piedmont (Browne 1899, 521). Soon thereafter, some in the Maryland government began to fear the Piscataway would ally with hostile tribes or French missionaries at their new town in Virginia and began making overtures to the Piscataway, asking them to return to reserved lands in Maryland where they could be more easily surveilled (Browne 1903, 243–244). The Piscataways were divided about returning to their homeland. A colonial envoy who visited the group in Virginia reported that many "Comon sort" were in favor of returning, but the Piscataway *tayac* and his great men refused (Browne 1899, 520–521).

Some Piscataway returned to southern Maryland, some dispersed among other tribes across the eastern woodlands, and others followed the *tayac* to Heater's Island in the Potomac River, well beyond the frontier of English settlement in Maryland in 1699. Tayac Othotamaqua, who led this contingent of Piscataway, agreed to legally relinquish claims to some fragments of the supposedly reserved Indian lands near Piscataway Creek for nominal compensation—reserved lands whose boundaries the English did not respect and colonial authorities did not enforce (Strickland 2015). It is this group of Piscataway whose history is best preserved in colonial records due to the *tayac*'s continued dealings with travelers and colonial officials.

In 1704, an outbreak of smallpox among the Piscataway at Heater's Island killed fifty-seven people, including Othotamaqua, and may have initiated a northward migration into Pennsylvania, although some Piscataway were at Heater's Island as late as 1712. A short time after this date, the remaining Piscataway abandoned the island and eventually resettled at Conoy Town on the Susquehanna River in 1718, where they remained until 1743, when encroaching English settlement and the related landscape change ruined the group's ability to hunt near their town. When the Piscataway left Conoy Town, some sixty-two years after initially leaving their homeland along Piscataway Creek, Tayac Old Sack sent a message to Pennsylvania's governor recounting the group's journeys: "our fforefathers came from Piscatua to an Island in Potowmeck to Conejoholo" (Kent 1984, 70). Old Sack's words indicate that even among those who left Maryland, "Piscatua" remained the ancestral home in the Piscataways' memories and geographies.

Displacement and Its Effects: Archaeological and Historical Evidence

The following discussion examines both historical and archaeological evidence for how removal affected two groups of Piscataway: those who left the Maryland colony and followed Tayac Othotomaqua northward in 1699 and those who remained in Maryland and lived among English settlers in a dramatically changing landscape.

Those Who Left

Comparative analysis of archaeological assemblages related to post-1680 Piscataway migrations allows us to examine diachronic change and to see how the Piscataways adjusted to new physical and social geographies after they were displaced from their homeland of "Piscatua." Although differences in excavation methods, analytical techniques, and level of detail in reporting for the related sites precludes direct quantitative comparisons, enough data are available to make observations regarding material change and continuity among the group. The sites we examined are Accokeek Creek/Moyaone (1300–ca. 1608), Posey (ca. 1660–1680), Zekiah Fort (1680–ca. 1692), Heater's Island (1699–1712), and Conoy Town (1718–1743) (figure 2.1).

The Accokeek Creek site, situated on the Potomac River near the mouth of Piscataway Creek, was a substantial Piscataway settlement that was occupied from the fourteenth century into the early seventeenth century (Stephenson, Ferguson, and Ferguson 1963). Sometime after 1608 but

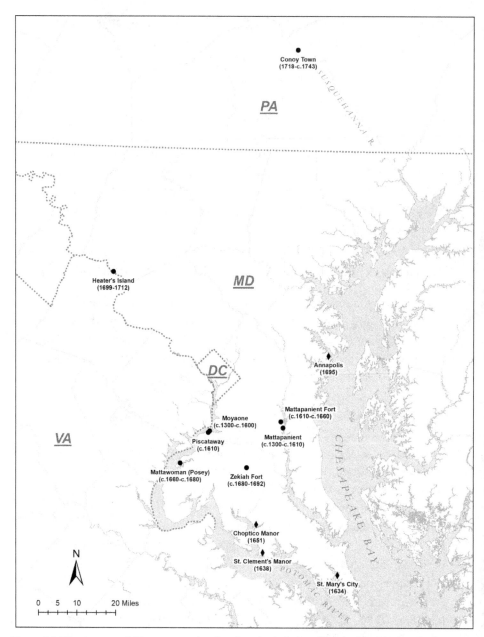

Figure 2.1. Piscataway and Piscataway-related archaeological sites discussed in this chapter. Image by Scott Strickland.

before 1634, the Piscataway moved further up Piscataway Creek to a more sheltered settlement. Although ossuaries containing mid-seventeenth century European material were later identified along Upper Piscataway Creek, the seventeenth-century settlement referred to as the Piscataway Fort has not been found (Curry 1999, 28–40; Ferguson and Stewart 1940). In the 1940s, avocational archaeologist Alice Ferguson excavated this site, the ancestral homeland of the Piscataway. Her methods of excavation have made it difficult to reconstruct artifact provenience and stratigraphy and it is not clear how much earth she moved in total.

The Posey site, located south of Piscataway Creek on Mattawoman Creek and believed to be home to the Mattawoman king or other elites in the period 1660–1680, may serve as a kind of rough proxy for the Piscataway Fort. In 1987 and again in 1996, archaeologists excavated a total of thirty-seven 1.5 × 1.5 meter units at the Posey site with limited feature excavation. In addition, archaeologists also collected and water-screened a 25 × 25 centimeter sample of the plow zone for each unit in an effort to recover beads and other small finds (Harmon 1999).

The Zekiah Fort site is located just south of Waldorf, Maryland, on the edge of Zekiah Swamp, which forms the headwaters of the Wicomico River. This site, located twelve miles southeast of Piscataway Creek, is the historically documented inland refuge where Lord Baltimore directed the Piscataway in 1680. In 2011, the authors, Scott M. Strickland, and Michael J. Sullivan identified the site, which contains a mix of typical Piscataway materials, ceramics associated with other groups, and European artifacts diagnostic of the fourth quarter of the seventeenth century. This evidence aligns well with the Piscataway abandonment of the site circa 1692–1695. Our team excavated forty-six 5 × 5 foot test units at the site, most of which consisted of a plow zone averaging about eleven inches in thickness overlying B-horizon subsoil, a common profile in the intensively farmed southern Maryland coastal plain. The team screened plow zone through 1/4-inch mesh and water screened a 1 × 1 foot sample from each unit through fine mesh (Flick et al. 2012).

The Heater's Island site, which the Piscataway occupied from 1699 to 1712, is situated in the Potomac River near Point of Rocks, Maryland, some fifty miles northwest of Piscataway Creek. After vacating Zekiah Fort and briefly settling in Virginia, some Piscataway erected a fort and cabins on the island, which was located a substantial distance away from colonial settlement. A team participating in a University of Maryland field school under the direction of Robert Schuyler identified the site in the 1960s. They excavated a total of 113 5-×-5-ft test units and screened plow zone through ¼-inch mesh. They also excavated pits, posts, and a long, trapezoidal trench-like feature believed to be the remains of a palisaded bastion (Curry n.d.).

The Conoy Town site is located in Lancaster County, Pennsylvania, roughly 100 miles north of Piscataway Creek. Conoy Town was occupied when several Piscataway migrated into Pennsylvania's Susquehanna Valley after leaving Heater's Island. Documentary evidence suggests that this settlement was occupied from about 1718 until 1743. Although artifact collectors had been aware of the Conoy Town archaeological site for decades, it was not professionally excavated until 1970, when Barry Kent of the Pennsylvania State Museum conducted work at the site. He stripped and shovel-scraped a large portion of the site's plow zone to subsoil and mapped pits, postholes, and burials before excavating them (Kent 1984).

The distributions of artifacts at these sites revealed a general decrease in the proportion of Native American–made ceramics and tobacco pipes over time (table 2.1). No materials of European manufacture were recovered at Accokeek Creek, and European ceramics and tobacco pipes were few in number at the Posey site (1660–1680). At Zekiah Fort (1680–ca. 1692), about 80 percent of the ceramics were made by Native Americans, but European ceramics formed a much larger portion of the assemblage than at earlier sites. European-produced clay pipes also outnumbered Native American–made counterparts at Zekiah. By the time Heater's Island was occupied (1699–1712), Native American–manufactured ceramics and tobacco pipes constituted a small minority of the artifact assemblage, and at Conoy Town (1718–1743), there is little evidence for vessels or pipes made by Native Americans. Closer analysis of the materials recovered from these sites suggests that territorial displacement, not assimilation or acculturation, influenced these material trends.

The majority of the ceramics recovered from Mattawoman and Zekiah Fort are Potomac Creek ceramics, a ware type that was tempered with crushed quartz and is commonly associated with the Piscataway and other Potomac Valley groups after 1300 CE (Egloff and Potter 1982; Potter 1993). At Heater's Island, both Potomac Creek–type and Camden-like (untempered) ceramics were recovered, although the Potomac Creek ceramics may be associated with an earlier Late Woodland occupation on the island (Curry n.d., 16). This means that the density of Native

Table 2.1. Decrease in the proportion of Native-made ceramics and tobacco pipes over time

	Posey (ca. 1660–1680)		Zekiah Fort (1680–ca. 1692)		Heater's Island (1699–1712)	
	Density/foot³	Count	Density/foot³	Count	Density/foot³	Count
Copper alloy projectile points	0.01	6	0.004	4	0.012	35
Native-made ceramics	4.4	2823	0.4	458	0.05	149
European-made ceramics	0.1	68	0.1	108	0.1	248
Native-made pipes	0.4	257	0.1	135	0.004	12
European white clay pipes	0.2	115	0.4	409	0.2	591
European flint debitage	0.1	92	0.4	369	0.02	47
Gunflints	0.003	2	0.01	13	0.01	31

American–made ceramics at Heater's Island may, in fact, be even lower than Table 2.1 shows.

The recovery of thousands of fragments of Native American–made ceramics from Posey along with what archaeologists have identified as ceramic wasters suggests a vibrant ceramic production economy that was probably driven by trade, including trade with Europeans (Hall 2012, 159–161). A similar pattern—large numbers of Native American–made ceramics and ceramic wasters—was observed at the Camden site, a mid- to late-seventeenth-century settlement on the south side of the Rappahannock River in Caroline County, Virginia (MacCord 1969). However, wasters were not found at Zekiah Fort or Heater's Island, both of which were extensively excavated. The trends revealed in table 2.1 and figure 2.1, then, suggest an interruption in ceramic production brought about by the relocation of Piscataway people to an area where knowledge of local clays was undeveloped. While data from Zekiah Fort indicate some limited continuation of Native American ceramic production, the numbers (in terms of both count and density) drop dramatically for Heater's Island. The greater numbers of untempered Camden-like wares at Heater's Island suggest that the precipitous decline in Native American ceramic production between the late seventeenth and the early eighteenth centuries was accompanied by a shift or experimentation in pot-making practices.

Both locally produced red clay tobacco pipes of Native American manufacture and European-made white clay tobacco pipes were recovered from all sites except Accokeek Creek, although in smaller proportions than at almost any contemporary, comparably excavated colonial site in Maryland. This suggests that Native American tobacco use may have continued for ritual rather than recreational purposes. However, red pipes were gradually replaced by white pipes. The latter predominated at Posey in the third quarter of the seventeenth century, but at Heater's Island in the early eighteenth century, they formed no more than a handful of fragments, and these few may be associated with the island's Woodland period occupation. Native American tobacco pipe production continued through the occupation of Zekiah Fort (although no wasters were recovered there), but their absence at Heater's Island suggests that Indians were no longer making tobacco pipes. European-made tobacco pipe fragments are present at Heater's Island in significant density, although they show a decrease relative to Zekiah Fort.

Quartz and quartzite debitage was present at Posey, Zekiah Fort, and Heater's Island. Quartz was the primary stone type used in the production of Potomac projectile points (1300–1700 CE) at the Accokeek Creek site (Stephenson, Ferguson, and Ferguson 1963, 145–146) and was among the most common materials found on Native American sites in southern Maryland (Wanser 1982). Significantly, however, European flint constituted the majority of stone debitage recovered from Zekiah Fort. The presence of flint debitage bearing remnant cortex (including some primary flakes) and some larger debitage suggests the possibility that Native Americans produced gunflints during this occupation. Although no flint cobbles or large core fragments were recovered, initial reduction may have occurred off site in coastal areas near English plantations, where European flint cobbles were often available as discarded ship's ballast. A 7:6 ratio of European-made gunflints (gunspall and French prismatic types) to Native American–made (bifacial and expedient type) gunflints at Zekiah contrasts with a 27:4 ratio at Heater's Island, suggesting a reliance on European-produced gunflints at the latter site. Although the plow zone density of gunflints is consistent at both sites, the density of flint debitage is significantly higher at Zekiah Fort than at Heater's Island.

Brass triangular points were present in the plow zone at Heater's Island at a density three times greater than at Zekiah Fort. Stone and brass points were produced contemporaneously at Posey and Zekiah. Three stone Madison points from Heater's Island may also indicate continuation of stone and brass point co-production; however, these points are more likely associated with an earlier occupation on the island. This same issue is also present at the Conoy Town site, where several Late Woodland stone points were recovered in addition to brass points.

In summary, there appears to have been a decline in traditional craft production following the move to Zekiah Fort and continuing after the Piscataway moved to Heater's Island. Based on sherd quantities and the absence of wasters, ceramic production declined sharply during these occupations. The manufacture of local clay tobacco pipes appears to have ceased entirely by 1700. Lithic data suggests that gunflints, which the Piscataway obtained through both Native American manufacture and colonial trade at Zekiah, were primarily obtained from European sources at Heater's Island. The decline of Native American craft production and increased use of European trade items should not be read as evidence of assimilation or acculturation. In fact, just the opposite was the case: even though English settlers harassed and displaced the Piscataway, prompting them to distance themselves from colonial settlements in the late seventeenth century, they continued to hunt in the traditional manner (presumably with bows and brass-tipped arrows) and to construct Native American–style cabins and tree-bark canoes. The Piscataway used traditional knowledge and skills to continuously adapt to colonial intrusion.

The decline of certain traditional crafts appears to have been a product of displacement. When they migrated, Piscataway individuals left a familiar homeland landscape and the accrued social knowledge it contained. While Zekiah Fort can be seen as the initial displacement of the Piscataway, the site was still within the group's larger coastal plain territory, and its resources would have been familiar to Piscataway families. However, the site was materially poorer than earlier "homeland" sites like Posey and Accokeek Creek. The 1699 migration to Heater's Island took the Piscataway from the familiar coastal plain to the junction of Maryland's Blue Ridge and Piedmont physiographic provinces. In this case, Piscataway migrants were not settling in a familiar environment. The move required the Piscataway to essentially re-create their home in a new landscape that did not have the accrued, localized knowledge of Moyaone and its territory. Their principal objectives after this migration were likely constructing shelter and securing a food supply rather than locating local clay or lithic raw material sources. Their use of European trade items may have initially been a pragmatic adjustment to the new landscape, a decision that probably intensified after a smallpox outbreak in 1705 killed fifty-seven Piscataway, likely stunting the transmission of craft production knowledge and technique.

Although apparent declines in traditional craft production suggest that the Piscataway adjusted how they created and re-created place in new landscapes, other lines of evidence are suggestive of practices that recalled the group's ancient home. At the cemetery of Conoy Town, which the Piscataway occupied from 1716 to 1743, archaeologists identified "71 interred packages or bundles of more or less disarticulated human skeletal remains" in 1970 (Kent 1984:392–393). Up to five bundles, in some cases packaged in fabric or skin bags (fragments of which were observed archaeologically), were present in a single pit. The differential decomposition of individual bundles within a single pit combined with the general lack of disturbance or evidence of pit reopening was interpreted as evidence for pre-burial decomposition of bodies in a charnal house or other location prior to burial. These small-scale, semicommunal burials are reminiscent of the larger, traditional ossuary burials of the Piscataway homeland (Curry 1999; Ferguson and Stewart 1940; Stephenson, Ferguson, and Ferguson 1963, 67–74). As Kent observes, however, true ossuary burial may not have been possible given the Conoy Town's smaller population and the shorter length of site occupation. Nonetheless, the similarities between the communal bundles at Conoy Town and earlier ossuaries in the homeland are suggestive of Piscataway attempts to re-create home in a distant place.

Those Who Stayed

The southern Maryland Native Americans who chose not to migrate out of the colony faced a very different displacement as English settlement and population growth brought dramatic changes to their homeland. Maryland's Indian reserves were intended to fix the Native American population in bounded space, thus opening what the English saw as unused land for settlement, even though Native American subsistence and social relations were based on seasonal mobility (King, Mansius, and Strickland 2016). The disposition and enforcement of reservation boundaries was subject to Maryland's colonial political upheavals. Beginning in 1695, royal governor Francis Nicholson actively attempted to dispossess the Piscataway and Pamunkey of their Potomac lands in order to boost tobacco production (Browne 1900, 282). Recognizing that earlier agreements guaranteed that the Piscataway would have access to reservation lands, Nicholson encouraged them to sell off their lands to the English as a remedy for boundary disputes (Browne 1899, 385). Nicholson also designated the Piscataway *tayac* the "commander" of all the Native Americans on Maryland's western shore (including the Pamunkey and the Choptico) and urged them all to relocate to live among the Piscataway (Rice 2009, 167; Browne 1899, 384–385). When the Piscataway *tayac* left the colony in 1697, however, those remaining were left with little voice or clout with colonial officials.

In the case of the Choptico, a tributary Piscataway group that lived along Choptico Creek, encroaching English settlement included a conflict with one colonist who demanded rent from the Indians and took "by Violence" some mats, bowls, and baskets (Browne 1899, 522). The encroaching English also destroyed the Choptico's sacred places. In 1707, an English colonist stole funerary goods from the Choptico "Queens Daughters Tomb" (Browne 1907, 29). These are just a few of the litany of complaints the Choptico made against their English neighbors (see King, Trussell, and Strickland 2014). Despite these issues, however, Choptico individuals appear to have maintained some place-making traditions in their homeland through continued production of objects such as bowls, mats, and baskets. Limited archaeological evidence from shovel-testing at the Choptico Indian Town site corroborates this, suggesting that manufacture of traditional ceramics continued at least into the early eighteenth century (King, Trussell, and Strickland 2014).

Anglo–Native American land disputes continued well into the eighteenth century, as the Indians who remained in southern Maryland in the 1730s continued to assert rights to reservation land. In one case, George Williams, the son of the queen of Pamunkey, argued that decades-old agreements with the colonial government guaranteed reservation lands that colonists were settling. Williams's primary dispute was with Charles Pye, although county court depositions list several others who had settled on reserved land. The 1733 deposition of 72-year-old John Ward indicates that the local Native Americans had maintained memory of the genealogy of the reservation land. Ward's deposition indicates that several Indians told him that before the king of Mattawoman died, he declared to his great men that he had given a reserved tract called Cornwallis Neck to the queen of Pamunkey.[2] Williams's complaint eventually came before the Governor's Council, which decided in Pye's favor in 1736 (Browne 1908, 93–96).

The George Williams case offers some of the best available insight on the eighteenth-century life of the Indians who remained in Maryland. Several county court depositions establishing Williams's claim of descent from the Pamunkey queen and vouching for his Indianness are suggestive of a shift in the relationship between the colonial government and the remaining Native Americans on the western shore. Davidson (1998) argues that in eighteenth-century Maryland, "Indianness" came to be seen administratively as a mutable, cultural category rather than a racial one. Indians were viewed as Indians so long as they outwardly acted in a way that met English expectations of Native American behavior or asserted treaty-granted rights. Otherwise, Indian individuals were de facto classified into the white/black/mulatto racial system.

Pye's complaint to the council indicates that Williams had adopted English animal husbandry practices, including keeping, grazing, and marking livestock (Cissna 1986, 206–207; Browne 1908, 95). Additionally, in Williams's initial petition to the county court, he indicated that he had received "the holy Sacrament of baptism according to the rights and Ceremonies of the Church of England."[3] The adoption of certain English customs may have been strategic as Native American groups displaced from or dispossessed of their lands historically used indigenized forms of European animal husbandry or religions to establish land claims (Cipolla 2011; Silverman 2003). However, the 1736 council decision seemed to indicate that the Maryland government would no longer protect the western shore reservation .

The migration of the political leadership of the Piscataway out of the colony and the atrophied relationship between western shore Native Americans and the colonial government left a politically displaced Native American population on the margins of English society. Changes in the landscape in the eighteenth and nineteenth centuries also furthered this displacement through the removal of the physical signs of the Native American past as Maryland's woodlands were transformed into agricultural fields. The widespread adoption of plow agriculture in the latter portion of the eighteenth century (Miller 1986) contributed to the reshaping of Native American places in the Chesapeake. The Rapidan Mound in Virginia, for instance, underwent substantial alteration as a result of plowing and looting that rendered this Native American landmark almost unrecognizable from its original form (Dunham, Gold, and Hantman 2003, 114–115).

At Moyaone, as at other Native American places, siltation of creeks and shoreline erosion began to reshape the Piscataway homeland. Alice Ferguson's archaeological work in the 1960s found that the stockade lines for the precolonial Piscataway town ran into the Potomac River, indicating that shoreline erosion had subsumed a substantial portion of the site. Likewise, the historic Piscataway fort on Piscataway Creek had largely vanished from the landscape by 1719, when local Englishman Francis Marbury described in a deposition that "the High hill w[hi]ch he shewed the Comiss[ione]rs near Piscattaway Creek is the hill topp on which the old Indian fort stood . . . [and] that the trenches belonging to the said fort were very fresh and visible in his time and memory" (quoted in Marye 1935, 209). Marbury also described a nearby stand of pine trees and brush that had formerly been an Indian field associated with the fort, "which in this Deponents time and memory had been full of sedge grass and clear of Brushes and trees" (quoted in Marye 1935, 210). Vegetative growth, erosion, and other natural forces contributed to the erasure of visible evidence of the indigenous landscape in southern Maryland when colonial policies forced the Piscataway to abandon these places.

Several other English practices effectively removed the traces of Maryland's Native American landscape. For instance, the English exploited many of the enormous shell mounds that had accrued through centuries of repeated visits to spots along the Potomac and Wicomico Rivers, including by the Piscataway, for use in lime kilns (e.g., Holmes 1907, 116, 121; Reynolds 1889, 256). English colonists also defaced Native American burials, as in the 1707 theft of grave goods from the "tomb" of the Choptico queen's daughter (Browne 1907, 29), part of a long-standing English practice of opening Native American graves that diminished visible markers of indigenous territories (Heany 2016, 644). As southern Maryland natives were displaced politically and spatially through colonial policies and English land tenure, the cultural shift in land use begin to erase the visible features of the Native American landscape.

Marginalization and dispossession of indigenous populations reshaped Native American relations with their homelands. Anthropologist Karen Blu (1996, 198) describes how Lumbee places in rural North Carolina had deliberately indistinct community boundaries to evade attempts by more powerful political or economic entities to control Indian affairs. She notes that a group's lack of control over the landscape often heightens social and community ties. While white society emphasized visual, bounded places in constructing the landscape, the Lumbee created meaningful places with blurry boundaries where "the unseen, the unmarked became a source of potential strength and resistance, an empowering counterconstruction" (Blu 1996, 218).

In southern Maryland, the family hunting unit emerged as an important form of social organization among the displaced Native American population, affording subsistence in marginal environments of the coastal plain (Porter 1980, 50). This arrangement physically and socially distanced Native American groups from the white population. Despite the efforts of English administrators to reclassify Maryland Indians into binary racial categories (Davidson 1998), twentieth-century anthropologists noted that the indigenous community in southern Maryland had developed a distinct social identity. Gilbert (1945, 244–245) notes, for instance, that the mid-twentieth-century Native American members of St. Ignatius Church in Port Tobacco, who sat in a separate section of the church, were buried apart from both white and black church members in the church's cemetery and celebrated seasonal events reminiscent of Indian customs.

While displacement relegated Maryland's remnant Native American population to marginal spaces within their homeland, ties to places that are important in indigenous history and cosmology persisted. Landscape changes stemming from forces of production and forces of nature may have blurred the boundaries of these places (to outsider's eyes) or removed their visible signs altogether. However, Piscataway memories of culturally meaningful places persisted through visitations and oral histories over centuries. The Indian man Swann, mentioned at the beginning of this chapter, recalled the apparently unmarked and "forgotten" location of the "old Indian Town" in Zekiah Swamp in the 1880s, nearly two centuries after the site had been abandoned (Reynolds [1883] 1968, 310–311). The location of this site was not confirmed by archaeologists until 2011, despite more than seventy-five years of efforts by several individuals and organizations. More recently, a Piscataway elder helped one of the authors identify the archaeological remains of the seventeenth- and eighteenth-century Choptico Indian Town based on an oral history about the name of an adjoining parcel that his great-great-grandmother, who was born at the town, had passed to future generations (King, Trussell, and Strickland 2014, 23).

Conclusion

By the mid-seventeenth century, Maryland government policies attempted to restrict mobile Native American populations to reservations or circumscribed villages so that productive lands could be freed for English settlement and cultivation. The delineation of reserved Indian lands did little to prevent the encroachment of English settlers and the resulting conflict with colonists. In 1695, Governor Nicholson advocated the usurpation of Native American reservation lands (Browne 1900, 282). Frequent harassment from colonists and a threatened subsistence compelled a large contingent of Piscataway to leave their ancient homeland and migrate north.

The effects of this displacement are archaeologically visible in the dramatic declines in Native American–made clay and stone items after migration. Producing pots, pipes, and stone points were routine acts of place making based on localized social knowledge. Such acts, repeated over time and space, created and recreated the Piscataway homeland by encoding memories and knowledge in the landscape for generations. The disruptive nature of displacement is evident in the diminished evidence for continued traditional craft production (ceramic pots, pipes, and stone tools) at Zekiah Fort, Heater's Island, and Conoy Town. New and unfamiliar environments draw into relief the limits of traditional knowledge and presented "new sets of possibility and constraint" (Cipolla 2014, 118). The Piscataway appeared to have adjusted to this through an increased reliance on European trade items. Despite this observation, documentary records indicate that other traditional practices, including hunting and wigwam and canoe construction, persisted long after initial displacement in 1680. Evidence from Conoy Town suggests that the Piscataway also continued to renegotiate their relationship to the southern Maryland homeland through mortuary practices that were reminiscent of their ancestors' practice of ossuary burial.

In southern Maryland in the eighteenth century, the Piscataway who remained on the margins of Anglo-American society in the homeland witnessed substantial environmental change, as their former towns, camps, and other places were subsumed in tracts of private property and were erased from the landscape by plows, lime kilns, erosion, and the acts of looters. These forces removed much of the visible evidence of Native American history in the landscape. In addition, Maryland authorities came to see "Indian" as a mutable characteristic, thus extending removal to identity (Davidson 1998). Despite the removal of the physical traces of the indigenous landscape, memories of culturally significant places persisted through acts of visitation and oral tradition by the Piscataway remaining in southern Maryland. These acts of memory resisted removal and preserved the ancestral Piscataway homeland.

Acknowledgments

The authors would like to express their appreciation to members of the Piscataway Indian Nation and the Piscataway Conoy Tribe of Maryland for their support. We are also grateful to Skylar Bauer, Gregory J. Brown, Edward E. Chaney, Dennis C. Curry, Paige Ford, D. Brad Hatch, Maureen Kavanagh, Maggie Lucio, Mary Kate Mansius, Alison Shepherd, Scott M. Strickland, and Michael J. Sullivan for their assistance with and support for this work.

Notes

1. The fall line is the geographic (and geological) break between the coastal plain and the Piedmont of the United States.

2. Charles County Court, Court Records, 1731–1734, MSA C658–631, p. 331, Maryland State Archives, Annapolis, MD.

3. Charles County Court, Court Records, 1731–1734, MSA C658–631, p. 331, Maryland State Archives, Annapolis, MD.

References Cited

Birch, Jennifer, and Ronald F. Williamson. 2015. Navigating Ancestral Landscapes in the Northern Iroquoian World. *Journal of Anthropological Archaeology* 39:139–150.

Blu, Karen I. 1996. "Where Do You Stay At?": Homeplace and Community among the Lumbee. In *Senses of Place*, edited by Steven Feld and Keith H. Basso, 197–227. Santa Fe, NM: School of American Research Press.

Bradley, Richard. 2003. The Translation of Time. In *Archaeologies of Memory*, edited by Ruth Van Dyke and Susan E. Alcock, 221–227. Malden, MA: Blackwell.

Browne, William Hand, ed. 1883. *Proceedings and Acts of the General Assembly of Maryland, January 1637/8–September 1664*. Archives of Maryland, vol. 1. Baltimore: Maryland Historical Society.

———. 1884. *Proceedings and Acts of the General Assembly of Maryland, April 1666–June 1676*. Archives of Maryland, vol. 2. Baltimore: Maryland Historical Society.

———. 1885. *Proceedings of the Council of Maryland, 1636–1667*. Archives of Maryland, vol. 3. Baltimore: Maryland Historical Society.

———. 1896. *Proceedings of the Council of Maryland, 1671–1681*. Archives of Maryland, vol. 15. Baltimore: Maryland Historical Society.

———. 1899. *Proceedings and Acts of the General Assembly, September 1693–June 1697*. Archives of Maryland, vol. 19. Baltimore: Maryland Historical Society.

———. 1900. *Proceedings of the Council, 1693–1697*. Archives of Maryland, vol. 20. Baltimore: Maryland Historical Society.

———. 1903. *Proceedings of the Council, 1696/7–1698*. Archives of Maryland, vol. 23. Baltimore: Maryland Historical Society.

———. 1907. *Proceedings and Acts of the General Assembly of Maryland, March 26, 1707–November 4, 1710*. Archives of Maryland, vol. 27. Baltimore: Maryland Historical Society.

———. 1908. *Proceedings of the Council of Maryland, April 15, 1732–July 26, 1753*. Archives of Maryland, vol. 28. Baltimore: Maryland Historical Society.

Cipolla, Craig N. 2011. Commemoration, Community, and Colonial Politics at Brothertown. *Midcontinental Journal of Archaeology* 36(2):145–171.

———. 2014. Resituating Homeland: Motion, Movement, and Ethnogenesis at Brothertown. In *Archaeologies of Mobility and Movement*, edited by Mary C. Beaudry and Travis G. Parno, 117–131. New York: Springer.

Cissna, Paul B. 1986. The Piscataway Indians of Southern Maryland: An Ethnohistory from Pre-European Contact to the Present. PhD diss., American University.

Creese, John L. 2013. Rethinking Early Village Development in Southern Ontario: Toward a History of Place-Making. *Canadian Journal of Archaeology* 37:185–218.

Curry, Dennis C. 1999. *Feast of the Dead: Aboriginal Ossuaries in Maryland*. Crownsville, MD: The Archaeological Society of Maryland, Inc. and The Maryland Historical Trust Press.

———. n.d. "We Have Been With the Emperor of Piscataway, at His Fort": Archaeological Investigations of the Heater's Island Site (18FR72). Ms. on file, Maryland Historical Trust, Crownsville, MD.

Davidson, Thomas. 1998. Indian Identity in Eighteenth Century Maryland. *Oklahoma City University Law Review* 23:133–140.

Dudley, Sandra. 2010. *Materialising Exile: Material Culture and Embodied Experience among Karenni Refugees in Thailand*. New York: Berghahn Books.

Dunham, Gary, Debra Gold, and Jeffrey Hantman. 2003. Collective Burial in Late Prehistoric Virginia: Excavation and Analysis of the Rapidan Mound. *American Antiquity* 68(1):109–128.

Egloff, Keith, and Stephen R. Potter. 1982. Indian Ceramics from Coastal Plain Virginia. *Archeology of Eastern North America* 10: 95–17.

Feld, Steven, and Keith Basso, eds. 1996. *Senses of Place*. Santa Fe, NM: School of American Research Press.

Ferguson, Alice L., and T. D. Stewart. 1940. An Ossuary near Piscataway Creek, a Report on Skeletal Remains. *American Antiquity* 6(1):4–18.

Flick, Alex J., Skylar A. Bauer, Scott M. Strickland, D. Brad Hatch, and Julia A. King. 2012. *"A Place Now Known Unto Them": The Search for Zekiah Fort*. St. Mary's City, MD: St. Mary's College of Maryland.

Gallivan, Martin D. 2007. Powhatan's Werowocomoco: Constructing Place, Polity, and Personhood in the Chesapeake, C.E. 1200–C.E. 1609. *American Anthropologist* 109(1):85–100.

———. 2012. Persistent Memories and Contested Heterotopias in the Native Chesapeake. Paper presented at the annual meeting of the Society for Historical Archaeology, Baltimore, Maryland.

———. 2016. *The Powhatan Landscape: An Archaeological History of the Algonquian Chesapeake*. Gainesville: University Press of Florida.

Gilbert, William H. 1945. The Wesorts of Southern Maryland: An Outcasted Group. *Journal of the Washington Academy of Sciences* 35(8):237–246.

Hall, Valerie M. J. 2012. These Pots Do Talk: Seventeenth-Century Indigenous Women's Influence on Transculturation in the Chesapeake Region. MA thesis, Illinois State University, Normal, IL.

Handsman, Russell G. 2008. Landscapes of Memory in Wampanoag Country—and the Monuments upon Them. In *Archaeologies of Placemaking: Monuments, Memories, and Engagement in Native North America*, edited by Patricia E. Rubertone, 161–193. New York: Left Coast Press.

Harmon, James M. 1999. Archaeological Investigations at the Posey Site (18CH281) and 18CH282. Prepared for Environmental Division, Indian Head Division, Naval Surface Warfare Center, Charles County Maryland. Report on file at Jefferson Patterson Park and Museum, St. Leonard, Maryland.

———. 2001. The Geographic Conditions of Contact: Native Americans, Colonists, and the Settlement Landscape of Southern Maryland, 1600–1695. PhD diss., University of Maryland, College Park.

Heany, Christopher. 2016. A Peru of Their Own: English Grave-Opening and Indian Sovereignty in Early America. *William and Mary Quarterly* 73(4):609–646.

Holmes, William Henry. 1907. Aboriginal Shell-Heaps of the Middle Atlantic Tidewater Region. *American Anthropologist* 9(1):113–128.

Ingold, Tim. 1993. The Temporality of the Landscape. *World Archaeology* 25(2):152–174.

Kammen, Michael G., ed. 1963. Maryland in 1699: A Letter from the Reverend Hugh Jones. *Journal of Southern History* 29:362–372.

Kelly, Kevin. 1979. "In Dispers'd Country Plantations": Settlement Patterns in 17th-Century Surry County, Virginia. In *The Chesapeake in the Seventeenth Century*, edited by Thad W. Tate and David Ammerman, 183–205. New York: W. W. Norton and Company.

Kent, Barry C. 1984. *Susquehanna's Indians*. Anthropological Series no. 6. Harrisburg, PA: Pennsylvania Historical and Museum Commission.

King, Julia A., Mary Kate Mansius, and Scott M. Strickland. 2016. "What Towne Belong Ye To?" Landscape, Colonialism, and Mobility in the Potomac River Valley. *Historical Archaeology* 50(1):7–26.

King, Julia A., Suzanne Trussell, and Scott M. Strickland. 2014. *An Archaeological Survey of Choptico Indian Town, Chaptico, Maryland*. St. Mary's City, MD: St. Mary's College of Maryland.

MacCord, Howard A., Sr. 1969. Camden: A Postcontact Indian Site in Caroline County. *Quarterly Bulletin of the Archaeological Society of Virginia* 24(1):1–55.

Marye, William B. 1935. Piscattaway. *Maryland Historical Magazine* 30(3):183–239.

Miller, Henry M. 1986. Transforming a "Splendid and Delightsome Land": Colonists and Ecological Change in the Chesapeake, 1607–1820. *Journal of the Washington Academy of Sciences* 76(3):173–187.

———. 2004. Archaeology of Colonial Encounters along Chesapeake Bay: An Overview. *Revista de Arqueologia Americana* 23:231–290.

Mills, Barbara J. 2008. Remembering while Forgetting: Depositional Practices and Social Memory at Chaco. In *Memory Work: Archaeologies of Material Practices*, edited by Barbara J. Mills and William H. Walker, 81–108. Santa Fe, NM: School of Advanced Research Press.

Pleasants, J. Hall. 1932. *Proceedings of the Provincial Court, 1663–1666*. Archives of Maryland, vol. 49. Baltimore, MD: Maryland Historical Society.

Porter, Frank W. 1980. Behind the Frontier: Indian Survivals in Maryland. *Maryland Historical Magazine* 75(1):42–54.

Potter, Stephen R. 1993. *Commoners, Tributes, and Chiefs: The Development of Algonquian Culture in the Potomac Valley*. Charlottesville: The University of Virginia Press.

Potter, Stephen R., and Gregory Waselkov. 1994. Whereby We Shall Enjoy Their Cultivated Places. In *Historical Archaeology of the Chesapeake*, edited by Barbara J. Little and Paul A. Shackel, 23–33. Washington, DC: Smithsonian Institution Press.

Reynolds, Elmer R. (1883) 1968. Memoir on the Pre-Columbian Shell Mounds at Newburg, Maryland and the Aboriginal Shellfields of the Potomac and Wicomico Rivers. In *Congrès International Des Américanistes: Compte-Rendu de la Cinquième Session, Copenhagen*. Nendeln, Liechtenstein: Kraus Reprint.

———. 1889. The Shell Mounds of the Potomac and Wicomico. *American Anthropologist* A2(3):252–259.

Rice, James D. 2009. *Nature and History in the Potomac Country: From Hunter Gatherers to the Age of Jefferson*. Baltimore, MD: John Hopkins University Press.

Silverman, David J. 2003. "We chuse to be bounded": Indian Animal Husbandry in Colonial New England. *William and Mary Quarterly*, 3d ser. 60:511–548.

Slattery, Richard G., and Douglas Woodward. 1992. *The Montgomery Focus: A Late Woodland Potomac River Culture*. Crownsville: Maryland Historical Trust.

Smolek, Michael A. 1984. "Soyle Light, Well-Watered and On the River": Settlement Patterning of Maryland's Frontier Plantations. Paper presented at the Third Hall of Records Conference, St. Mary's City, Maryland.

Stephenson, Robert L., Alice L. L. Ferguson, and Henry G. Ferguson. 1963. *The Accokeek Creek Site: A Middle Atlantic Seaboard Culture Sequence*. Anthropological Papers no. 20. Ann Arbor, MI: Museum of Anthropology, University of Michigan.

Strickland, Scott M. 2015. An Investigation of Two 1701 Land Transfers: John Accatamacca, also Known as Octomaquath, Emperor of Piscataway to Several Englishmen. Prepared for the Maryland Historical Trust. Ms. on file, St. Mary's College of Maryland, St. Mary's City, MD.

Strickland, Scott M., Virginia R. Busby, and Julia A. King. 2015. *Defining the Indigenous Cultural Landscape for the Nanjemoy and Mattawoman Creek Watersheds*. Prepared for the National Park Service, Chesapeake Bay, Annapolis, Maryland. St. Mary's City: St. Mary's College of Maryland.

Strickland, Scott M., Julia A. King, G. Anne Richardson, Martha McCartney, and Virginia Busby. 2016. *Defining the Rappahannock Indigenous Cultural Landscape*. Prepared for the National Park Service Chesapeake Bay, the Chesapeake Conservancy, and the Rappahannock Tribe of Virginia. St. Mary's City: St. Mary's College of Maryland.

Sullivan, Kristin M., Erve Chambers, and Ennis Barbery. 2013. *Indigenous Cultural Landscapes Study for the Captain John Smith Chesapeake National Historic Trail*. College Park, MD: University of Maryland.

Tayac, Gabrielle. 1999. "So Intermingled with This Earth": A Piscataway Oral History. *Northeast Indian Quarterly* 5(4):4–17.

Wanser, Jeffrey C. 1982. *A Survey of Artifact Collections from Central Southern Maryland*. Maryland Historical Trust Manuscript Series no. 23. Annapolis, MD: Maryland Historical Trust and the Coastal Resource Division, Tidewater Administration, Department of Natural Resources.

3

Mapping Chickasaw Removal

TERRANCE WEIK

> Mappings beckoned into being . . . do work in the world in thoroughly
> contingent ways through complex networks of knowledge, discourse, me-
> dia forms, technologies and networks of power and patronage.
>
> Rob Kitchin, Justin Gleeson, and Martin Dodge,
> "Unfolding Mapping Practices," 494

Since Paleolithic times, humans have been depicting landscapes on rocks
and other natural media (Utrilla et. al. 2009). Over the last 2,000 years,
maps have been a means of controlling access to land, structuring ex-
changes (e.g., rent or taxes), locating people, illustrating human land uses,
identifying resources, and tracking transportation routes (Smith 2007, 3).
For archaeologists, maps are one of the most popular means of present-
ing data and one of the most useful types of primary sources of evidence
(see Davidson 1986). Maps are members of a family of value-laden images
(Harley 1988, 278–279). They are products of collective beliefs, vehicles
for social relations, and politically valent artifacts. Maps are not simply
objective spatial knowledge. Like other sources, they contain errors and
biases that archaeologists and other scholars try to interpret and analyze
(Davidson 1986; Smith 2007). Maps can also be works of art, whether
as representations of propertied accomplishment or as representations of
refugees' memories (Shanaathanan 2015; Smith 2007, 84). For example,
the Chickasaw Nation's geospatial division won an award at an 2012 GIS
(geographic information systems) conference for their "Historic Map of
the Unconquered and Unconquerable Chickasaw People." This award-
winning image integrated iconography and themes ranging from colonialism to the Chickasaw astronaut who rode the space shuttle. The map

includes pre- and post-removal Chickasaw territories. The title of this map raises an important question: What would explain how Chickasaw people and their enslaved Africans moved from what became Mississippi to Oklahoma by the nineteenth century?

The goal of this chapter is to answer this question by exploring the cultural significance and social impact of historical and modern maps for both archaeologists and participants in the process of historic US "Indian removal." Maps of Chickasaw removal were created during processes that involved the clash of epistemologies, the exercise of rhetorics, the commodification of environmental features, and the forced transfer of land. These processes operated alongside the spiritual chaos, anguish, and physical toll that dispossession took on Native American people (Paige, Bumpers, and Littlefield 2010; see Akers 1999, 63). This chapter was written to help readers understand the materiality of maps and the roles that cartography played in human displacement.

A Synopsis of Chickasaw Cultural History

The Chickasaws had been living in southeastern North America for centuries before Europeans settled and colonized the area. Indigenous oral traditions and early chronicles place Chickasaw genesis in the north-central part of what is today the state of Mississippi. However, their origins, travels and influence reached over the Lower Mississippi River Valley and into what became Tennessee, Alabama, South Carolina, and Florida.

Archaeological research in these areas has documented the Chickasaws' emergence from precolonial Mississippian societies of antiquity and their association with sacred sites such as the Nanih Waiya mound. Starting in the sixteenth century, they went through centuries of transitions, shifting between clustered and dispersed settlements, settling along ridges and waterways of the Black Prairie region (e.g., Chiwapa Creek and the Tombigbee River). They traveled along centuries-old indigenous trails and invasive Euro-American routes such as the Natchez Trace, engaging in diplomacy, warfare, exchange, kinship networks, governance, and spiritual practices. Archaeological fieldwork and archival research has documented Chickasaw villages, summer and winter homes, corncribs, kitchens, yards, storage sheds, homes, burials, fences, croplands, hunting grounds, corrals, refuse pits, ballfields, battlegrounds, and workspaces (Atkinson 1985, 2004). Their heritage sites include locations such as Ackia, Yaneka, Big Town (Chokkilissa), Pontotoc, Pankitakili, and Buzzards Roost (Colbert's Ferry).

Ethnographic and archival research provides observations that constitute a synthetic model of the fundamental structuring relationships and social practices of the colonial and removal eras. Like their Choctaw neighbors, Chickasaws spoke a western variant of the Muskogean language family. Their primary organizing principles coalesced around exogamous totemic clans, local house groups, town affiliations, moieties (dualistic governing divisions of diplomacy and social order or war), and specialist societies (e.g., warrior sodalities) (Cegielski and Lieb 2011, 28–31). Ritual Chickasaw specialists provided healing, taught about cosmology, facilitated communication with ancestors and spirits, provided leaders with spiritual guidance, consecrated ceremonies, and officiated at rites of passage. Subsistence activities involved hunting, fishing, farming, and trade.

The Chickasaw population, which amounted to 6,000 or less during the colonial and removal periods, was the smallest of the major southeastern Native American societies. However, their communities had a regional influence that transcended their numbers.

They are famous for their martial skills, which they used against more numerous and better-armed colonial and indigenous wartime adversaries, particularly the French colonists and the indigenous Choctaws or Creeks. Their service to the English army and later the US army gained them important allies and sources of arms. Chickasaw diplomacy, networking, and long-distance exchange facilitated the flow of deerskins, slaves, guns, needles, cloth, and many other goods that Native Americans, Europeans, and Africans sought in what became the southeastern United States.

Maps are an important source of evidence for some of the historic generalizations that have been outlined above and the centuries of Chickasaw movements across the region. But before the cartography of Chickasaw removal can be analyzed, methodological considerations must be addressed that frame the alternative ways we can remap the Chickasaw's later experiences of migration and dislocation.

Archaeological Approaches to Maps

Maps are a central mode of archaeological knowledge production and truth claims (Kidder 2002; Smith 2007, 81). They are effective tools for relocating long-forgotten buildings and informing predictive human settlement models (Beaudry and Mrozowski 1988, 8; Weik 2009; Wood 1990). Typically, archived maps are used to interpret the historical context and landscape relationships of archaeological sites (Rotman and Nassaney 1997). Historical maps also can be used in conjunction with excavations as a means of delineating the relative scope of various landowners' impacts and shifts in land-use strategies (Beaudry 2002, 132–133, 136–137). The Ordnance Survey maps the UK created in the nineteenth century are popular sources. Archaeologists such as Wright (2015, 34) have laid them under feature maps to track the material integrity of ancient ditches, which were used as property boundaries over centuries.

Maps, along with censuses, have been important tools of colonial and modern state formations and nationalistic land and population control (Greene 2011, 54). Archaeologists have used US General Land Office maps to track precolonial Native American land impacts, changes in residence of indigenous people and settlers, and changing environmental cover (Peacock et al. 2008). Ironically, maps generated from the same system that mapped settlers' land claims and helped them legally take Chickasaw lands are the templates for modern United States Geological Survey topographic maps that are the primary means of spatial representation cultural resource managers use to reinscribe heritage on cartographic sources. Archaeologists and state officials in Oklahoma and Mississippi use these maps to document Chickasaw artifacts and historical place locations (Brooks 1996, 270; Morgan 1996, 27; Sims 2001, 10, 31).

Archaeological research in the Caribbean has been particularly attuned to the importance of archived maps. For instance, Delle's (1998, 2014) exploration of slavery and colonialism in Jamaica shows how the slaveholders' control of and capacity to represent space and capital were essential for their exercise of power over non-elite and enslaved people. Colonial maps have been used to link archaeological site locations with tax records (Armstrong, Hauser, and Knight 2009, 95). Armstrong and colleagues (2009, 106–107) note how tax records contradict maps of the island of St. John, showing how free Black people obtained land in regions that maps represent as undivided properties of previous large landholders. This interdisciplinary analysis of the changing status of St. John laborers (e.g., from enslaved to free) also showed the utility of GIS for linking maps with archaeological site features and other sources (e.g., photos) in an integrative heritage program. They also show how more recent plantation feature maps created with GPS can be used to rectify Historic American Building Survey architectural plan maps and older archaeological maps.

The archaeological approach I take to mapping Chickasaw removal weds anthropologists', historians', and geographers' theories of critical cartography and landscape practice. I emphasize the epistemology, rhetoric, representational dimensions, and materiality of maps. These themes guide my analysis of how archaeologists have used maps, how maps shape relationships between people, and how people and maps are engaged.

Maps invoke and derive from epistemologies shaped by experience, socialization, and cultural practice. My conceptualization of mapping draws on the idea of maps as dynamic, evolving iterations (Kitchin, Gleeson, and Dodge 2012, 482). I draw on Kitchin, Gleeson, and Dodge's (2012, 494) perspective: "mappings unfold through a plethora of contingent, relational and contextual practices and do diverse work in the world through discursive events and material sites in conjunction with other modes of communication (such as text, images, spoken word, interactive new media) and forms of practice (such as collaboration, presentation, publication, debate)." Following this approach to maps as practices, my goal is to track how archaeologists, indigenous people, settlers, government officials, and technicians co-created, used, and interacted with maps. For example, I will examine how surveyors re-created both the environment and the territorial imperatives of a political system (see Harley 1988, 278).

Maps are culturally specific epistemological statements that invite dialogues and debates about space and place. Over centuries, western maps and land survey sciences have desocialized space, reduced amorphous entities to linear images, disembodied viewers and landscape features, and concealed forces that represent and impose geographical order (Blomley 2003, 127). In contrast, Native Americans have produced their own maps, in oral or physical forms, that have been as much concerned with being in the land as with asserting territoriality (Zedeno, Hollenback, and Grinnell 2009, 106–132).

One particular locus for the social analysis of maps that follows is the discursive force, the cultural logic, and the human deployments of grids, central features of Cartesian and capitalistic mappings of earth and people (see Blomley 2003, 129). In the early twentieth century, proponents of a European or Asian origin for the grid plan pointed to archaeological findings at Mohenjo-daro and Rome. But more recent geographical and anthropological studies have shifted the focus away from single-source arguments for origins toward more nuanced analyses of how different cultures around the world have used grids (Low 2000). Grids are a central feature of the General Land Office maps and surveying behaviors I examine in this chapter in terms of how they affect the quality of our evidentiary sources and the ways they are used to enact forced displacement, reshape relationships with land, and reallocate resources.

I propose more interculturally inclusive handlings of place and space in this chapter through a consideration of the rhetoric of removal and place making. St. Jean's examination of Chickasaw cartographers on deerskin maps (ca. 1720s–1730s) suggests that they illustrate spiritual and social proximities, networks of international relations, and paths to political-economic resources (St. Jean 2003, 769–770). St. Jean's view of these maps as rhetorical strategies is another useful conceptual tool that encourages us to consider what new or nineteenth-century Chickasaw spatial practices influenced their relationships with maps, land, and material culture. If we set aside the issue of a map's authorial provenience and consider General Land Office maps as sites of contestation, it is possible to rethink the instruments and processes of removal with attention to subaltern powers to act (see Horning, this volume).

Black's study of rhetorics of removal suggests another way to examine maps of dislocation through considering Native American responses to and initiatives related to US nationalist ideologies. The rhetorical tools US authorities used to enact removal included some core ideas: erasure (e.g., viewing Native American lands as devoid of people and Native American people as devoid of civilization); paternalism; national territoriality (racially and culturally homogeneous); republican citizenship, which had to be demonstrated through transforming landscapes into geometrically ordered or agriculturally oriented built environments; and Eurocentric godly authority (Christianized destiny) (Black 2009). Finally, it is important to note Native American objections to US removal policies. This type of opposition compares well with other contemporaneous cases of colonial displacement, such as local protests against soldier-surveyors in nineteenth-century Ireland (Smith 2007, 88–89).

Tania Li's (2010) critique of the management of capitalism, dispossession, and indigeneity provides a methodology for looking at the microscale of settler and Chickasaw land claims in a way that challenges homogenizing macroperspectives on Native American removal. Li argues that scholars need to avoid essentializing indigenous views and initiatives that emerged as colonialism and modern state formation imposed land titling and partition in Europe, Africa, and Asia. Doing so deromanticizes representations of indigenous land use and landscape ideals. It also avoids overemphasizing the local movements that championed collectivist land holding and territorialism at the expense of ignoring subaltern actions that have attempted to work within the colonial systems or try capitalistic approaches.

Archaeological Analyses of Chickasaw Removal Maps

Chickasaw settlements and battles are visible in a few colonial period maps (e.g., Atkinson 1985, 2004, 53). In what follows, I examine US General Land Office maps of the nineteenth century, as they are some of the most readily available maps from archives, digitized archival sources, and virtual government repositories such as the Bureau of Land Management's General Land Office records website.[1] These maps were constructed to enable the removal of the Chickasaws, the imperialistic takeover of their land, and their resettlement from 1818 to 1850.

Pre-Removal General Land Office Plat Maps and Archaeology of Levi Colbert's Prairie, Mississippi

Newer research on a removal-era settlement at Levi Colbert's Prairie, located in northeastern Mississippi (Monroe County), illustrates the potential methodological and interpretive issues facing archaeologists who use historic maps. From 1816 to 1838, enslaved Africans and Chickasaw slaveholders resided at Levi Colbert's Prairie, tended crops, and cared for livestock (Weik 2013). In the 1830s, a US surveyor designated the place "Colbert's Prairie" and archaeologists have continued to use the label. Levi Colbert was one of the most influential forces in early nineteenth-century Chickasaw politics and economic activities (e.g. ferries). He was a powerful leader who had a major role in the Chickasaw Nation's negotiations with the US government concerning removal.

Levi Colbert's Prairie first appears on maps of Chickasaw cessions, some of the earliest US government maps of the area. Government officials saw the maps as a means to facilitate land sales and legal property ownership. Chickasaw removal was directly connected to expanding slavery-based economies, driven by US citizens who saw profits in new cotton fields on Chickasaw lands (Paige, Bumpers, and Littlefield 2010). The maps and accompanying surveyors' notes were part of a wider body of knowledge and discourse that informed the competing land claims of Native Americans and settlers (Walls 2015, 72–75, 140–146). These maps were constructed in the aftermath of treaty negotiations (e.g., the 1832 Treaty of Pontotoc Creek) as part of the General Land Office's national Public Land Survey System (Conover 1923, 5–22). Cession maps were constructed largely from surveyors' notes, observations about land forms, measurement points, vegetation, soil types, hydrological features, and cultural features (e.g., roads).

The locations of the artifacts found at Levi Colbert's Prairie help resolve a contradiction between the notes of US surveyor E. J. Bailey, and a Chickasaw cession map for Township 12, Range 6 East, that John Bell made in 1835. While the Chickasaw cession map locates Levi Colbert's house south of the nearest east-west-running section line, Bailey's surveyor notes place the house north of that same section line (figure 3.1). Most of the subsurface and surface finds marked with GPS (e.g., daub, brick, pottery, beads, bone, nails, and bottle glass) locate the habitation areas twenty or more meters west of where the surveyor's notes say a house was situated. Ground-penetrating radar (GPR) data collected from around this area, which suggests a rectanguloid feature at 9–18 centimeters below the surface, hints at another possible line of evidence that the house was where both artifacts and the surveyor's notes place it. However, subsurface testing needs to be done to confirm whether GPR data correlates with the presence of artifacts and soil residues of human activity. This example demonstrates how archaeologists must be sure to check the paper trail that accompanies maps and be aware of cartographic errors and interpretive biases (see Smith 2007, 84–85). On the other hand, archaeologists working on Chickasaw sites elsewhere note that surveyors' notes sometimes lack details that are present on maps (e.g., Brooks 1996, 272).

Surveyors' notes have proven themselves useful at Levi Colbert's Prairie in helping locate not only the position of settlement remnants but also other land features that are no longer visible. For instance, metal detecting was done in one area around where a surveyor's notes suggest that a nineteenth-century road crosses the closest north-south running section line. A horseshoe and chain links were found in this area. As with other parts of the world, road building was a major means of clearing paths

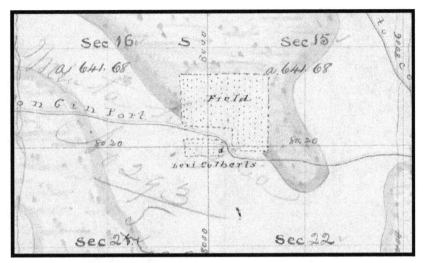

Figure 3.1. Levi Colbert Prairie Settlement on an 1835 U.S. "Chickasaw Cession" Map excerpt. Courtesy of the Bureau of Land Management.

for the flow of commodities, settlers, troops, and missionaries that advanced nation-states and colonies at the expense of indigenous people, poor squatters, and maroon societies. At the same time, roads were both Levi Colbert's pathways to profit (e.g., from his cattle) and the eventual routes of the removal of his kin and enslaved laborers.

As one moves from the regional-scale matter of settlement location to the local-scale issue of settlement configuration, questions arise as to what the Chickasaw land cession map and surveyor's notes are telling us and what they are silent about. Surface finds, artifacts detected with metal detectors, subsurface architectural remains, and recently excavated pits suggest that Levi Colbert's Prairie was not a compact homestead populated by a single dwelling or a barracks. It was most likely a multihome farm settlement whose material footprint covers nearly a hectare (figure 3.2). If that is the case, what would explain the lack of detail about other potential structures in the surveyor's notes? Was the surveyor simply focused on the few cultural and natural features that were relevant to property claims and the boundaries (e.g., section lines) of a grid system? And were the challenges of pulling chains and using a compass in this semiforested and partly marshy environment a further deterrent to detailed documentation of all major buildings? Alternately, was the surveyor engaged in a mode of documentary erasure? In other words, was he driven by male,

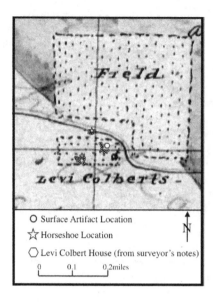

Figure 3.2. Surface finds and archivally identified nineteenth-century architecture at Levi Colbert's Prairie. Image by Terrance Weik.

elite, racist, or Eurocentric documentation biases that ignored the residences of non-elite Native Americans (who were not designated household heads like Levi Colbert) and enslaved people (see Gonzales, Kertész, and Tayac 2007)? Or did how the land was used change in the years after the survey was completed and create archaeological features that we have discovered? In other words, were other buildings (which are suggested by the artifacts and features we have found) and the larger settlement built after the surveyor had passed through on his documentation mission? Conversely, were buildings built, abandoned, and then demolished before the surveyor visited (1833), leaving no visible traces for him to map (see Brooks 1996, 272; Elliott and Wells 2003, 93–95)?

The first option, the surveyor deciding to document only what he saw as cartographically necessary and legally important features, seems more likely than the alternative explanations. It seems unlikely that Colbert and his agents or laborers would have made a major investment in constructing new buildings after the surveyor came through (1833–1837), in light of the fact that they knew that their imminent emigration would force them to leave behind valuable constructed assets. Further, a geographer's assessment of General Land Office maps in the region suggests that while cession maps are useful sources for general cultural landscape analysis, they lack significant attention to built environments and material culture (Walls 2015, 269). The geographer's study suggests a low correlation between previously discovered archaeological sites and cultural features on General Land Office maps (Walls 2015, 255, 264).

Although many surveyors were skilled in the science of land observation, different types of mapping errors were created for a variety of reasons, such as miscalculations by surveyors, the limitations of their survey and cartographic instruments, distortions caused by the aging and warping of map parchment, and errors introduced during map reproduction (Agnew 1941, 375; Bragg 2004; Davidson 1986, 28; Walls 2015, 18). Similarly, Peacock et al. (2008, 248) note how nineteenth-century surveyors of Mississippi had biases regarding environmental features. For instance, some surveyors avoided conifers with sticky sap. Finally, historians and geographers recognize that the US government's policy was to get lands mapped by the General Land Office to market as quickly as possible, as "proceeds from land sales [were] an important part of federal revenue" (Carlson and Roberts 2006, 489). Thus, it is likely that surveyors faced great pressure to facilitate this process (see Walls 2015, 152, 165). In fact, some surveyors were land speculators themselves (see Bragg 2004, 68–69).

What did Levi Colbert think about the process of removal that surveyors were participating in? The answer to this question is informed by historians' changing views of the Colberts and the removal period. Decades ago, historians viewed them as opportunists, who were profiteering from treaties. This activity coincides with Li's (2010, 400) concern with "dispossessory and accumulative practices of 'indigenous' elites and 'customary' authorities" in colonial situations around the world. Similarly, Levi Colbert benefited from treaties in the form of monetary compensation and land, as did other Chickasaw leaders. The US government paid Colbert $4,500 for the losses of Chickasaws who were displaced by land sales (St. Jean 2011, 11). We do now know to what extent he distributed the money to those who were dispossessed. More recent views of Colbert see him as either a resistant defender of Chickasaw interests or as someone who both enriched himself at the expense of his people and strongly advocated for the Chickasaws. By 1830, the Chickasaws were seeking to keep leaders in check by outlawing cash payments to their treaty representatives (St. Jean 2011, 11).

However, Colbert did attempt to protest and forestall removal through various means. His rhetoric in diplomatic meetings in the 1820s referred to ancestral ties to land: "We never had a thought of exchanging our land for any other, as we think that we would not find a country that would suit us as well as this we now occupy, it being the land of our forefathers" (quoted in Black 2009, 73). Yet by the 1830s, after the United States allowed the state of Mississippi to intervene in Chickasaw affairs and disregard their property and human rights, Colbert and others were more amenable to establishing terms for relocation. But even after he conceded that invading US military and political-economic powers were making removal inevitable, Colbert attempted to help the Chickasaws make the most of land sales by bargaining hard for the best price and structure of land compensation for the Chickasaw Nation.

Postremoval Chickasaws at Novotny, Oklahoma

Postremoval Chickasaw maps and archaeological sites are just as relevant to our inquiry as pre-removal sites. Unfortunately, Brooks's (1996, 265) decades-old observation that archaeologists have not given adequate attention to postremoval Chickasaws still rings true. Novotny, a site the federal Works Progress Administration originally excavated in the 1940s, is one of few excavated Chickasaw sites in Oklahoma. A few neighboring sites were examined as part of a project that discovered middens and graves (Brooks 1996). The assemblage at Novotny consisted of refined earthenware pottery, faunal remains, lithics, bottles, artifacts for preparing and consuming food (e.g., a coffee mill), metal items (e.g., knives), and pipes.

The handmade pots used at Novotny, which are similar to southeastern colonowares, are striking evidence that ceramic skills persisted through the forced migration (figure 3.3). This is no small feat in light of the way that removal to a new location disrupted intergenerational knowledge tied to material culture production, such as the location of raw materials (see Flick and King, this volume). Chickasaw potters who were forced to relocate to Oklahoma would have had to exert effort to discover new environmental resource banks, such as clay outcrops. Low-fired earthen pottery is also present in Levi Colbert's Prairie and the few other nineteenth-century Mississippi settlements that have been investigated to date.

Removal also impacted the Chickasaws' acquisition of European-made dishes in ways that implicated local pottery production. For instance, the geographic location of postremoval Chickasaw settlements in relation to the Choctaw who preceded them in that part of Oklahoma is

Figure 3.3. Locally made cup excavated from Novotny. Courtesy of Sam Noble Oklahoma Museum of Natural History, the University of Oklahoma. Photo by Terrance Weik.

part of Brooks's explanation for why local handmade pottery outnumbered imported ceramics in the ceramic sub-assemblage at Novotny; the Chickasaw lived in an area that was farther down the line on regional trade routes. In other words, the Chickasaw in this area may have relied more on their indigenous pottery because of the lower availability of imports that resulted from their remoteness from traders and supply chains. In contrast, their Choctaw neighbors were likely to buy more and better factory-made ceramics because they were advantageously positioned to see the traders before the Chickasaw did.

General Land Office plat maps are the earliest archival evidence for buildings at the Novotny archaeological site. Domestic artifacts were located where the square icons near the center of section 7 suggest that Novotny's buildings, including a "deserted house," were located (figure 3.4). Land patent books indicate that in 1906, Lulu Kemp was the earliest Chickasaw resident to officially claim the land where the site is located.

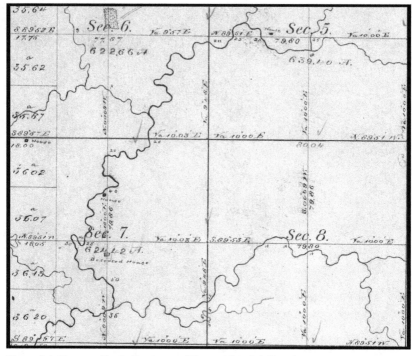

Figure 3.4. Novotny Site in Section 7 of General Land Office plat map excerpt. Courtesy of the Bureau of Land Management.

Brooks suggests that the 1870 General Land Office plat map provides evidence that the same family may have occupied the land since the Chickasaw were removed from areas east of the Mississippi River around 1837. Brooks (1996, 273) also explores the social ties that Lulu Kemp had with neighbors based on their shared surnames: he suggests that patent recipient Jemima Kemp, whose land was ½ mile north of Novotny, was kin to Lulu Kemp.

A number of caveats apply to Brooks's assessment of the Novotny site. Although his interpretation is clearly provisional, it lacks an accounting of the frequency of postremoval migrations to the area and a full set of criteria for establishing the residential duration of the Kemps or other families (or individuals) in the area. Brooks points out that a Choctaw family that received a patent at the same time as the Kemps lived just three miles to the east. The fact that the Choctaw had removed to this region (from Mississippi) before they agreed to turn over this area to Chickasaws raises questions about the strength of an ethnically exclusive interpretation of

Novotny. Census documents provide more clues about the sociocultural complexity of local groups. For instance, the Dawes rolls list Choctaws with the Kemp surname, possibly indicating family ties across cultural lines. The Dawes rolls were created as part of the execution of the General Allotment Act, (also known as the Dawes Act for its vocal supporter, member of Congress Henry Dawes). This legislation was part of the US campaign to destroy indigenous governments, assimilate people designated as Indians, and extinguish communal land ownership through individual land allotments (Krauthamer 2013, 141).

Other descendants of Native Americans who were removed from the southeast hint at twentieth-century indigenous discourses on land and dispossession. For example, Dewitt Duncan (a Cherokee) expressed his outrage about the Dawes Act and Euro-American double standards by pointing out how the US government would never send "survey compan[ies]" to divide the "earth into sections," "annullying all title" in states with white majorities, the way they did to Native American lands in Oklahoma. Duncan's statement was made before a US senate committee during the same year that Lulu Kemp's land patent was finalized (quoted in Black 2015, 134). Duncan and like-minded indigenous peers protested a variety of factors that separated Native Americans from their homes, including land speculators' unscrupulous deals, indigenous people's misunderstandings about what legal documents meant, and Native Americans' need for money in a cash economy.

While maps may have served as a means of erasure in the past, more recent maps produced by Native American organizations have used cartographic countermeasures. For instance, the Chickasaw Nation's (Oklahoma) Geospatial division has constructed a *Map of Chickasaw Treaty Cessions & Removal Routes of Chickasaw Indians* that not only includes ancient settlements but also large areas encompassing trade routes and hunting grounds.[2] This significantly redefines the scope of their pre-removal homelands and challenges Euro-American, US, and state (e.g., of Mississippi) maps that circumscribe Chickasaw territory more narrowly.

A Microhistorical Anthropology of Pre-Removal Land Competition

A final example of the role of maps in removal involves the ways the General Land Office and its agents managed and accommodated the claims of settlers and Chickasaws to land twenty miles southeast of Levi Colbert's

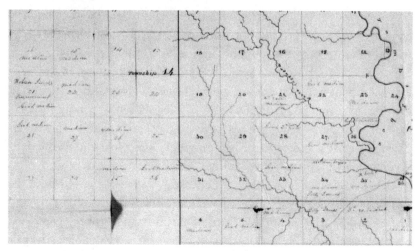

Figure 3.5. US plat map attached to letter from Benjamin Reynolds to Lewis Cass, August 28th, 1835. Courtesy of National Archives and Records Administration.

Prairie (Monroe County, Mississippi). The power of grids, the way dispossession was managed, and the rhetoric of land claims is visible on a General Land Office plat and documents related to a dispute involving at least four parties who struggled to own section 35 of Township 14 South, Range 7 East (figure 3.5). Letters exchanged between Indian Agent Benjamin Reynolds and an unnamed superior in the US War Department (September 1835) will serve as a point of departure because they briefly summarize the main claims on section 35.[3] Other evidence that is part of US Indian Affairs records will be brought in to explain the outcome and illustrate what it says about the rhetorics of Chickasaws, settlers, and US government officials.

According to the Treaty of Pontotoc Creek and other agreements the US government and the Chickasaws negotiated from 1816 to 1834, factors such as the number of household members and the number of enslaved residents in a household determined how many sections (each of which was one square mile of land) were allocated to household heads. The logic of the grid that was used to create the General Land Office plat maps also shaped US land allotment procedures. People were given whole or part sections, always in square or rectangular portions of the Public Land Survey System grid. Chickasaw clan or house-group lands were disconnected as the area was rectilinearly partitioned, creating a need for the Chickasaw to develop different travel routes and renegotiate how they used and accessed land (e.g., for subsistence or spiritual rites).

The Chickasaw candidate who claimed section 35 was Roberson James. James was a bicultural Chickasaw (his mother was Chickasaw, and his father was English) who was the grandson of Levi Colbert. Benjamin Reynolds's letter to the War Department stated that as the head of a household and a slaveholder, James was entitled by treaty to 2½ sections of land.[4] Reynolds argued that James's claim to section 35 was invalid because the treaty did not guarantee him the option of a "reservation" that was contiguous to his mother's land. Moreover, Reynolds argued that James had to choose sections that included land he already "improved." Reynolds sent the War Department a draft plat map containing three townships that features "Robinson James improvements" in section 21 of neighboring Township 14, Range 6 East.[5] These improvements are over 8 miles northwest of section 35 (figure 3.5). The US surveyor's notes indicate that the environment on the section lines around the edges of this improved land was "2nd rate prairie" that was swampy in areas. The surveyor also noted that indigenous trees such as black oaks, post oaks, and blackjacks were growing on this land. Neither the surveyor notes nor the map specifies whether the noted improvements indicated land cleared of trees, land that had buildings on it, or some other form of modified environment. So it is puzzling why a generic but explicit notation for improvements would be listed on Reynold's draft map and not in the official surveyor's notes (see Walls 2015, 225, 244). But the surveyor was half a mile from the center of the section, so it is possible that the improvements existed out of his sight or were in areas obscured by vegetation. But who else would have been in a better position to observe them? Did Roberson James communicate these improvements to the surveyor or to Reynolds or the map maker?

The second contender for section 35 was Richard Humphries, "a white man married to a Chickasaw woman."[6] A letter from Reynolds to Lewis Cass, head of the War Department (which oversaw the General Land Office), described Humphries's "settlement on sections 34 & 35" and noted that by November 1834 Humphries had cultivated 50 acres of crops in section 35.[7] Benjamin Reynolds's letter to the War Department denied Humphries's claim by referring to the 1834 treaty, which allotted the land to someone else.[8] The farmland that Humphries tended, one of the hallmarks of ideal republican citizenship, failed to gain rhetorical traction in this US land claim process. This illustrates how the exercise of Eurocentric land use was not always enough to secure a claim, as treaties between two (allegedly) consenting national powers could override individual demonstrations of prior settlement and agriculture.

William Cooper and James Davis's claim on section 35 was not given much explanation outside of Reynolds's reiteration that under article 10 of the 1832 Treaty of Pontotoc Creek, they were assigned one section that could not interfere with "Indian reservations."[9] The 1834 US-Chickasaw treaty granted one section "jointly to William Cooper and James Davis, lawyers of Mississippi who have been faithful to the Indians, in giving them professional advice, and legal assistance, and who are to continue to do so, within the States of Tennessee, Alabama and Mississippi, while the Chickasaw people remain in said States" (Kappler 1904, 421).

Robert Gordon's claim to section 35 was given preference over all the other "floating claims," according to Benjamin Reynolds's September 1835 letter to the War Department.[10] Gordon was an immigrant from Scotland who had married a resident of Cotton Gin Port. He became a successful merchant at his various regional stores and a skilled speculator who profited nicely from the Chickasaw land cessions (Elliott and Wells 2003, 83, 100). Reynolds's letter to the War Department quoted the (unnamed but likely US) attorney general regarding the 1832 and 1834 treaty provisions. Reynolds confirmed Gordon's right to locate anywhere in the Chickasaw cession that did not interfere with land that the Chickasaws or any other person had claimed, inhabited, or occupied. On one level, the language of land allocation that the attorney general used confirmed the power of treaties to regulate choice and access. But why would the attorney general rule in Gordon's favor with regard to section 35 specifically? An argument could be made for political favoritism. Gordon had extra leverage because he had established a business partnership with John Bell, the US surveyor general (Elliott and Wells 2003, 100). It remains to be seen if John Bell was any relation to deputy surveyor James H. Bell, who approved the survey notes for section 35. But as the following treaty excerpt suggests, Gordon's leverage was also built on economics: it was part of bond note that he agreed to take on from James Colbert, a Chickasaw. Colbert issued the bond to fellow Chickasaw debtors. According to the 1832 Treaty of Pontotoc Creek:

The Chiefs of the nation represent that they in behalf of the nation gave a bond to James Colbert for a debt due to him, of eighteen hundred and eleven dollars, ninety-three and three fourth cents principal, that James Colbert transferred said note to Robert Gordon and that said note, and the interest thereon is yet due and unpaid, and the said Robert Gordon has proposed to take a section of land for said note, and interest up to this date. It is therefore agreed by the nation to grant him a section of land, to be taken anywhere in the nation, so as not to interfere with any reserve which has been provided as a residence for the Chickasaws, which shall be in full for said note and interest. (quoted in Kappler 1904, 363)

Debts to merchants were a common justification that the colonial powers in what became the United States used to rationalize or legitimate claims on indigenous lands. From the perspective of a merchant or a lender, compensation for goods or loans was crucial to the integrity of the economic system.

In an August 1835 petition letter to Lewis Cass, Roberson James invoked a republican notion of the ownership and improvement of section 35.[11] James declared that he had had trees "deadened" (cut by his enslaved laborers) and had had his initials carved into trees that were left standing. James employed the trope of improvement, a central component of the ideology of nineteenth-century US republicanism. Ironically, James's mission education equipped him to work the removal system while at the same time arguing for a Chickasaw alternative and criticizing the justness of US land rights. For instance, James protested the amount and location of land that was available to indigenous people, arguing that the US policy of allocating only sections (or fractions) in one location conflicted with the common practice of "natives" in "the [Chickasaw] nation" of having land in two locations. More research is necessary to see if James's argument that it was the policy of Indian agents to recognize multi-location Chickasaw claims is supported by evidence. James also pointed to the problem he saw involving Cooper and Davis, lawyers whom the treaties rewarded with land for protecting "Indians' rights." James argued that the lawyers were violating his rights by taking land that he saw as his possession.

For Roberson James, the issue was as much about place and residence as it was about property.[12] Reynolds's letter to Lewis Cass stated that James had been living on section 35 since the "later part of winter" of 1835.[13] Roberson James's claim on section 35 was also based on the rationale that this land was adjacent to sections selected for his mother, where he had grown up. Thus, his claim could be seen as an assertion of nostalgia for Roberson's birthplace, his home space (see Battle-Baptiste 2011). One might also wonder whether James hoped to persuade officials by appealing to the sanctity of the mother-son bond. It might have also been driven by a notion of security or labor cooperation that could be gained from kin-based co-residence or proximity in rural or frontier environments.

As the Chickasaw were historically matrilineal, it is also possible that Roberson was leveraging a mode of rhetoric consistent with indigenous kinship or matrilocality. James's mother, Charlotte "Lotty" James, was Levi Colbert's daughter. Lotty's house and two sections (west and southwest of section35) are marked on the map and affirmed by the final US land patent she was granted (figure 3.5). She also received a patent on section 34, which effectively removed Richard Humphries from that land.

Examining Reynolds's draft plat map as an artifact (see Smith 2007) opens up more possibilities for interpretation.[14] One possible line of inquiry could examine whose agency is behind the pen that put the name "R. James" on section 35 of the draft plat map (figure 3.5). No other person with the surname James is listed in Reynolds's letter to the War Department, which describes contenders for section 35.[15] So it is possible that Reynolds, another administrator, or a surveyor saw a justification for listing James in section 35. Alternately, a map draftsman could have used his personal knowledge or the observations of an acquaintance to guide the addition to the map (see Walls 2015, 244). More archival research may reveal whether James lobbied the cartographer or an official to place his name on the map. In the end, Roberson James's US land patents suggest that he fared well. Even though he did not get section 35, he claimed Section 36 and Sections 1 and 2 of Township 15, adjacent to his mother's lands.

Another burning question is why section 35 was so coveted. From an economic perspective, it was an alternative port on the Tombigbee River that could build on the success of nearby towns such as Cotton Gin Port. It emerged to serve the growing demand for transportation infrastructure to move crops and livestock and to facilitate the flow of settlers and their wider trade networks. An affidavit from a settler named Moses Collins supported Roberson James in his land dispute with Robert Gordon.[16] Collins's affidavit statement, given under oath, declared that Roberson lived on section 35 by 1830, that a man enslaved by James "deadened timber" and carved James's initials on a beech tree, and that he knew that the claims of the widow James (Roberson James's mother) did not conflict with those of her son. However, Robert Gordon's land patent (#417) is proof that he prevailed by 1836, despite James's support in affidavits that settlers and Chickasaws submitted.[17] Gordon's patent is one reason why he can be credited with the founding of what has become the city of Aberdeen, Mississippi. The modern town extends westward and eastward from section 35.

Further Questions, Future Research

Many contradictions and questions remain that further complicate our understanding of the removal process. For instance, removal didn't just involve the displacement of Chickasaws from their territory. US troops removed some white settlers who flooded into Native American lands ahead of US approval, before they had legally purchased property. This form of squatting has provided an archaeologist with the opportunity to study US military establishments such as Fort Hampton, Alabama (1809–1816). Fort Hampton exhibits characteristics (e.g., less defensive features) that are different from other regional forts (e.g., Fort Mitchell). Fort Hampton was built to protect white settlers and regulate Native American activity (Chandler 2014, 25, 95, 100; Chase 1974).

Some Chickasaws benefited from the (short-term) removal of other Chickasaws. Affidavits sent to the War Department on behalf of Roberson James suggest that other Chickasaws, kin, and settlers all approached his family, the nearest residents, about claiming section 35. Roberson James's petition asking Lewis Cass to intervene regarding his claim to section 35 mentions that he abandoned his claim to other lands in the vicinity. This could be the reason why another Chickasaw, Imnubby, who received US land patent 408, claimed section 21 (figure 3.5), 8 miles west of section 35, the area containing Roberson James's former "improvements."[18] Did James encourage Imnubby to claim section 21? Or was it like other cases where the US government removed Chickasaws from land allocated to other Chickasaws (Kirk Perry, personal communication, December 28, 2015)?

Another set of issues that archaeologists of Chickasaw removal will have to address are the points of travel, provisioning, and rest along the literal Trail of Tears. Before the forced Chickasaw exodus, parties of

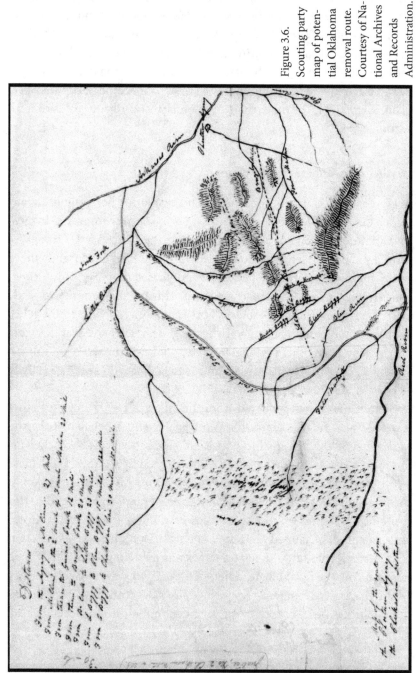

Figure 3.6. Scouting party map of potential Oklahoma removal route. Courtesy of National Archives and Records Administration.

leaders, including Levi Colbert, visited prospective relocation lands in Oklahoma (e.g., in 1828). Some of these maps list key landscape features such as Clear Boggy River from which removal stopover points such as Boggy Depot derived their name (figure 3.6) (Wright 1927). Boggy Depot contains surface artifacts that could be the focus of future removal archaeology (Kirk Perry, personal communication, December 28, 2015). Some maps leave sparse but informative snapshots of the trails Chickasaw scouting parties and their accompanying US agents took.

Figure 3.6 and the field notes from the Bureau of Indian Affairs that accompany it focus on primary travel paths, barriers (e.g., rivers), soil quality, potential pasturage for migrating livestock and horses, and the distances that separated stopover points. These issues remind us that removal to reservations was a process, not a single journey. It is parallel to twenty-first-century forms of human removal such as the deportations from Somalia featured in Peutz's (2006) ethnography, which involve troubling illegalities, a web of profiteers, flexible and low-cost staging points (for human containment and transport), traumatic (dis)embodying experiences, and various forms of violence. Chickasaws, like other Native American groups, moved to Oklahoma territory in search of protection from alienated western indigenous people and Texas settlers. They also sought sovereignty in the face of the attempts of the US government to merge them with neighboring Choctaws (old kin and enemies). Because vivid descriptions exist for some staging points of Chickasaw removal, archaeologists may one day recover remnants of the materiality of these dislocating migrations.

Conclusion

The investigation of Levi Colbert's Prairie, lands claimed by the James family, and the Kemp homesteads of Oklahoma point to the potential uses of maps, archival texts, and archaeological finds to help illustrate removal. Because the archaeology of Chickasaws in the nineteenth century is still in an early stage of development, much remains to be learned about the materiality of forced human displacement and changes in the relationship between people and land. My analysis has shown that the archival record is as subject to criticism and interpretive challenges as the archaeological record. Maps were artifacts and tools of removal, institutional mediators of land management, and bases for intercultural and interpersonal contention.

The material effects of forced relocation I have mentioned in this chapter parallel what happened in other groups such as the Seminole, whose members continued to make and use indigenous handmade pottery after removal (Quimby and Spoehr 1950). More research is necessary to understand how long these traditions continued west of the Mississippi River. It remains to be seen if the tempo and scale at which locally made potting disappeared from Chickasaw communities in Oklahoma was similar to what happened among other indigenous groups such as the Piscataway (see Flick and King, this volume) or among African American colonoware producers. Cultural practices such as Green Corn rites, which involved the destruction of worn baskets and pottery as part of the cleansing and purification rituals, constitute one challenge to studying pottery. Despite these examples of disrupted material heritage, it is important to note that Chickasaw descendants are revitalizing potting and other crafts and are passing relearned skills to young people. The legacies and rediscovery of potting practices are being transmitted across the modern Chickasaw Nation and the world via the Internet and heritage programs.[19]

Perhaps Lotty and Roberson James's Mississippi homelands or their postremoval destinations will one day be explored through archaeological and archival research. While Levi Colbert died before the Trail of Tears, he participated in expeditions that explored potential relocation lands in Oklahoma where the James family and others removed to. That type of expedition has produced a body of primary evidence that illustrates removal. His wife and enslaved Africans did make it to Oklahoma, a fact that is evident in photos and documentary sources. My examination of postremoval Native Americans shows us that they were not relocated to culturally homogenous territories, even when their natal ethnonational group governed the postremoval region.

Cartographers, historians, chroniclers, and archaeologists are showing us that removal was not a single event. It was a series of negotiations, conflicts, explorations, and projections that played out over various landscapes. My discussion suggests that competition for property and the management of land claims was not simply a top-down process, even though it was heavily pushed by nationalistic US forces. At times, settlers aided Chickasaws in their land claims against other settlers. In the final analysis, Chickasaws borrowed from Euro-American ideology and employed their own forms of rhetoric to pursue their interests before, during, and after removals.

Notes

1. U.S. Department of the Interior Bureau of Land Management, General Land Office Records, http://www.glorecords.blm.gov/default.aspx.

2. *Map of Chickasaw Treaty Cessions & Removal Routes of Chickasaw Indians,* Voices: Native People's Concepts of Health and Illness, https://www.nlm.nih.gov/nativevoices/ assets/timeline/000/000/307/307_w_full.jpg.

3. Benjamin Reynolds to War Department, September 29, 1835, National Archives Chickasaw Agency, 1824–1870, Letters Received by the Office of Indian Affairs, 1824–1881, Record Group 62 (hereafter RG 62), National Archives and Records Administration, Washington, DC (hereafter NARA), Microfilm Publications no. 234, Roll 136, Frames 710–712.

4. Reynolds to War Department, September 29, 1835.

5. Map transmitted by Benjamin Reynolds on claim of Robert Gordon and R. James, September 1835, RG 62, NARA, National Archives Microfilm Publications no. 234, Roll 136, Frames 713–714.

6. Benjamin Reynolds to Lewis Cass, War Department, August 28, 1835, RG 62, NARA, National Archives Microfilm Publications no. 234, Roll 136, Frames 706–708.

7. Reynolds to Cass, August 28, 1835.

8. Reynolds to War Department, September 29, 1835.

9. Reynolds to War Department, September 29, 1835.

10. Reynolds to War Department, September 29, 1835.

11. Roberson James to Lewis Cass, War Department, August 5, 1835, RG 62, NARA, National Archives Microfilm Publications no. 234, Roll 136, Frames 721–727.

12. James to Cass, War Department, August 5, 1835.

13. Reynolds to Cass, August 28, 1835.

14. Map transmitted by Benjamin Reynolds, September 1835.

15. Reynolds to War Department, September 29, 1835.

16. Moses Collins, affidavit statement given to D. H. Morgan, August 1835, RG 62, NARA, National Archives Microfilm Publications no. 234, Roll 136, Frame 737.

17. U.S. Land Patent #417, granted to Robert Gordon, October 19, 1842, U.S. Department of the Interior, Bureau of Land Management, General Land Management Records, https://glorecords.blm.gov/details/patent/default.aspx?accession=MS2720__.417&doc Class=STA&sid=bloyz05k.skv#patentDetailsTabIndex=1; Moses Collins. affidavit statement given to D. H. Morgan, August 1835, RG 62, NARA, National Archives Microfilm no. 234, Roll 136, Frame 737.

18. U.S. Land Patent #417, granted to Imnubby, November 9, 1842, U.S. Department of the Interior, Bureau of Land Management, General Land Management Records,https:// glorecords.blm.gov/details/patent/default.aspx?accession=MS2720__.408&docClass=S TA&sid=3qzathky.qgz#patentDetailsTabIndex=1.

19. "Pottery," *Thrive*, Season 1, Episode 1, https://www.chickasaw.tv/episodes/thrive
-traditions-season-1-episode-1-pottery.

References

Agnew, Dwight L. 1941. The Government Land Surveyor as a Pioneer. *Mississippi Valley Historical Review* 28(3):369–382.

Akers, Donna L. 1999. Removing the Heart of the Choctaw People: Indian Removal from a Native Perspective. *American Indian Culture & Research Journal* 23(3):63–76.

Armstrong, Douglas V., Mark Hauser, and David Knight. 2009. Variation in Venues of Slavery and Freedom: Interpreting the Late 18th Century Cultural Landscape of St. John, Danish West Indies Using an Archaeological GIS. *International Journal of Historical Archaeology*. 13(1):94–111.

Atkinson, James R. 1985. The Ackia and Ogoula Tchetoka Chickasaw Village Locations in 1736 during the French-Chickasaw War. *Mississippi Archaeology* 20:53–72.

———. 2004. *Splendid Land, Splendid People: The Chickasaw Indians to Removal*. Tuscaloosa: University of Alabama Press.

Battle-Baptiste, Whitney. 2011. *Black Feminist Archaeology*. Walnut Creek: Left Coast Press.

Beaudry, Mary C. 2002. Trying to Think Progressively about 19th-Century Farms. *Northeast Historical Archaeology* 31: 29–142.

Beaudry, Mary C. and Stephen A. Mrozowski. 1988. The Archaeology of Work and Home Life in Lowell, Massachusetts: An Interdisciplinary Study of the Boott Cotton Mills Corporation. *Industrial Archaeology* 14(2): 1–22.

Black, Jason Edward. 2009. Native Resistive Rhetoric and the Decolonization of American Indian Removal Discourse. *Quarterly Journal of Speech* 95(1):66–88.

———. 2015. *American Indians and the Rhetoric of Removal and Allotment*. Jackson: University Press of Mississippi.

Blomley, N. 2003. Law, Property, and the Geography of Violence: The Frontier, the Survey, and the Grid. *Annals of the Association of American Geographers* 93(1):121–141.

Bragg, Don C. 2004. General Land Office Surveys as a Source for Arkansas History: The Example of Ashley County. *Arkansas Historical Quarterly* 63(2):166–184.

Brooks, Robert L. 1996. Reexamination of WPA Excavations at Novotny Site. *Chronicles of Oklahoma* 74(3):264–283.

Carlson, Leonard A., and Mark A. Roberts. 2006. Indian Lands, "Squatterism," and Slavery: Economic Interests and the Passage of the Indian Removal Act of 1830. *Explorations in Economic History Explorations in Economic History* 43(3): 486–504.

Cegielski, Wendy, and Brad R. Lieb. 2011. Hina' Falaa, "The Long Path": An Analysis of Chickasaw Settlement Using GIS in Northeast Mississippi, 1650-1840. *Native South* 4 (1): 24–54.

Chandler, Tonya Danielle Johnson. 2014. An Archaeological and Historical Study of Fort Hampton, Limestone County, Alabama (1809–1816). MA thesis, University of West Florida.

Chase, David W. 1974. *Fort Mitchell: An Archaeological Exploration*. Special Publication of the Alabama Archaeological Society, No. 1. Moundville: Alabama Archaeological Society.

Conover, Milton. 1923. *The General Land Office: Its History, Activities and Organization*. Baltimore, MD: Johns Hopkins Press.

Davidson, Thomas E. 1986. Computer-Correcting Historical Maps for Archaeological Use. *Historical Archaeology* 20(2):27–37.

Delle, James A. 1998. *An Archaeology of Social Space: Analyzing Coffee Plantations in Jamaica's Blue Mountains*. New York: Plenum Press.

———. 2014. *The Colonial Caribbean: Landscapes of Power in Jamaica's Plantation System*. New York: Cambridge University Press.

Elliott, Jack D., and Mary Ann Wells. 2003. *Cotton Gin Port: A Frontier Settlement on the Upper Tombigbee*. Jackson, MS: Quail Ridge Press for the Mississippi Historical Society.

Gonzales, Angela, Judy Kertész, and Gabrielle Tayac. 2007. Eugenics as Indian Removal: Sociohistorical Processes and the De(con)struction of American Indians in the Southeast. *Public Historian* 29(3):53–67.

Greene, Lance. 2011. Identity in a Post-Removal Cherokee Household, 1838–1850. In *American Indians and the Market Economy, 1775–1850*, edited by Lance Greene, Timothy K. Perttula, and Mark R. Plane, 54–66. Tuscaloosa: University of Alabama Press.

Harley, J. B. 1988. Maps, Knowledge, Power. In *The Iconography of Landscape: Essays on the Symbolic Representation, Design, and Use of Past Environments*, edited by Denis E. Cosgrove and Stephen Daniels, 277–312. Cambridge: Cambridge University Press.

Kappler, Charles J., ed. 1904. *Indian Affairs: Laws And Treaties*. Vol. II, *Treaties*. Washington: Government Printing Office.

Kidder, Tristram R. 2002. Mapping Poverty Point. *American Antiquity* 67(1):89–101.

Kitchin, Rob, Justin Gleeson, and Martin Dodge. 2012. Unfolding Mapping Practices: A New Epistemology for Cartography. *Transactions of the Institute of British Geographers* 38:480–496.

Krauthamer, Barbara. 2013. *Black Slaves, Indian Masters: Slavery, Emancipation, and Citizenship in the Native American South*. Chapel Hill: University of North Carolina Press.

Li, Tania. 2010. Indigeneity, Capitalism, and the Management of Dispossession. *Current Anthropology* 51(3):385–414.

Low, Setha M. 2000. *On the Plaza: The Politics of Public Space and Culture*. Austin: University of Texas Press.

Morgan, David W. 1996. Historic Period Chickasaw Indians: Chronology and Settlement Patterns. *Mississippi Archaeology* 31(1):1–39.

Paige, Amanda L., Fuller L. Bumpers, and Daniel F. Littlefield. 2010. *Chickasaw Removal*. Ada, OK: Chickasaw Press.

Peacock, E., J. Rodgers, K. Bruce, and J. Gray. 2008. Assessing the Pre-Modern Tree Cover of the Ackerman Unit, Tombigbee National Forest, North Central Hills, MS, Using GLO Survey Notes and Archaeological Data. *Southeastern Naturalist* 7(2):245–266.

Peutz, Nathalie. 2006. Embarking on an Anthropology of Removal. *Current Anthropology* 47(2):217–241.

Quimby, George I., and Alexander Spoehr. 1950. Historic Creek Pottery from Oklahoma. *American Antiquity* 15(3):249–251.

Rotman, Deborah L., and Michael S. Nassaney. 1997. Class, Gender, and the Built Environment: Deriving Social Relations from Cultural Landscapes in Southwest Michigan. *Historical Archaeology* 31(2):42–62.

Shanaathanan, Thamotharampillai. 2015. Commemorating Home: Art as Place Making, an Artist's Narration. *Journal of Material Culture* 20(4):415–428.

Sims, Douglas C. 2001. Guidelines for Archaeological Investigations and Reports in Mississippi. Mississippi Department of Archives and History/Mississippi State Historic Preservation Office. http://www.mdah.ms.gov/new/preserve/archaeology/archaeological-survey/.

Smith, Angèle. 2007. Mapped Landscapes: The Politics of Metaphor, Knowledge, and Representation on Nineteenth-Century Irish Ordnance Survey Maps. *Historical Archaeology* 41(1): 81–91.

St. Jean, Wendy. 2003. Trading Paths: Mapping Chickasaw History in the Eighteenth Century. *American Indian Quarterly* 27(3/4):758–780.

———. 2011. *Remaining Chickasaw in Indian Territory, 1830s–1907.* Tuscaloosa: University of Alabama Press.

Utrilla, P. C., M. C. Mazo, M. Sopena, M. Martínez-Bea, and R. Domingo 2009. A Palaeolithic Map from 13,660 calBP: Engraved Stone Blocks from the Late Magdalenian in Abauntz Cave (Navarra, Spain). *Journal of Human Evolution* 57:99–111.

Walls, Michael David. 2015. Rediscovery of a Native American Cultural Landscape: The Chickasaw Homeland at Removal. PhD diss., University of Kentucky. http://uknowledge.uky.edu/geography_etds/37/.

Weik, Terrance. 2009. A First Look at the Archaeology of African Americans at Strawberry Plains. *Mississippi Archaeology* 41(1):3–32.

———. 2013. Chickasaw-African Transitions. Report Submitted to the Mississippi Department of Archives and History. January 3rd.

Wood, Raymond W. 1990. Ethnohistory and Historical Method. *Archaeological Method and Theory* 2:81–109.

Wright, Duncan. 2015. Early Medieval Settlement and Social Power: The Middle Anglo-Saxon "Home Farm." *Medieval Archaeology* 59(1):24–45.

Wright, Muriel. 1927. "Old Boggy Depot." *Chronicles of Oklahoma* 5(1): 4–16.

Zedeno, Maria Nieves, Kacy Hollenback, and Calvin Grinnell. 2009. From Path to Myth: Journeys and the Naturalization of Territorial Identity along the Missouri River. In *Landscapes of Movement: Trails, Paths, and Roads in Anthropological Perspective*, edited by James E. Snead, Clark L. Erickson, and J. Andrew Darling, 106–132. Philadelphia: University of Pennsylvania Press.

4

Whitewashing an African American Landscape

The Impact of Industrial Capitalism on the Removal of Rural People

STEFAN WOEHLKE AND MATTHEW REEVES

Removal has deep roots in the history of humanity. However, since the beginning of the capitalist system, it has been a primary tool for shaping the global cultural landscape (Canterbury 2012). This is evident in processes of enslavement, indentured labor, immigration, human trafficking, gentrification, riots, and genocide. The amount of labor needed to fuel European colonial expansion and industrialization was quickly met through enslaving African captives and removing them to the plantations and mines of the Americas. Their labor fueled the formative period of global capitalism (McMichael 1991, 326). This diasporic removal shaped both sides of the Atlantic. It destabilized the social and political topography of the African continent. Diverse African peoples were forced onto lands where indigenous populations were being removed through disease, physical force, and cultural genocide (Alvarez 2014). Enslaved Africans and their descendants continued to become victims of removal as they were repeatedly sold to meet the demand for agricultural workers that spread westward across what became the United States (Berlin 2010). Eventually, the legal system of slavery ended. This limited the ability of wealthy people to use violence to forcibly move Africans and their descendants across the Americas. The powerful needed to develop new strategies and modify old ones to remove people as the demands for land increased and the availability of labor decreased in the context of industrializing agriculture.

Archaeology is critical to understanding how these removal strategies developed over decades and how they were adapted to diverse social, economic, and ecological contexts (Mullins 2006). Perhaps more important, archaeology and anthropology can help identify the tactics that were best suited for resisting removal in diverse situations across multiple spatial and temporal scales. Some resilient communities have limited the effects of undesired social, environmental, and economic changes. In this chapter, we use a historical materialist analysis of western Orange County, Virginia, to better understand how migration was imposed on the county's African American residents, resulting in multiple periods of removal operating at different scales through time. Then we relate them to similar forces operating at the global level today.

Five processes common in capitalist systems are largely responsible for the forced and coerced forms of removal that African Americans experienced in Orange County: unfair competition due to economies of scale, the command of spatial relations, fracturing of class consciousness, deskilling of the workforce, and the removal of farmers from their means of production (Harvey 1989). These processes are identifiable through combining information from archaeological surveys and excavations, historic maps and aerial imagery, government documents, and newspapers. These sources also provide the details needed to understand how economic processes intersected with, adapted to, relied on, and reproduced other systems of oppression, especially racism (Collins 2000).

In Orange County, the strategy of coerced removal was implemented to maintain control of spatial relations and reproduce power structures following dramatic changes in social, economic, and legal systems brought about by the US Civil War, emancipation, and the enfranchisement of African American men. Elites accomplished this through manipulating biases and structural inequalities in society. This process appears to have resulted in a great migration of people who "freely" chose to move from rural to urban settings in the late nineteenth and early twentieth centuries in search of wealth. This surficial interpretation whitewashes the complex systems that produced a context in which the choices of African Americans were limited to the illusory opportunities of urban life. Given this, they made the best choice they could to improve their own lives and those of their families. This process ultimately resulted in the removal of entire communities.

Orange County is an appropriate starting point for identifying global patterns because the structural elements that shaped its historical trajectory after emancipation were exported across the globe during the green revolution of the twentieth century. This global agricultural movement, which the United States and its western allies led, brought modern capitalist forms of agriculture to developing countries (Pilcher 2017). The process resulted in millions of farmers losing control of their property and moving to cities to seek a wage as wealthy planters incorporated new technologies such as hybrid seeds, irrigation, fertilizers, pesticides, and machinery. Similar efforts in the twenty-first century have continued the dispossession of smallholder farms around the globe, putting people at risk of similar removals from their ancestral lands (Tucker 2014). Today, small-scale farmers must develop strategies that counter the economic and social forces behind large-scale intensive agriculture if they want to continue to control their homelands and their agricultural heritage (Linder 2010; Jokisch 2002).

Project Background: Synthesizing Evidence of Coerced Removal in Orange County, Virginia

Orange County, Virginia, was carved out of the western portion of Spotsylvania County in 1734, shortly after enslaved Africans and Europeans began moving into this section of the Virginia Piedmont to establish plantations (Scott 1907). The Rapidan River runs along its northwest boundary up to the Rappahannock River, which feeds the Chesapeake Bay to the east. It is approximately twenty miles north of Charlottesville, Virginia (figure 4.1). The terrain is made up of degraded ridgelines where jagged mountains stood billions of years ago. Today it consists of farmland, small towns, and a few nationally significant historic sites. Our work centers on one such site, Montpelier, the home of President James Madison. It is currently owned by the National Trust for Historic Places and is managed by the Montpelier Foundation. The property covers an area of approximately 2,700 acres.

After the property was donated to the National Trust for Historic Places in 1984, archaeological, architectural, and historical research began. Over

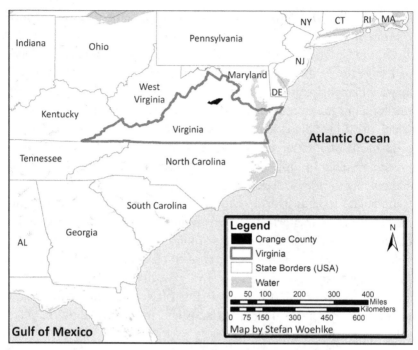

Figure 4.1. Map showing the location of Orange County in the Piedmont region of Virginia.

the last three decades, over 100 archaeological sites have been identified on the property. Some date back to a time before the colonial era, but most are from the eighteenth through the twentieth centuries. This data includes evidence needed to identify occupation periods, functions, and boundaries for each site. The recovered artifacts contribute to our understanding of people's lives in the past. Detailed material evidence of past lifeways comes from large-scale excavations of select sites on the property that are ongoing.

Historical research has also been an important part of the work of the Montpelier Foundation. For example, foundation researchers have identified and researched historic documents from the three generations of the Madison family that lived on the property. Researchers have collected other documentation as part of the foundation's effort to understand how the property and its owners have fit into the larger context of Orange County, the state of Virginia, and the United States. They have compiled massive amounts of historical data that is still being analyzed today.

Architectural research has also been a major component of the Montpelier Foundation's work since its establishment. The first major task was an architectural survey to document the dozens of buildings and ruins that were visible on the landscape. After this, the architectural history of the Madison home was completed to assess the potential for restoring the mansion to the way it was during the president's retirement years.

All the research conducted by Montpelier Foundation researchers and associated scholars from other institutions has produced a wealth of data that has made detailed analysis of social, economic, and landscape changes possible. This chapter builds on that foundation. We primarily rely on a few data sets for our analysis of movement, changing spatial relations, and African American removal: metal detector surveys, federal population censuses, agricultural censuses, historic maps, and photographs.

Metal Detector Surveys

Metal detector surveys have become an integral part of interpreting the history of activities on the Montpelier landscape from the eighteenth through the nineteenth centuries. Metal detector use on the property goes back decades, well before the property was given to National Trust for Historic Places. Some employees of Marion duPont Scott used the devices to search for Civil War materials across the property. The first large-scale application of this technology was made to identify Civil War encampments on the property during a project the American Battlefield Protection Program funded (Reeves and Trickett 2009). The success of this project resulted in an expansion of the survey in which skilled operators with experience in the region conducted a targeted survey focusing on road traces, hilltops, and floodplains perceived as having the potential to contain archaeological sites (Woehlke and Trickett 2015). After the targeted survey was completed, analysis showed that earlier, more ephemeral, eighteenth-century sites were being missed. A new, systematic grid-based survey methodology was put in place that identified additional nineteenth- and twentieth-century sites and a few eighteenth-century domestic sites (Woehlke and Reeves 2015). This systematic approach is continuing across the property; it identifies additional sites every survey season.

Historical Documentation

Our analysis also relies heavily on US population and agricultural censuses of the area. These provide valuable information about households and farmers. Household data from population censuses includes names, relationships, and occupations. Agricultural censuses provide information on property value, crops, livestock, soil improvements, and agricultural equipment. Specific spatial locations have not been determined for all the households included in the censuses, but we have combined the known locations and paths of the census agents to determine coarse-grained spatial relationships. This process was started as part of a Montpelier Foundation project conducted by Matthew Reeves and Susanna Lewis and continues to be expanded as part of the authors' research (Reeves and Lewis 2005). Lastly, historical photographs from descendants, local organizations, and aerial surveys have provided additional evidence related to the material culture and settlement systems at different times in the past.

Orange County and Montpelier: A Landscape Shaped by Removal

Orange County is a landscape that has been shaped by a series of removals that began before Europeans occupied this territory. Its significance to English colonists increased as the tobacco fields of the Tidewater region were depleted of nutrients through overuse. Before white settlers could exploit the rich soils of western Virginia, they had to remove the indigenous Monocan peoples from their ancestral lands. Many Monocans left decades before whites established the first plantations in the area. Some may have moved to the James and Rappahannock Rivers to participate in the deerskin trade with Europeans, others moved to the mountains to live in isolation, and some may have integrated with similar cultural groups to the north, south, and west (Hantman 2010).

One of the early tobacco plantations in this region was called Mount Pleasant. It was owned by Ambrose and Frances Madison, the grandparents of President James Madison (Reeves and Fogle 2007). The first non-indigenous people to live there were enslaved Africans and some overseers. The majority of enslaved Africans who arrived in Orange County in the first few decades of the eighteenth century were most likely forced onto slave ships in West Africa, primarily from ports in the Bight of Biafra.

This theory is based on the fact that names from this region appear in the historic record and on general trends identified through analyzing shipping records from the transatlantic trade in captive Africans (Chambers 2005). Other members of the enslaved community in Orange County would have come from West Central Africa or from other colonies in the Americas.

Mount Pleasant: Frances Madison (1720–1761)

Artifacts that Monocan peoples likely manufactured were found at Mount Pleasant (Reeves and Fogle 2007, 110). This suggests that there may have been some interaction between the ten to fifteen enslaved Africans who first arrived to build a plantation in the 1720s and the former residents who had mostly abandoned the area by that time. The initial labor required to establish the plantation during this first phase of colonial occupation included clearing fields and processing timbers to build Mount Pleasant and the related buildings necessary to run a successful tobacco plantation. The landscape would have been covered by an oak, hickory, and pine forest (Druckenbrod, Shugart, and Davies 2005, 38). Early historical records document a range of tree species, including red, white, and Spanish oaks; pines; dogwoods; chestnuts; black gums; and yellow poplars (Druckenbrod and Shugart 2004, 208). Because of the expansive network of roots related to recently felled trees, fields could not have been sown using the aid of the plow. Instead, the tobacco would have been grown using hoes to loosen and build the mounds of soil necessary. It would have been many years before the root systems decayed enough that they could have been removed, so it is believed that the fields were not plowed until after they were exhausted and had gone through their first fallow period (Druckenbrod and Shugart 2004). The lack of plowing and the persistence of root systems prevented rapid erosion during the early years of settlement, although the steep slopes of the Piedmont hills are susceptible to erosion with only small amounts of stress related to human activity (Sherwood 2010). Using hoes also meant a greater demand for labor, since plows dramatically speed up the tilling and hilling of the soil.

Ambrose and Frances Madison finally moved to the property in 1732. It was undoubtedly difficult for the enslaved community to adjust to the new proximity of their captors. Ambrose Madison died within six months of arriving. Three enslaved people were found guilty of conspiring to kill him. Only one was executed, the enslaved medicine man of a neighboring plantation named Pompey. Turk and Dido returned to the custody of Frances Madison. They appear to have lived out the rest of their lives at Mount Pleasant and their names were repeated in children's names in later generations (Chambers 2005). The enslaved laborers who built the plantation also had to adjust to an influx of additional people of African descent into their group. In 1733, twenty-nine enslaved Africans and African Americans were recorded as living at Mount Pleasant, fifteen of whom were sixteen or older (Chambers 2005). This shows the presence of enslaved children, which means that families in some form existed by that time.

After Ambrose died, Frances Madison ran Montpelier as a tobacco plantation for the rest of her life. She didn't transfer the property to her eldest son, James Madison Sr., as was customary at the time (Reeves and Fogle 2007). This decision forced James to seek other ways of establishing himself and building his wealth. He engaged in a variety of social, political and economic activities. He became a member of the local Anglican vestry and a colonel in a local militia. He also earned money as a merchant and profited from selling the labor of enslaved people skilled in carpentry. Perhaps his most significant business investment was a large blacksmithing operation on the Mount Pleasant property where enslaved blacksmiths built and repaired tools for nearby Piedmont planters. James Madison Sr.'s industrial developments are important to consider since it means that people he enslaved were being trained in valuable trades. In addition to blacksmiths, many other skilled laborers could be found among the enslaved Africans and African Americans on the property, including carpenters, masons, and gardeners. Enslaved people with skills in high demand had potential access to a meager personal income by doing extra work while they were rented out to nearby planters for extended periods of time.

Our knowledge of the distribution of archaeological sites during the period Frances Madison owned and ran Mount Pleasant is limited. Most people and activities were clustered in the home house quarter. Another concentration of enslaved laborers and an overseer were living at Black Level quarter, but its location has not yet been identified (Chambers 2005). One concentration of early eighteenth-century material was found through a metal detector survey in the spring of 2014, but it is not clear that it is Black Level, since it is near the Madison family's property boundary and may be outside it. This is likely a domestic site for enslaved field laborers. Additional excavation is needed to gain a better understanding of the relationship between this isolated site and the dense concentration of people around the Mount Pleasant home house quarter. We expect that more sites from this period will be identified through grid-based metal detector surveys that provide greater coverage than testing along transects or targeting areas perceived to have a high probability of containing a site (Woehlke and Reeves 2015). The population of the enslaved community and the sites associated with them increased through the end of the eighteenth century. As the labor force grew, the amount of land brought into tobacco cultivation increased as well.

Montpelier: Col. James Madison (1761–1801)

The first major transitions in the organization of Montpelier's plantation operations took place when Frances Madison died and Col. James Madison inherited the plantation. This occurred in the 1760s, when Montpelier, a Georgian-style brick mansion, was constructed a few hundred yards northeast of Mount Pleasant, adjacent to the blacksmithing complex. A former tobacco field that had been depleted became an area where domestic sites associated with the enslaved community were clustered. This was just east of the Mount Pleasant site, which continued to be occupied by members of the enslaved population and an overseer for many decades (Reeves and Fogle 2007).

Other crops also needed to be grown at Montpelier because of high transportation costs arising from poor access to navigable waterways. Providing a sustainable food supply was essential for life in Orange County. Corn was the second most important crop for the first decades after English migration to the region. By the 1760s, wheat became more important. The theory that grain production expanded at this time is supported by an increase in grist mills across the county (Schlotterbeck 1980). It is likely that many of the first fields cleared in the area had already gone through a fallow period and that the old roots were no longer impeding plows. This transition also followed the establishment of Col. Madison's blacksmithing complex. His industrial operation, which produced and repaired farming equipment, was essential to the earliest mechanization of Orange County agriculture. The extent of African influence on the practice of smithing is still unclear.

Economic diversification in Orange County extended beyond agricultural products. A social economy developed in which planters exchanged resources to meet local demands for products and labor. Enslaved craftspeople continued to be hired out to neighbors for short and extended periods. Often these were specialists, such as carpenters, who might be needed for a long-term construction project. Other industries that developed in the eighteenth and nineteenth centuries involved harvesting lumber; milling; carding; tanning leather; manufacturing saddles and harnesses, boots and shoes, clothing, barrels, and furniture; and construction. Diversified tasks meant many things for the enslaved community. For example, more skilled artisans were trained in valuable crafts, and there was something for everyone to do all the time. As the importance of tobacco declined, diversified agricultural regimes helped balance the demand for labor throughout the year (Schlotterbeck 1980).

Archaeological surveys have identified an increase in the number of sites within a few hundred yards of Montpelier during the years that Col. Madison lived there. It is not clear how the Black Level quarter changed, since it has not yet been identified through survey. It may be located on a portion of Madison property that the Montpelier Foundation does not own today. A better understanding of these eighteenth-century shifts in settlement patterns will depend on an expansion of the multiyear, grid-based metal detector survey that is still under way across the property.

Montpelier's Second Phase: James and Dolley Madison (1801–1844)

James Madison Sr. died in 1801. This triggered major change in the management of the plantation. James Madison Jr., who would later become president, inherited the property. Some of the enslaved population remained under the ownership of Nelly Madison, his mother, while control of others was transferred to President Madison and his siblings. This undoubtedly sent shockwaves through the enslaved community as some people were forced to leave Montpelier to work for other Madison relatives. As a result, the population of the enslaved community shrank. It did not reach its late-eighteenth-century numbers for twenty years (Chambers 2005).

James Madison Jr. made many changes to the landscape over the next three and a half decades. First, he moved the blacksmithing complex to the far southern end of his property. He also continued to transition from monocrop tobacco agriculture toward a mix of tobacco and grain, a change that made the plantation more responsive to market fluctuations (Schlotterbeck 1980). The excavation of a tobacco barn complex in 2012 revealed a dramatic shift toward mechanized grain agriculture. A former tobacco barn with a smoking pit and trenches around the interior edges that doubled as an out-of-season domestic site was converted to a threshing barn. The hand-wrought teeth of a threshing machine were recovered in the yard around the barn and the two large postholes that held it in place were also excavated (Trickett 2013). The fact that these teeth were hand wrought reinforces how important the blacksmith complex was for the mechanization process that Madison's father had started decades earlier. This early nineteenth-century expansion of mechanization occurred as wheat became the main export crop for the county (Schlotterbeck 1980).

Madison also experimented with methods to increase soil fertility and land productivity. He acquired new tools and had blacksmiths modify others, including the reinforcement of a moldboard plow to cut through the heavy Piedmont clay. Enslaved laborers were instructed to rotate crops and plant grasses after harvest to reduce erosion. The overseer was told to set aside plots to test different fertilizing methods that combined manure and plaster. Fields were also manured during fallow resting periods to help restore depleted nutrients (Schlotterbeck 1980).

In addition to the technical and agricultural transitions, huge social changes came to Orange County. Westward expansion and the rise of the Cotton Belt in the South drove white migration in waves, but the African American migration was even greater. This is what Ira Berlin calls the second great migration of African Americans (Berlin 2010). It impacted the entire Upper South because of the huge demand for labor and capital that it spurred. Enslaved families were torn from one another to feed the tremendous need for labor that the planting and harvesting of cotton required. Once again, enslaved African descendants experienced a traumatic removal like those their grandparents and great grandparents had experienced when they were taken from Africa. In both the 1820s and the 1830s, over 2,000 people of African descent left Orange County—doubtless sold to "negro traders" who beat a steady transport of enslaved individuals in chained lines of human coffles leading to and from the major slave-trading centers of Richmond, Charleston, and New Orleans (Baptist 2014). This is about double the net migration of whites, and it continued at a disproportionate rate for decades after the 1830s (Schlotterbeck 1980).

At Montpelier, the plantation population stayed together during Madison's life. During that period, the distribution of sites associated with the plantation became more evenly distributed across the landscape. This would have maximized production by reducing the amount of time needed to travel to the fields. It also suggests that there may have been a shift in the management of the enslaved population and social relations. Sites dating to this period are easily found through metal detector surveys, since the mechanization of nail production meant that members of the enslaved community had ready access to them and they left clear traces of human activity in the archaeological record (Woehlke and Reeves 2015). These widely distributed sites loosely consolidate in three areas of the Montpelier Foundation's property. The first is the area around the mansion. A second area of domestic and agricultural structures is located east of the mansion in an area that is currently wooded. A third cluster of domestic structures dating to this period is located northwest of the mansion across modern-day Route 20, the historic plank road (Woehlke and Trickett 2015).

The End of Slavery at Montpelier (1844–1864)

The African American community in western Orange County experienced the pain of removal as the decline in demand for labor in the region combined with an increase in demand to the west and south. After Madison died in 1836, the portion of the community living at Montpelier began to experience removal. Many could still remember when the community had been divided thirty-five years earlier, after the death of the president's father (Chambers 2005). This time they were being split among members of the Madison family and many others. Dolley Madison was forced to sell Montpelier in 1844 because of the debts her husband had accrued. She sold the mansion, the majority of the land, and most of the enslaved population to Henry Moncure. She had already sold the rest of the land in smaller parcels leading up to the final sale. After that, she moved to

Washington, DC, where she sold Madison's papers to Congress in 1846 for $25,000 (Madison 1886).

After Moncure purchased Montpelier, the area was made up of smaller farms cut from the Madison family property. Initially, this led to a more evenly dispersed population across the landscape because of the smaller parcels. However, many of the sites were quickly abandoned. This likely represents the removal of the enslaved population previously held by the Madison family. In the period 1844–1860, the mechanization of mixed grain agriculture resulted in the abandonment of over half the sites in the Montpelier Foundation's east woods and about a third in the north woods (Woehlke and Trickett 2015). New barns were also constructed at Montpelier, signifying an investment in capital-intensive projects and equipment at the same time that the enslaved community was sold away to southern plantations. The homes of the enslaved community around the plantation were demolished and replacements were constructed near the new barns, which were located much farther northeast (Reeves and Marshall 2009).

Federal censuses show the stagnation and frequent declines in the African American population in Orange County in the first half of the nineteenth century. Federal censuses show that population increased slightly from 1820 to 1830 (7,661 to 8,181 people), followed by a sharp decline that brought the population below 1820 levels. In 1840, 7,335 African Americans were recorded in Orange County. There was a slight increase in each of the following years until emancipation. This period of decline and stagnation in the population is a result of forced removal that targeted the youth. This can be seen in the population tree of the 547 enslaved people living around Montpelier in 1860, where the lower portions of the tree (younger people) were considerably smaller compared to the number of individuals over thirty-five years old (Reeves and Lewis 2005).

During the Civil War there were multiple periods when the Confederate army camped in Orange County. Confederate officers took over domestic sites occupied by enslaved African Americans (Reeves and Trickett 2009; Reeves 2014). Many of the enslaved community may have taken this opportunity to escape north across to the Rapidan River into Culpepper County, which was the line between the Union and Confederate armies in the winter of 1863–1864. Escaping to Union territory provided a degree of freedom, but Union soldiers commonly took advantage of African

Americans fleeing enslavement by robbing them of their possessions or food (Dunaway 2003). Dramatic shifts in the social fabric of the county continued after the sale and removal of enslaved people to the Cotton Belt and then their emancipation following the Civil War.

Emancipation: New Opportunities for African Americans (1865–1900)

In the decade from 1860 to 1870, the African American population decreased by 36 percent. It is likely that many of the African Americans who lived in Orange County in this period had been sold further south by the start of the Civil War, while others likely took advantage of the disruption of Confederate troop occupation to leave Orange County for territory federal troops occupied during the war. Some left the area after emancipation in search of friends and family who had been victims of forced removal and had been taken away before the war. Others went in search of more freedom and jobs than could be found in the land where they were raised (Reeves and Lewis 2005). There was also movement within the county, primarily to the local towns of Orange Courthouse and Gordonsville, that led to a restructuring of voting districts so the white residents could maintain political control of the county after the 1870 census (Scott 1907, 163–164).

Emancipation also affected family life. Free from the fear that their spouses or children would be forced farther south, the African American community experienced a small baby boom in the five years after emancipation. Licensed marriages in the African American community also increased after the end of the war (Reeves and Lewis 2005).

It took time for African American communities to become established, but Jacksontown, located just southwest of Montpelier, was well on its way by 1870 (Reeves and Lewis 2005). This community, which consisted of nuclear families, may have been a popular location for African Americans since it was centrally located between large farms where community members could find work as laborers and domestic servants. Over time, many of the families that lived there were able to purchase land. By 1900, twenty-six families in this community owned land. This was the highest concentration of African American landowners in the county (Reeves and Lewis 2005).

The domestic sites associated with African Americans on the Montpelier Foundation's property had decreased dramatically by 1900. Surveys conducted across the property indicate that African Americans lived on only nine sites on the property after the Civil War (Woehlke and Trickett 2015). One belonged to the Gilmore family, who mortgaged their property and eventually regained full ownership in 1901 (Reeves 2010). The Walker and Taylor families both purchased 5.5-acre lots from Col. Willis, their former captor, for $1 in 1886. In another portion of Orange County, William Lee inherited forty acres after serving by the side of the man who claimed ownership of him during the Civil War. When Lee returned home with the body of his former owner, he was given forty acres of land, which he gave to his mother (Perdue, Barden, and Phillips 1976). In the last decades of the nineteenth century, the few other African Americans living on current Montpelier Foundation property were either day laborers paying rent or tenants, as were most other African Americans in the county (Reeves and Lewis 2005).

Most African Americans living in Orange County in 1870 were farm laborers. Additionally, 7 percent were classified as laborers and another 7 percent as domestic servants. Given the low wages for this class of worker it would have been extremely difficult to raise the capital needed to purchase the land or livestock required to build wealth. Only 3 percent of African Americans were listed as farmers, and only some of them owned their land. This contrasts dramatically with the white population, of which 57 percent were classified as farmers and only 5 percent as farm laborers and 2 percent and 1 percent were classified as laborers and domestic servants, respectively. The rest of the white population were skilled laborers, clerks, doctors, merchants, and railroad workers (Reeves and Lewis 2005). African Americans in Orange County who were unable to find jobs as skilled laborers had no power to bargain with property owners over contracts since their labor could easily be replaced by that of other members of their community who were also looking for work.

From 1870 to 1880, the African American population surrounding Montpelier increased by 39 percent. Personal property values also grew to an average range of $10–20. However, there were some outliers in the African American community who skewed these numbers. A select few households accumulated hundreds of dollars of wealth, while most were recorded as having no private property or just a few dollars.

During this period another African American settlement known as Slabtown was established outside the town of Orange, less than five miles up the road from Montpelier. By 1880, 132 African Americans were living there. These were mostly nuclear families living on small lots. The residents were predominantly laborers and domestic servants who likely worked in the town of Orange (Reeves and Lewis 2005).

Jacksontown also grew during this decade. As more families had more children, the population rose to 182 in 1880. This African American community also increased its rate of ownership and pooled resources to construct some community buildings, including a schoolhouse, a community store, and a meeting hall (Reeves and Lewis 2005). These resources undoubtedly contributed to the attractiveness of this community to other African Americans in the region.

Some African Americans lived outside these neighborhoods, scattered across the countryside. These households tended to have more wealth than those living in the towns or little villages in the area. This is mostly related to the livestock and farm equipment that many of them used to produce food for their families and the market (Reeves and Lewis 2005). Another interesting contrast is the higher average age in these more rural households. This may be related to the tendency for children to leave the area for work once they became adults. Similarly, the children in Jacksontown and Slabtown tended to be younger in 1880, as older teenagers left the area for work.

In 1880, the employment patterns remained very similar. Laborers and farm laborers made up 57 percent of the African American workforce. The number of farmers grew from 3 percent to 11 percent, which is likely related to the amount of time that had passed since emancipation but could also relate to changes in who the census takers considered to be farmers. Very few African Americans had the money to acquire property immediately following the Civil War, but by 1880 more families could pool resources to purchase their own farmland. Interestingly, white farmers made up proportionately less of the white labor force, falling from 57 percent in 1870 to 47 percent in 1880. The types of work both populations did diversified. Skilled labor outside agriculture continued to be an important sector of the economy. The railroad had become a major employer for everyone by 1880, especially in Gordonsville. A small percentage of African Americans found work in hotels or as merchants. The white community occupied a wider range of the workforce, becoming doctors, clerks, and teachers. The rate of domestic servitude for whites held steady during the decade (Reeves and Lewis 2005).

The wealth gap between whites and African Americans living in the western portion of Orange County persisted, including between land-owners. According to the federal agricultural census, in 1880, the average value of an African American's farm was $270, while for whites it was $4,174 (Reeves and Lewis 2005, 11). Similarly, the difference in the amount of land they owned was significant. African Americans owned about twenty acres on average, while white farmers owned an average of around 300. This discrepancy in the size of farms also affected how they were managed. Due to the smaller size of their farms, African Americans had to work about 70 percent of their property, as opposed to 36 percent for whites. This contributed to differences between the productivity of land. White farmers were able to produce three to five more bushels of grain per acre than African Americans. This is a result of the poor-quality soils in areas where African Americans could afford land. Furthermore, their small size meant that they lacked the acreage needed to let fields rest and rotate effectively. Compounding this factor was the ability of many white farmers to purchase the chemical fertilizers that were beginning to be industrially produced at this time. Only one African American farmer is reported to have purchased fertilizer in 1880 (Reeves and Lewis 2005).

Similarly, white and black farmers used different amounts of outside wage labor. Only one African American farmer was recorded as paying any wages in 1880. Noah Wales paid $18 in wages for the year. He owned fifty-two acres and had the highest property assessment among the African Americans in Orange County, $3,600. He produced the second-largest amount of wine of anyone in Orange County (Reeves and Lewis 2005). He also produced fruit, wool, timber, and butter from his property (Reeves and Lewis 2005).

The demand for agricultural labor was linked to the amount and variety of crops a farm produced. Since most farms African Americans owned were small, less than twenty acres, they had little demand for labor beyond the nuclear family. When necessary, local communities banded together, sharing equipment and labor or bartering crops in exchange for help on the land.

After 1880, African American land ownership continued to grow at a slow and steady rate. By the 1900 census, almost one-third (254 of 616 households) of the African Americans in this part of Orange County owned land (Reeves and Lewis 2005). This trend was possible because families continued to pool their resources. As children grew into adults and were able to contribute to household savings, families purchased their first plots of land.

The Gilmores were one African American family that lived on the Montpelier Foundation's property after emancipation. After the Civil War, they got a mortgage to purchase the land from Dr. James Madison, the president's nephew. Archaeology confirmed that George and Polly Gilmore built their first home with material salvaged from abandoned winter huts the Confederate army had built (Reeves 2010). The Confederates most likely cleared the Gilmore property when it devoured forests to use for firewood and to construct its camps (Reeves and Trickett 2009). The Gilmores saved for years before they were able to purchase large timbers to build a more substantial cabin in 1873 (Reeves 2010). The family's first home on the property continued to stand for decades and appears behind the current structure in a photograph from the early twentieth century (figure 4.2).

George Gilmore farmed his own land and supplemented his income by working additional jobs. The family did not have enough land to provide everything it needed. In 1880, George was listed as a farmer with twelve acres of tilled land and four acres that were unimproved. His two eldest sons, Jerry and Philip, were listed as laborers; their wages supplemented what the family earned from its harvests (Reeves and Lewis 2005). According to the 1880 agricultural census, the farm's value was $26. This was primarily attributed to one pig and one hog who had a combined value of $15. As George and Polly grew older, their youngest son, William, began to take over responsibility for the farm. As George became unable to work his land, William supported his parents through his labor. In 1901, just before Dr. James Madison passed away, George Gilmore purchased the land for $560. This was a steep price for the total acreage of the property and suggests that race had an impact on property values.

Two other African American families who lived on the Montpelier Foundation property after the Civil War were the Walkers and the Taylors. Charles and Rebecca Taylor were tenant farmers who rented forty-five acres of land from John Willis. They bought almost six acres from Willis in 1886 for $1. This was shortly before John Willis passed away and was the same deal Willis gave the Taylors' neighbors, the Walkers. Peter and Hannah Walker's property contained one structure where initial excavations have been conducted. It appears to have been occupied just after the

Figure 4.2. A 1920 photograph of the Gilmore cabin with an earlier structure present in the background. Courtesy of Al Mills.

Civil War and may have been constructed using salvaged materials, like the first Gilmore cabin. The farms and other property of the Walkers and Taylors are both valued over $100 in 1880. Both properties were sold to William duPont within a year of each other. The Walkers sold their property for $100 in 1900 and the Taylors sold theirs for $150 in 1901. This was the same time that George Gilmore paid $560 for sixteen acres (Reeves and Lewis 2005).

The Taylors seem to have moved in with their children after they sold the house. Rebecca signed her name, which suggests that she was literate to some degree by 1900. Charles signed with an X. Charles Taylor's will was recorded in the Orange County Court House in 1918. It is unclear what happened to Peter and Hannah Walker after they sold their home and moved off the land.

William duPont and other wealthy white landowners continued to buy up properties around Montpelier in the early twentieth century. William duPont, who was independently wealthy, did not depend on the land to produce a profit. He used Montpelier as a place to raise thoroughbred horses. Over time, he purchased almost 5,000 acres of land surrounding the mansion. He bought land from white and black families, resulting in the removal of more African Americans from the county. Eventually, he acquired the Gilmore family's land through a court-ordered auction intended to settle a dispute between the remaining siblings in 1920. This was a common practice that disproportionately impacted African American estates. After parents passed away, siblings usually acquired equal shares of a property under a legal framework called tenancy in common. If one person wanted to sell their share, they could sell it to another buyer. If they can't find another buyer or if the new shareholder wanted to sell the property, the court could force a sale of the property. This strategy contributed significantly to the loss of African American farmland throughout the late nineteenth and twentieth centuries (Gilbert, Sharp, and Felin 2002) and continues to impact African American families today. In the case of the Gilmores, William duPont quickly ended the auction with a bid of $5000, far more than George and Polly's son William could raise.

Over the course of the twentieth century, the last of the remaining African Americans who lived on property that currently makes up the Montpelier Foundation were bought out or were forced out when their landlords sold their property to William duPont. Some African Americans worked as laborers for the duPonts and rented out rooms or houses on the property. Eventually, the property was transferred to the National Trust for Historic Places after Marion duPont Scott passed away in 1984. The last African American residents left the Montpelier property after this transfer. In 2000, no African Americans lived on this land.

Economic inequality prevented African Americans from building wealth and acquiring property in Orange County after the end of slavery. Many African Americans still live there, but their numbers have continued to shrink as the white population has grown at an increasingly rapid pace. Racism was a significant contributing factor, resulting in intimidation that increased the ability of wealthy whites to exploit the labor and fears of their African American workers. According to articles in *The Native Virginian*, a paper printed in the town of Orange, the Ku Klux Klan had significant support and was harassing African Americans in the county before 1870.[1] This intersection of economic inequality and racism exacerbated the obstacles the African American community needed to navigate. The relationship between Orange County and other rural communities is key to understanding how similarly coercive economic structures led to the removal of people in diverse contexts. Racism also played a role in supporting a system that embraces economic exploitation and enabled a small minority to consolidate wealth.

The Impact of Industrial Capital on Rural Removal

The foundations of industrial capitalism were being laid by the end of the eighteenth century. The demand for cheap labor grew as industrialization spread across Europe and then the United States in the first half of the nineteenth century. Initially, enslaved workers played a significant role in southern industry. At the Tredegar Iron Works in Richmond, one of the leading industrial manufacturers in the South in the antebellum period, the labor force transitioned from a mix of enslaved black and poor white laborers to an entirely enslaved workforce in 1847 after a strike by white workers (Trotter 2000, 20). Following the Civil War, a new mass of free blacks moved to cities in search of wage labor. This migration led to a rapid expansion of the surplus labor force, enabling industrial capitalists to push down wages and expand their profit margins.

The process of urbanization David Harvey describes is influenced by five capitalist forces that shape the landscape (Harvey 1989). The first is an unfair competition due to economies of scale. Second is a command of spatial relations. Third is a fracturing of class consciousness, which limits the ability of the working class to organize. Fourth is the deskilling of the workforce, which makes individual workers replaceable and reduces their ability to demand fair wages. Last is the removal of workers from their means of production, which eliminates their ability to control production. These same forces operate in rural agricultural settings.

Unfair Competition Due to Economies of Scale

It is an obvious statement that many white Orange County residents benefited from an economy of scale following the Civil War, but it is important to take a moment to describe the impact this advantage had on the removal of African Americans from the landscape. Immediately after emancipation, African Americans rarely had any wealth. The departure of half of the African Americans in Orange County between 1860 and 1870 is likely tied to this transition to a modern capitalist form of poverty and the desire to flee an area where they had experienced violent oppression.

The few who were able to acquire a small portion of local property faced a steep competitive disadvantage compared to former slaveholders, who still controlled the majority of farmland.

Large farms could produce a profit while being managed in a way that encouraged consistently higher yields. White-owned farms had enough land to produce timber through managed woodlots and could sustain extended fallow periods. A fallow period kills diseases and insects that are tied to specific crops and nourishes fields through a resting period. Larger farms also supported livestock that grazed in fallow fields, dumping their waste along and its nutrients back into the soil.

On small farms, most or all of the acreage had to be cultivated to produce enough food to last a family through the year and a small surplus that could be sold at market. This position manifests itself in the fact that African Americans tilled 70 percent of their land on average, compared to 36 percent for white farmers (Reeves and Lewis 2005). This agricultural reality reduced nutrients and the long-term productivity of the farms African Americans owned. The negative impacts of overfarming contributed to the inability of African American farmers to compete with larger farms throughout the twentieth century.

Economies of scale negatively affect small farmers in another way. James C. Scott describes how the development of mechanized agricultural equipment for rice production in Malaysia greatly increased the amount of grain that could be produced with fewer hours of human labor. However, farmers needed to have enough property in tillage to be able to afford the equipment (Scott 1985). As large farmers take advantage of their scale, increasing the food supply, the price for agricultural products declines. There is a constant push to purchase more land and bigger and better pieces of equipment to increase profit under these conditions. Even when owners of small farms can afford to rent equipment, they lose a greater portion of their profit than large land owners. This makes the transition to mechanized agriculture risky and often impossible for small operators.

Ultimately, the financial benefits of farming small plots decrease. For small farmers and their families, the lower profits they earn from any surplus production becomes less than the income they could earn from wage labor. When farmers believe they can earn more money to feed and support their families through wage labor, they are more likely to transition to a wage-based position.

The Command of Spatial Relations

The economy of scale resulted in large industrial farming operations maintaining command of spatial relations. This is evident in the small fraction of African American farmers who were present in Orange County compared to the number of white farmers after the Civil War. Unequal access to land put the African American community at a disadvantage. Because of their lack of property, they were forced to work as wage laborers, tenant farmers, or sharecroppers. This hindered their ability to build the capital necessary to obtain their own land, since white farmers paid them only enough to attract their labor.

The command of space in late nineteenth-century Virginia can also be seen in the location of African American population clusters in western Orange County. The landowners were spread thinly throughout the more rural parts of the county, but they could generally only afford marginal agricultural land. This resulted in poor harvests in relation to the white farmers. The African American settlements are directly related to where there was demand for labor. Jacksontown was in the center of a cluster of large farms. This placed them near enough that their labor could be extracted for agricultural and domestic tasks. Slabtown was located on the outskirts of the town of Orange. Most African Americans there worked as laborers in town or as domestic servants, but they were kept separate from the white homes in the center of town. Similarly, in Gordonsville there was an African American community that was built around demands of the railroad industry. Equal portions of African Americans and whites worked for the railroad, which would have enabled the companies to exploit the competition between races to push down wages and maximize profits.

Harvey explains how this control of spatial relations relates to time and the extraction of the maximum amount of labor possible. By having workers nearby, capitalists can maximize the amount of laborers' time that they can exploit, since workers can be summoned easily and quickly arrive at their place of employment (Harvey 1989). This leads to an increase in the amount of capital that can be consolidated by organizations such as the railroad in Gordonsville and the individuals that own it.

This control of space is also important when considering how capital and space were managed by communities of African Americans. For example, in Jacksontown, African Americans pooled their resources so they could construct a schoolhouse and a community meeting hall (Reeves and Lewis 2005). Communal architecture became an attractive feature for African Americans who were looking for a place to settle in the decades after the war. By working together, the community members in Jacksontown countered the elite domination of space that ignored the educational and social needs of black communities (Du Bois 1953). Despite these efforts, Jacksontown gradually dissolved in the twentieth century as individuals in the community succumbed to pressures to sell their land or to leave the area in search of more stable wage labor and opportunities that provided upward mobility.

Control of space continues to be an essential component of large-scale agriculture and continues to impact rural communities around the globe. Ronald Nigh describes how international corporations purchase huge tracts of land for agricultural purposes. They use unsustainable methods that maximize profits through the application of chemicals that lead to the destruction of the soil, then they move on to another region or another country (Nigh 1999). They can do this efficiently because of the ease with which capital can move between countries. This style of agriculture increasingly contributes to the migration of smallholder farmers away from their homelands around the world (Jokisch 2002).

Fracturing of Class Consciousness

Large landholders prevent the agricultural working class and smallholders from building solidarity that can move the working class toward a balance of power in society. Racism was key to maintaining divisions in Orange County, but gender, nationality, religion, and sexuality are also frequently exploited to create divisions within the working class. In *The Urban Experience*, David Harvey focuses on the fracturing of class consciousness among the working poor and the managerial classes. Both groups are at the mercy of elite capitalists. But he acknowledges the effects of specific historical contexts in his definition of class relations. Specifically, "residual" social and economic classes that were created under specific economic conditions of the past occasionally persist into new modes of production because they are still useful for the dominant class (Harvey 1989, 112).

Racism operated as a system that created a gulf between members of the working class when emancipation occurred in the United States. There was no need for elites to change the racial structure of social relations after the Civil War because racism divided the working class into manageable groups of competing labor. This is what happened in 1847 at the Tredegar Ironworks in Richmond as described above (Trotter 2000, 20). It is a pattern that can be seen in industrial centers across the United States, as in Baltimore, where immigrants were able to block the access of African Americans to attractive wage labor positions (Fields 1985, 47).

Deskilling of the Workforce

Another impact of industrial agriculture is the deskilling of the workforce. At Montpelier, this began when President Madison introduced plow agriculture and threshing machines. But, it occurred across the United States and expanded with the adoption of chemical fertilizers and insecticides. In the twentieth century, seeds were modified through hybridization and genetic modification in ways that contribute to the deskilling of the workforce (Fitzgerald 1993; Stone 2007). Industrialization of agriculture increases production while reducing the demand for labor and for specialized agricultural knowledge (Nigh 1999). Non-agricultural skills that support the agricultural infrastructure have also been impacted. This can be seen in a reduction in the demand for teamsters and trucking as railroads come into prominence or the closing of local mills as large-scale industrial milling increased at agricultural transport hubs.

In Orange County, the enslaved community generally consisted of three subclasses of laborers: field workers, domestic servants, and skilled craftsmen. Following emancipation, this division of labor could still be seen in the local African American community of Orange County in 1870, when 73 percent of the workforce was employed as unskilled or agricultural laborers, 7 percent were employed as domestic servants, and only 6 percent were employed as skilled laborers (Reeves and Lewis 2005). This contrasted starkly with the white community in Orange County in 1870: 57 percent were landowners farming their own land and the rest filled positions in the categories skilled labor and management. Only 8 percent of the white population worked as laborers, farm laborers, or domestic servants.

In some respects, the situation improved for African Americans over the next decade, but they were still far behind the white community in terms of their ability to access skilled jobs. Concurrently, the demand for unskilled labor fell as agriculture began to become increasingly mechanized. Fifty-seven percent of the African American community was employed as farm or other laborers in 1880. In the white population, the proportion of laborers decreased to 6 percent. Meanwhile, the proportion of skilled laborers increased for both the white and black communities (Reeves and Lewis 2005). This was likely related to jobs the railroad industry provided in Gordonsville and Orange, bringing new development in both towns. Railroads were essential components of the agricultural infrastructure, and their absence often resulted in the death of small towns (Fennell 2011; Shackel 2011). The mechanization of agriculture decreased the demand for labor in the rest of the nineteenth century and into the twentieth century. This resulted in a relative increase in the amount of skilled labor in the area, but it also contributed to the migration of unskilled or unemployed laborers out of the county toward urban centers, where the prospects of finding employment were thought to be higher.

Removing Farmers from Their Means of Production

The structural benefits for large-scale farmers made it difficult for small farmers to stay in operation. Throughout the twentieth century, the fundamental base of agriculture began to be privatized. Production of seed and experimentation through hybridization shifted from the responsibility of individual farmers to the private intellectual property of agricultural seed companies (Fitzgerald 1993). This impacted all farmers who owned their own farms and the people who worked on those farms. This situation was compounded by genetically modified crops. Today in the United States, farmers are sold only annual licenses for genetically modified seed and are thus legally blocked from producing their own seed for the future.[2] Seed corporations use this legal framework to remove all farmers from the means of production.

There are cases where the introduction of genetically modified crops have spurred interest and experimentation between farmers. In Warangal, India, genetically modified cotton has led farmers to breed new strains. This is possible because the Indian legal system does not remove farmers from the means of production. Genetically modified seeds are more expensive than the hybrid seeds agricultural companies in India produce, but they are purchased instead of licensed, so farmers maintain the right to collect seed for future harvests or create their own hybrids (Stone 2007). The types of regulations large agricultural corporations impose greatly impacts the ability of farmers to maintain ownership of their land.

Conclusion

Removal has been a part of rural landscapes for centuries. In the Americas, it began when Europeans removed indigenous people during colonization and replaced them with enslaved Africans from across the Atlantic. Their enslaved descendants continued to be divided and moved around the landscape at the will of slaveholders, whose actions were fully supported by federal law. Mechanization began in the eighteenth century, resulting in a reorganization of the national landscape. The cotton gin increased labor demands in the South and West as the wheat thresher reduced demand in the Mid-Atlantic; enslaved people were forcibly removed from their homes and their families so that their white captors could chase a greater profit margin. When legalized slavery ended, the forces of capitalism coerced the removal of African Americans from rural landscapes. The dramatic decline in sites associated with African Americans at Montpelier highlights how racism and economic pressures combined to force people away.

The globalization of industrial agriculture has expanded the impact of the economic forces behind rural removal. The demand for skilled labor has declined, as has the demand for agricultural labor. Small farms owned by families and individuals are unable to compete with large corporate operations. Even the industrial farming operations are losing power to corporations through the privatization of seed. Eventually these forces coerce rural people to remove themselves.

These economic pressures are global. To counter the impact of these processes it is important to understand their historical trajectory and the physical patterns that are associated with them. Archaeology highlights the dynamic shifts in rural settlements where the industrialization of agriculture occurs. Additional research into the African American community in Orange County will help identify the tactics that helped people maintain their land throughout the nineteenth century and into the twentieth century. These findings can contribute to the global debate over how to maintain the diverse agricultural traditions people practice around the globe and their right to property.

Notes

1. "The Ku Klux Klan," *Native Virginian*, April 3, 1868, 2.
2. Bowman *v.* Monsanto Co., 59 U.S. 278 (2013).

References Cited

Alvarez, Alex. 2014. *Native America and the Question of Genocide.* Lanham, MD: Rowman & Littlefield Publishers.

Baptist, Edward E. 2014. *The Half Has Never Been Told: Slavery and the Making of American Capitalism.* New York: Basic Books.

Berlin, Ira. 2010. *The Making of African America: The Four Great Migrations.* New York: Penguin Books.

Canterbury, Dennis C. 2012. *Capital Accumulation and Migration.* Leiden: Brill.

Chambers, Douglas B. 2005. *Murder at Montpelier: Igbo Africans in Virginia.* Jackson: University of Mississippi Press.

Collins, Patricia Hill. 2000. *Black Feminist Thought: Knowledge Consciousness, and the Politics of Empowerment.* Boston: Unwin Hyman.

Druckenbrod, Daniel L., and Herman H. Shugart. 2004. Forest History of James Madison's Montpelier Plantation. *Journal of the Torrey Botanical Society* 131(3):204–210.

Druckenbrod, Daniel L., Herman H. Shugart, and Ian Davies. 2005. Spatial Pattern and Process in Forest Stands within the Virginia Piedmont. *Journal of Vegetation Science* 16(1):37–48.

Du Bois, William Edward Burghardt. 1953. Negroes and the Crisis of Capitalism in the United States. *Monthly Review* 54(11):478–485.

Dunaway, Wilma A. 2003. *The African American Family in Slavery and Emancipation.* Cambridge: Cambridge University Press.

Fennell, Christopher C. 2011. Examining Structural Racism in the Jim Crow Era of Illinois. In *The Materiality of Freedom: Archaeologies of Post Emancipation Life*, edited by Jodi A. Barnes, 173–189. Columbia: University of South Carolina Press.

Fields, Barbara Jeanne. 1985. *Slavery and Freedom on the Middle Ground: Maryland during the Nineteenth Century.* New Haven, CT: Yale University Press.

Fitzgerald, Deborah. 1993. Farmers Deskilled: Hybrid Corn and Farmer's Work. *Technology and Culture* 32(2):324–343.

Gilbert, Jess, Gwen Sharp, and M. Sindy Felin. 2002. The Loss and Persistence of Black-Owned Farms and Farmland: A Review of the Research Literature and Its Implications. *Southern Rural Sociology* 18(2):1–30.

Hantman, Jeffrey L. 2010. Monocan Archaeology of the Virginia Interior, A.D. 1400–1700. In *Societies in Eclipse: Archaeology of the Eastern Woodlands Indians, A.D. 1400–*

1700, edited by David S. Brose, C. Wesley Cowan and Robert C. Mainfort Jr., 107–123. Tuscaloosa: University of Alabama Press.

Harvey, David. 1989. *The Urban Experience*. Baltimore, MD: The Johns Hopkins University Press.

Jokisch, Brad D. 2002. Migration and Agricultural Change: The Case of Smallholder Agriculture in Highland Ecuador. *Human Ecology* 30(4):523–550.

Linder, Patrick. 2010. The Long Decline of the Family Farm. *Anthropology Now* 2(3): 74–80.

Madison, Dolley. 1886. *Memoirs and Letters of Dolley Madison: Wife of President James Madison, President of the United States*. Boston: Houghton, Mifflin, and Co.

McMichael, Philip. 1991. Slavery in Capitalism: The Rise and Demise of the U. S. Antebellum Cotton Culture. *Theory and Society* 20(3):321–349.

Mullins, Paul R. 2006. Racializing the Commonplace Landscape: An Archaeology of Urban Renewal along the Color Line. *World Archaeology* 38(1):60–71.

Nigh, Ronald. 1999. Agriculture in the Information Age: The Transnational Ecology of Corporate versus Smallholder Farming. *Urban Anthropology and Studies of Cultural Systems and World Economic Development* 28(3/4):253–298.

Perdue, Charles L. Jr., Thomas E. Barden, and Robert K. Phillips. 1976. *Weevils in the Wheat: Interviews with Virginia Ex-Slaves*. Charlottesville: University of Virginia Press.

Pilcher, Jeffery M. 2017. *Food in World History*. London: Routledge.

Reeves, Matthew B. 2010. Historical, Archaeological, and Architectural Research at the Gilmore Cabin. Technical Report. Montpelier Station: Montpelier Foundation.

———. 2014. Home Is Where the Woods Are: An Analysis of a Civil War Camp Complex in Virginia. In *From These Honored Dead: Historical Archaeology of the American Civil War*, edited by Clarence R. Grier, Douglas D. Scott, and Lawrence E. Babits, 141–158. Gainesville: University Press of Florida.

Reeves, Matthew B., and Kevin Fogle. 2007. Excavations at the Madison's First Family Home, Mount Pleasant (1723–1800): Summary of Archaeological Excavations 1997– 2004. Technical Report. Montpelier Station: Montpelier Foundation.

Reeves, Matthew B., and Susana R. Lewis. 2005. Orange County African Americans: Success and Hardship in the Decades Following Emancipation. Technical Report. Montpelier Station: Montpelier Foundation.

Reeves, Matthew B., and A. Marshall. 2009. Center for the Constitution Expansion. Technical Report. Montpelier Station: Montpelier Foundation.

Reeves, Matthew B., and Mark A. Trickett. 2009. Landscape Inventory of Civil War Sites in the "North Woods," James Madison's Montpelier and Cultural Resource Management Plan for their Preservation. Technical Report. Montpelier Station: Montpelier Foundation.

Schlotterbeck, John Thomas. 1980. Plantation and Farm: Social and Economic Change in Orange and Greene Counties. PhD diss., Johns Hopkins University.

Scott, James C. 1985. *Weapons of the Weak: Everyday Forms of Peasant Resistance*. New Haven, CT: Yale University Press.

Scott, William Wallace. 1907. *A History of Orange County, Virginia: From Its Formation in 1734 (o.s.) to the End of Reconstructions in 1870*. Richmond: Waddey Co.

Shackel, Paul. 2011. *New Philadelphia: An Archaeology of Race in the Heartland*. Berkeley: University of California Press.

Sherwood, Cullen W. 2010. Soils and Land Use in Montpelier's Landmark Forest. Technical Report. Montpelier Station: Montpelier Foundation.

Stone, Glenn Davis. 2007. Agricultural Deskilling and the Spread of Genetically Modified Cotton in Warangal. *Current Anthropology* 48(1):67–103.

Trickett, Mark A. 2013. Can See to Can't See: Excavations of the Field Slave Quarters at the Home of James Madison, 2012–2013. Technical Report. Montpelier Station: Montpelier Foundation.

Trotter, Joe William, Jr. 2000. African Americans and the Industrial Revolution. *Organization of American Historians Magazine of History* 15(1):19–23.

Tucker, Bram. 2014. Rationality and the Green Revolution. In *Applied Evolutionary Anthropology: Darwinian Approaches to Contemporary World Issues*, edited by Mhairi A. Gibson and David W. Lawson, 15–38. New York: Springer-Verlag.

Woehlke, Stefan F., and Matthew B. Reeves. 2015. Grid-Based Metal Detector Survey: Montpelier Foundation Department of Archaeology 2012 Field Survey. Technical Report. Montpelier Station: Montpelier Foundation.

Woehlke, Stefan F., and Mark A. Trickett. 2015. Echoes Past: Landscape Inventory of Archaeological Sites Identified by Metal Detector Survey, 2010–2011. Technical Report. Montpelier Station: Montpelier Foundation.

5

Worth(Less)

Value and Destruction in a Nineteenth- and Twentieth-Century Quarry Town

ADAM FRACCHIA

The nineteenth- and twentieth-century quarry town of Texas, Maryland, is fading away; it is being destroyed by a quarry and by commercial development. One by one the houses are being torn down and the land on which they sit is being graded and repurposed. Although Texas was the source of stone for the monuments of Baltimore and the nation and it produced the lime that fueled industries that propelled America into a world power, the town has proven hard to preserve. As the last of the early quarry homes is vacant and no effort has been made to protect it, this chapter asks why preservation of this home (figure 5.1) and the heritage of the wider town has been so neglected and silenced when the products of the workers who lived in these homes have become iconic symbols and memorials.[1]

The logic by which preservation decisions are weighed is dependent on the same processes that determined value in the past and led to destruction of both property and people. In the capitalist process, the accumulation of capital is regarded as a paramount goal and value is measured in relation to the ability to contribute to the maximization of capital. This logic justifies the continued destruction of older configurations of space and other impediments to accumulation. To facilitate this process, removal and destruction rely on a dispossession of rights and assigning value to people, their material culture, and ultimately their history in

Figure 5.1. John Landragan House, ca. 1984. Photograph by John McGrain, photo courtesy of the Baltimore County Department of Planning.

reference to the accumulation of capital. Existing stereotypes and patterns of racism are drawn upon to support the capitalist process through the reinforcement of inequality. Thus, the same patterns of discrimination and segregation are used to justify the removal of people, the removal of the built environment, and ultimately, the erasure of undesirable or threatening histories.

In Texas, categories such as black and white, immigrant and native born, skilled and unskilled were used to stratify people deemed to be worth less and were a pretext for their exploitation. Patterns of segregation often became patterns of removal when people were no longer needed or were in the way of new forms of accumulation. Evidence of this hierarchy of ethnicity, race, religion, and class still lies in the material culture and the built environment of Texas. Understanding how this contrast in value and the subsequent removal of people was maintained and perpetuated is necessary to understanding the history of Texas and the fate of its people and its future existence.

Value and Preservation

Part of the problem of preservation in Texas lies in the current popular history of the town, which draws upon a romantic and stereotypical narrative—about a town of Irish immigrants who had fled famine and were full of fighting and hard drinking. These Irish workers fought against blocks of stone but ultimately and inevitably faded away with their town into the larger melting-pot of America (Bertram 1954).[2] This seemingly inevitable story masks a more complicated reality. Accepting such a simplified narrative inhibits a full understanding of why the town is so devalued today.

Viewing the town in terms of production value offers an opening for alternative discourses that expose a more complex and contested town. By studying value in relation to production, one can see an ongoing process that is relevant to the present and that allows for a consideration of class as a relational analytical term rather than a gradational category where material culture is used as an indicator of wealth (Wurst 1999, 2006; Wurst and McGuire 1999).

In the town of Texas, social categories were continually exploited over the decades to allow the hazardous quarry industry to prosper by manipulating social stratification, residential differentiation, and ultimately removal, depending on what the needs of the quarry industry dictated. Social categories were tied to notions of value formulated within a capitalist process, a process that always sought to maximize the accumulation of capital and that based an individual's worth on his or her relation to that accumulation. This maximization was drawn from the exploitation of others, whereby laborers created surplus value for capitalists in exchange for a living wage (Harvey 1985, 1). To continue this unequal relationship, the capitalist class has to reproduce itself and maintain its domination over labor (Harvey 1985, 1; Harvey 1989).

In the capitalist process, the overall health of society is seen to be contingent on the maximization of profit. Conditions that satisfy the maximization of profit, even if they have negative consequences, are tolerated or promoted. For instance, in Baltimore in the 1950s and 1960s and even as recently as the 2010s, urban renewal maps classified the quality of housing and housing markets in neighborhoods. Based on value judgements, such maps were used to justify renewal and invoke eminent domain to seize and demolish homes and communities. These actions were taken with the stated goal of supporting wider economic development, but they resulted in the destruction of the fabric of communities. This same pattern of valuation was used in Texas, Maryland.

Devaluation is also evidenced in the treatment of people. As members of society, workers are an essential part of the chain of production. In this regard, although they are seen to have the capacity and obligation to further the accumulation of capital, the unequal relationships between the capitalist and worker needs to be maintained and the capitalist devalues the latter to justify inequity. Furthermore, if the conditions that would ensure people's preservation impede the maximization of profit and labor power, they are deemed to be in the way and thus must be devalued and removed. Devaluation allows the capitalist to reduce people to a condition where their lives can be ultimately seen as expendable, placing them in a state that the Italian philosopher Giorgio Agamben (1998) calls bare life. When a person is reduced to this state, he or she can be expunged from society and deprived of any and all rights. Likewise, the environment, buildings, and even history can be sacrificed for the health of society or the state.

Patterns of devaluation and subsequent marginalization are predicated on physical and cultural differences or abnormalities that are tied to production. These categorizations correlate physical differences with stereotypes and prevailing social ideals. In the late nineteenth century and the early twentieth, systematic racial categorizations were detailed in period reference works such as the *Dictionary of Races or Peoples* (Folkmar and Folkmar 1911) and *The Races of Europe* (Ripley 1899). The taxonomies such books generated were used to create or illustrate hierarchies of workers based on social and physical qualities. Using origin, customs, and physical traits as prescriptive, these books defined a worker's fate as inherently linked more to a natural law than to an exploitative process, thus masking the exploitation of capitalism. Further, since workers were said to own their labor power, they were deemed responsible for their own well-being. In Texas, this rhetoric is seen in the language and perspectives of journalists who denigrated the Irish and later African Americans for their supposed lack of industry and intemperance. In reality, the material conditions of working people are heavily influenced by or are a result of their relation to the capitalist process and the conditions set by the individuals who purchase their labor (Rockman 2009, 11).

Preservation often reflects the same dominant discourse about what is valuable in terms of the accumulation of capital and similar notions of devaluation. According to the National Park Service (2017), preservation is the act or process of applying measures necessary to sustain the existing form, integrity, and materials of a historic property. The preservation of properties is tied to the significance of what is valued, and buildings are removed or destroyed when there is a perceived lack of value. This value is most commonly established by weighing the property against the accumulation of capital. When a perception of limited or no value exists, then insufficient capital is applied to maintain or sustain properties over time.

Preservation can also be seen as a threat to the capitalist process. The existence of a physical remnant that narrates the realities of capitalism can be construed as impeding the accumulation of capital either by illustrating the effects of capitalism or standing in the way of new spatial configurations of capitalism (Harvey 1989). If preservation is viewed as a potential threat, then the past may be buried to hide or destroy the evidence (Gonzalez-Ruibal 2008). As Paul Shackel (2009) notes, even industrial ruins can be used to remember or recall working-class history and thus may be purposely removed from the landscape or contested. For example, the Ludlow Tent Colony Site, which was the scene of an attack in 1914 by the Colorado National Guard and company guards on a tent colony of 1,200 striking coal miners and their families at Ludlow, Colorado, serves as a memorial and part of the working-class identity in southern Colorado as well as a symbol of power in labor struggles (Saitta 2007, 94). Possibly because of this identity and because of anti-union sentiment, the Ludlow Monument that honors the victims of the Ludlow Massacre was vandalized in 2003 (Saitta 2007, 97–98). Thus, if preserved, sites like the Ludlow Tent Colony Site, now a National Historic Landmark, or Texas, Maryland, can show the effect and contradictions of capitalism.

Texas, Maryland

The town of Texas, Maryland, is located about twelve miles north of Baltimore in Baltimore County (figure 5.2). From the 1840s to the twenty-first century, Texas was the site of multiple limestone quarries and kilns around a town where the quarry workers and their families lived (figure 5.3). Although one active quarry still remains and continues to grow, the other quarries have been filled in and most of the quarry outbuildings have been destroyed.

The town of Texas has always been tied to the limestone industry. The

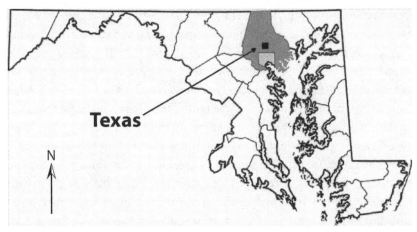

Figure 5.2. Location of the town of Texas in Baltimore County, Maryland. Baltimore is denoted in the lightest color. Image by Adam Fracchia.

Figure 5.3. Workers in a Texas quarry and adjacent limekilns in 1892. The photo shows the dangerous nature of the industry's extractive infrastructure. The chimney stacks of seven lime kilns are visible in the top of the photograph along with a series of lean-to shelters and sheds. Perched on the edge of the quarry is a pump house to keep the quarries from filling with water. Source: Harry T. Campbell Sons' Corporation, *The Campbell Story—75 Years of Growth* (Towson: Harry T. Campbell Sons' Corporation, 1967), 1.

combination of the arrival of the railroad in the area in the late 1830s, abundant shallow limestone deposits, and cheap immigrant labor led to growth of the quarry industry by native-born entrepreneurs. The industry quickly grew after the 1840s. In the 1850s, the amount of mineral wealth in Texas was compared to the potential wealth in the gold regions of California.[3] Stone was blasted out of the quarries and burned in the nearby kilns to make lime to fertilize fields and for industrial applications. Building stone was also quarried in Texas and nearby quarries for notable buildings such as the Washington Monument and United States Capitol in Washington, DC; the spires of St. Patrick's Cathedral in New York; and City Hall and the Peabody Institute in Baltimore (Williams 1893, 136). Although the industry waned around the 1880s, the demand for stone never disappeared.

For much of the nineteenth century, the quarry work was done by hand. A student paper written in the 1980s contains an interview with Lloyd Parks, who worked for a quarry owner in 1915 and described the lime-burning operation.[4] Limestone was quarried by seven to eight men. Two men would take it from the quarry in a cart drawn by three mules. A worker known as a breaker would use a ten-pound hammer to crush the limestone into eight-inch pieces at the top of the kiln while two men filled the kiln with fuel and stone and emptied out the lime. Workers labored in two shifts, from 6 am to 2 pm and from 2 pm to 6 am. The process Lloyd Park described shows the demanding and labor-intensive nature of the work of extracting and burning limestone into lime.

Mechanization and capital improvements were key to the industry of extracting building stone because they made it cheaper and faster to extract limestone. In and around Texas, as in other industrial locations, mechanization and consolidation continued into the twentieth century, and technology drove the expansion of the unskilled labor force (Jones 1999, 156; Rodgers 1978). In the quarries from which building stone was extracted, the stone work became largely mechanized. Diamond drills could drill a hole one inch in diameter and two feet deep in the span of five minutes. Doing the same work took three men with hammers and drills two to three hours.[5] The nearby Beaver Dam and Cockeysville Marble Works were also using steam powered saws and other dressing machinery at this time.[6]

Even though the burning of lime became less important and the industry became consolidated in the first decades of the twentieth century, the industry eventually expanded through mechanization. In the lime-burning industry, mechanization brought large-scale extractive operations that grew in size and scope throughout the twentieth century. The trend toward automation and mechanization has continued into the present, leading to operations that remove thousands of tons of stone daily in an ever-expanding quarry that has removed a large portion of the town.

For much of the town's history, a supply of disposable workers was needed because quarry work was labor intensive and dangerous. Numerous newspaper articles documented industrial accidents in the town (Fracchia and Brighton 2015), and the US federal population census from 1850 to 1900 recorded an increase in the incidences of widowhood in Texas. The intensive, physically dangerous work was not the only risk for quarry workers. Inhaling airborne contaminants resulting from the quarrying and processing of limestone and lime also contributed to the death of residents as well. According to interment records from St. Joseph's Church in Texas, from 1896 to 1924, the cause of death of 62 percent of the people buried in the church's cemetery (142 of 229) was a respiratory ailment such as tuberculosis or pneumonia. Silicosis, a lung disease caused by inhaling silica particles, increased the susceptibility of Texans to these illnesses and possibly others because silicosis destroys the lymph channels in the lungs, forming nodules and scarring the lungs and leading to increased vulnerability to infection (Foster 1985, 273–274). The link between dust and this "miner's disease" was known, and that knowledge could have been used to protect workers (Foster 1985, 268). However, the level of safety in the working environment was often more related to industry priorities and class relations, as Janet Siskind (1988, 203) found in her study of the intersection of class and silicosis in a nineteenth-century axe-grinding factory. The focus on the maximization of profit in Texas meant that a minimal amount was spent on the safety of the labor force.

In the second half of the nineteenth century, Irish immigrants met the quarry's need for unskilled workers. Quarry owners regarded the Irish, who were escaping oppression, famine, and poverty, as a source of cheap and expendable labor. The famine of 1845 to 1852, known as the Great Famine or the Great Hunger (An Gorta Mor), claimed more than a million lives and led to mass emigration from Ireland (Dolan 2008, 68; Kinealy 2014). The British poor law exacerbated this exodus through evictions and by compelling tenants to turn over their land to their landlord

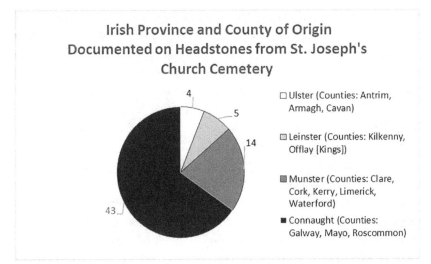

Figure 5.4. Distribution of the provinces and counties in Ireland listed on headstones in the St. Joseph's Church cemetery in Texas, Maryland. Image by Adam Fracchia, adapted from McGrain 1971.

(Dolan 2008, 70). As a result of this removal, 1.5 million Irish sailed for the United States in the period 1846–1851.

Based on headstone inscriptions in St. Joseph's Church cemetery in Texas, the province of Connaught in the west of Ireland saw the highest number of immigrants to Texas, followed by Munster in the southwest, then Leinster and Ulster. Eighty-six percent of the inscriptions with a home county listed mentioned Connaught or Munster (figure 5.4) (McGrain 1971). This wave of Irish immigrants was equally divided between males and females. More than half were unskilled laborers and as many as 90 percent were Catholic (Dolan 2008, 75; O'Donnell 1997, 16). In one sense, the Irish immigrants, who were mainly from the poor and rural west and south of Ireland, were leaving one landscape of removal for another.

Separation and Hierarchy

From the inception of the town of Texas, class and ethnic differences were established and reinforced. The quarry owners were originally native-born American entrepreneurs and landowners, while the first source of workers were predominantly Irish immigrants. The quarry owners created a landscape that separated them from and stratified the Irish. As a small, largely Irish town in a predominantly agricultural area of Baltimore County, the town of Texas was fairly unique. This case study of Texas is also distinctive because while the archaeology of the Irish diaspora has been studied in urban settings (Brighton 2008; Reckner 2004; Rotman 2010; Yamin 2001), the diaspora has been researched to a lesser degree in small industrial towns such as Texas.

The archaeological record provides evidence of the processes of marginalization and segregation in the material culture differences and spatial relationships within Texas. The industry, and subsequently the town, was segregated first by class and ethnicity and later by race. In the early years of the town, a largely Irish immigrant population was effectively made into "good workers" and commodities, who in turn were consumers absorbing surplus goods. All the while, the bonds of community and shared religious and ethnic identity were minimized or restructured.

The spatial landscape reinforced the industrial order for much of the second half of the nineteenth century, as is evident on historic maps. The native-born American entrepreneurs occupied the more spacious outskirts of the community, the skilled Irish workers lived closer to the center of town, and the unskilled laborers lived farther away from town and closest to the hazardous quarry and kilns. Further supporting the notion that unskilled laborers were seen as disposable is a county map from 1877 that depicts the unmarked homes of laborers as unlabeled boxes next to the railroad tracks using the same symbol that was used to mark the lime kilns (figure 5.5).

Since the town was largely Irish and Catholic for most of the nineteenth century, the town came under attack from outside as well. In Ireland, the Catholic Irish were marked as inferior to support the unequal tenant-landlord relationship, and this pattern of marginalization continued in the United States (Allen 1994; Orser 2007, 92). In the United States, newspapers often promoted stereotypes of the Irish as drunk, unproductive, and belligerent. Such attitudes contributed to the alienation of the Irish community and helped fuel physical attacks by members of the anti-immigrant and anti-Catholic Know Nothing Party. According to the Catholic Editing Company (1914, 109), on several occasions men in Texas had to stay up all night to guard their homes and the church from Know Nothing rioters. The *Baltimore County Advocate* also notes that residents

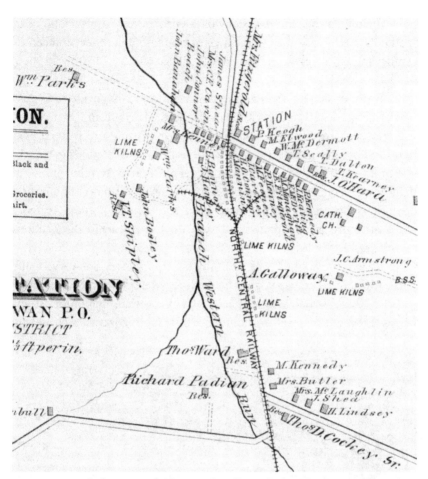

Figure 5.5. Detail of an 1877 map showing the village of Texas. The center of the community lies at the intersection of the railroad tracks and main road at the location of the station. Quarries were located in the unlabeled space adjacent to the kilns labeled on the map. *Atlas of Fifteen Miles Around Baltimore Including Anne Arundel County, Maryland* (Philadelphia: G. M. Hopkins, 1877). Image courtesy of the Sheridan Libraries of the Johns Hopkins University.

of Texas were often assaulted in Baltimore.[7] This violence and efforts to intimidate Irish workers segregated them from other workers and other communities.

Within the town of Texas, class-based segregation existed on the landscape among the Irish that reinforced the industrial hierarchy. Evidence of this separation is reflected in the architecture and patterns of private property ownership. Differences based on class are visible in the size, location, ornamentation, and proximity of the residences. Similar patterns of spatial hierarchy inscribed in architecture are found in other nineteenth-century industrial towns such as Lowell, Massachusetts (Mrozowski 2006, 74).

In Texas, unskilled laborers typically lived in two-bay-wide rowhouse blocks along the railroad tracks. Skilled laborers lived in similar two-bay-wide housing units, but they had more space, privacy and were located in a slightly safer area farther from the trains and quarries (figure 5.6). The homes of quarry operators and owners were free standing and were built using a completely different design from the two-bay configuration of workers' homes. The quarry operators' and owners' homes had more space and more ornamentation and were situated in more idyllic locations on the outskirts of town near major roads (figure 5.7).

To learn more about the effect of the quarry industry on everyday life in the town, three archaeological field schools were conducted from 2009 to 2011.[8] This research was supplemented by a reexamination of assemblages recovered from several home sites in Texas by contract archaeology

Figure 5.6. Poe-Burns duplex. Photograph by Herbert Harwood Jr., 1987; used courtesy of the Baltimore County Public Library.

Figure 5.7. Thomas Fortune House. Photograph by John McGrain; used courtesy of the Baltimore County Department of Planning.

that had been conducted in the 1980s and 1990s. Using both of these data sets, the research focused on the archaeological remains of several residences of quarry workers and their families that date to the second half of the nineteenth to the first half of the twentieth century.

The archaeological sites investigated were the homes of unskilled and skilled Irish workers and their families. The first site, a large rowhouse block next to a quarry, was built in 1854. For much of the building's history, laborers in the lime and quarry business rented the rowhouses in the block. The rowhouse block was documented to have sixteen households until 1897, when it was improved to just eight households. By the end of that year, the entire rowhouse block had burned down. The second site, a rowhouse home closer to the center of town, was built sometime around the 1850s and was owned by storekeepers until the 1860s, when skilled and unskilled workers occupied the property. Workers occupied this site until it burned down in 1904. Located near the center of town, the third site was a home of unknown design that was likely built around the 1850s and was occupied by a skilled laborer and his family into the twentieth century. The fourth site was a nearby duplex home built around the 1850s and occupied by two skilled workers and their families into the beginning of twentieth century.

The artifacts found at these four residential sites in the form of mass-produced consumable items indicate that the occupants of these homes were paying attention to the social norms and behaviors of the period and were trying to gain acceptance in a society that was openly hostile to them. Acceptance would have been appealing because it offered a degree of value and inclusion and thus protection.

The archaeological research also provided evidence that the material culture reinforced patterns of stratification and marginalization between the skilled and unskilled Irish workers who lived in Texas during the second half of the nineteenth century (Fracchia 2014; Fracchia and Brighton 2015). Differences in the quality and quantity of the material assemblages were observed across the four sites and correlate to the workers' place in the industry. Social status made these industrial divisions seem like a reflection of one's own effort rather than a reflection of the industrial hierarchy and residential differentiation that limited opportunities for mobility because of unequal access to resources. In this way, everyday objects, such as glassware, ceramics, medicine bottles, buttons, and smoking pipes reinforced the values of the autonomous and privatized individual (Leone 2005) who was responsible for his or her own condition and thus, the degree of bare life to which he or she was reduced.

The dining ceramics and glassware from the four sites illustrate attempts to adhere to period dining practices. In the nineteenth century, genteel dining etiquette dictated that people use specialized vessels for specific functions (Fitts 1999; Lucas 1994). Thus, observing an increase in the number of complex vessel forms and servingware found at a site suggests a change over time in the dining rituals to those prescribed as more appropriate by the wider society (Brighton 2009; Wall 1994, 2000). The decoration styles on these ceramics can indicate the ability to participate in wider social trends, integration into the market, and social differentiation. Comparisons of the quantity of decorated styles and vessels forms indicate that unskilled workers in Texas had few matched ceramics. In contrast, the skilled worker's sites yielded more matched ceramics and ceramics that were more contemporary with the time period. Yet all the

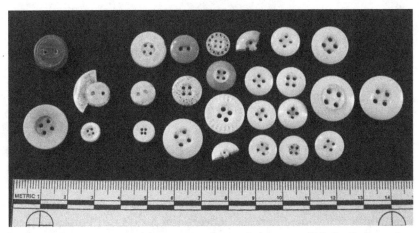

Figure 5.8. Buttons recovered from one residence of a laborer and his family. Image by Adam Fracchia.

sites indicate attempts to follow period dining practices with the number and quality of ceramics differentiating these households.

Buttons indicate a similar pattern of social stratification. Buttons found at the Texas sites represent much of the only evidence of the dress of the individuals in a household, since virtually no fragments of clothing were recovered. While the choice of clothing (and thus buttons) may represent one's individual identity, this choice may also be a reflection of one's group identity (Cunnington 1964; Entwistle 2000; McCracken 1988; White 2008). Thus, while buttons are functional, they also represent how people or a group have chosen to communicate and express ideas and identity.

The buttons found at the Texas sites indicate the efforts of individuals within a household to differentiate themselves while following appropriate standards of dress (Figure 5.8). The analysis examined 413 buttons, of which 118 (29 percent) were decorated, 288 (70 percent) were undecorated, and 7 (2 percent) were classified as other. The four sites exhibited similar ratios of decorated to undecorated buttons. Overall, the main difference observed between the buttons found at the four sites is in the quality of the material, which is a reflection of social differentiation among the sites. Although the analysis is limited, the buttons demonstrate that while the people at all of the houses attempted to adhere to notions of display and respectability, they did so with differing abilities.

In addition to the ceramics and buttons found at the four sites, the medicines recovered show disparities in health care that is consistent with the pattern of residential differentiation across the sites. Medicine during the nineteenth century included those prescribed by physicians or druggists, proprietary medicines, and home remedies. Home remedies consisting of plants are largely absent from the sample due to the lack of floral data but both proprietary and prescribed medicines were recovered through the identification of glass medicine bottles. Bottles for proprietary medicines or possible proprietary medicines were found at all four of the sites. These medicines ranged from basic remedies for constipation, such as castor oil and citrate of magnesia, to treatments for worms and genital diseases. One difference between the sites is that bottles for prescribed medicines were not found in the residences of unskilled workers. This difference may reflect a disparity in their ability to afford doctors even though the doctors were nearby, and fits with the general pattern of residential differentiation observed in Texas. Without access to doctors, even though doctors were just outside of town, the health of the unskilled workers would have been adversely affected, which would have reinforced the pattern of residential differentiation.

Personal items suggest that residents of Texas may have internalized class divisions. For example, pipes were found at all four of the sites, which indicates that smoking was common among individuals in all the households. The same white clay pipes were found in all of the workers' sites, but the pipe decoration varied according to class position. The homes of unskilled laborers contained some pipes with Irish symbols and slogans, for example "Home Rule," whereas the homes of skilled laborers and homeowners contained some pipes with American imagery, such as the eagle. Toward the last quarter of the nineteenth century, the Home Rule campaign of Ireland advocated for Irish self-government (Brighton 2009, 109), while in the Unites States, the Home Rule movement also was linked to labor struggles (Foner 1978; Reckner 2004). Unskilled laborers may have adopted such symbols as an expression of Irish heritage or nationalism or possibly in support of the labor movement. In contrast, skilled workers may have supported American imagery on their pipes as an effort to gain acceptance in American society.

Material culture suggests that patterns of marginalizing and stratifying workers persisted through the second half of the nineteenth century and into the twentieth century. During the 1880s and 1890s, evidence exists of increased strikes by the mostly Irish lime burners in Texas (Fracchia 2014, 120–121). This labor activism happened during a period where the community saw an increase in the arrival of Eastern and Southern European immigrants and African Americans who likely migrated from the South. The experiences of these groups in Texas during this time period are largely absent in the historical record of the town.

By the turn of the twentieth century, African Americans occupied the same locations as the Irish laborers. Artifacts from laborers' houses of this period are similar and nearly impossible to separate by race. Both black and Irish men were employed as laborers in the quarry industry. Yet African Americans do not appear in the local history of the town. For instance, African Americans are not mentioned in the documents of the local Catholic church and its school during this period, centers of social life in the community. This distinctive lack of documentation of African Americans in Texas town life supports the notion that the spatial separation of whites and blacks on the landscape became more pronounced in the twentieth century.

Segregation and Removal

The categorization and racialization of the Irish in the nineteenth century is one example of the creation of divisions that allowed them to be stratified and viewed as worth less than others and disposable. In Texas, immigrant workers and their families were attacked for being Irish and Catholic. Newspaper articles of the mid-nineteenth century depicted the Irish workers of Texas as lazy, drunk, and belligerent—traits that were used as justification for their marginalization and their segregation. Since sobriety was linked to the virtue of hard work and, ultimately, compliance with industry, it is notable that all of the descriptions of instances of violence and inappropriate behavior in town that were documented in the newspapers were tied to the consumption of alcohol. During the nineteenth century, drinkers were generally labeled as outcasts and outlaws. Characterizing Irish workers in this way opened the door for the use of legal authority in exercising control over this group (Tropman 1986, 30–31).

At the beginning of the twentieth century, the rhetoric of discrimination shifted as Irish immigrants and Irish identity were gradually accepted. During that time, the same stereotypes of being drunk, lazy, and belligerent were used against African Americans, who increasingly were employed in the quarry industry in Texas. African Americans occupied the lowest position in the industry and were paid the least, followed by Italians, then by general laborers (Weeks 1886, 38). One newspaper example used the pretext of alcohol consumption to depict African Americans as primitive. The article, titled "His Indian Blood Tamed: Big Negro Meets His Waterloo in Texas Deputy," described how a large African American who was said to be under the influence of alcohol and showing off his "war whoop" was put in his place with a shot to the chest, then arrested.[9] While there is some documentation of the stratification of African Americans in Texas in this time, there is less evidence of the experience of Italian immigrants during this time since they generally did not appear in the newspapers. However, the Italians in Texas fared better than the African Americans and eventually became part of the community, likely due to their shared Catholic identity with the established Irish residents.

As Irish identity become increasingly accepted in the early twentieth century, African Americans were confined to the west side of the railroad tracks next to the quarry, in the worst housing conditions in the town. A local resident who moved to Texas in the 1930s remembers that Irish and Italian families lived in town but African Americans lived in an enclave down by the railroad tracks (Deboalt 1993). Legal means aided in this separation and order. For example, a 1926 housing covenant on a parcel of land on the north side of the town's main road excluded "persons of negro extraction" from living on the main road. Thus, as the Irish had been in earlier decades, African Americans were physically segregated and were forced to live next to the quarry. African Americans in Baltimore experienced similar patterns of spatial separation and marginalization under practices of redlining and blockbusting and other discriminatory policies (Olson 1997).

Around the 1940s, new mining technology made the presence of a ready reserve of workers living next to the quarries significantly less necessary. Instead, quarry owners began to see the land in the town of Texas as more valuable for its mineral resources and increasingly valuable for the growing residential and commercial needs of the suburban population of Baltimore County. The profit from the quarry industry and its expansion were valued over the well-being of African Americans living in town. Authorities labeled the homes of African Americans on the west side of the tracks in Texas as rat-infested slums and used this rhetoric to justify the removal of the homes and people living there.[10] The lack of documentation about the removal of these homes makes it unclear where these individuals moved to and where they subsequently worked.

Destruction of the town and community in Texas was further accomplished through the slower process of disinvestment, including a lack of updates to basic infrastructure and denial of community development funds. This neglect explains why an observer commented in the late 1950s that the main street looked like the Germans had bombarded it (Bertram 1954). Thus, the town of Texas was slowly destroyed by a pattern of financial starvation and physical collapse because the town and the dwindling number of workers who lived there were no longer needed to serve the maximization of profits for the quarry industry. Although many residents sought work outside town, the town continued to shrink. The town could be sacrificed because of its lack of value in relation to the accumulation of capital and its reduction to bare life.

Weighed against the logic of capital accumulation in this manner, preservation efforts in Texas have generally failed. Attempts to nominate the town as a historic district met resistance and were blocked. In recent years, government agencies have used eminent domain to seize and destroy parts of the town. For example, in the 1990s, historic homes and a tavern along the railroad were demolished in order to build a road that would alleviate traffic congestion and a light rail line. According to a report that was conducted to comply with Section 4(f) of the National Transportation Act of 1966 (EA Associates 1986, 3–8), the homes had to be demolished because quarry operations could not be impeded and it would be too costly to move the homes a few feet to preserve them. In more recent years, other historic Texas homes that were deemed protected by the limited preservation ordinances of Baltimore County were illegally demolished with little repercussions because they were in the way of proposed commercial development. This myopic and sanctioned destruction has resulted in the removal of the town's history through physical demolition and, along with it, the evidence of the influence of capitalism on the lives of workers and their families.

The value of the few remaining homes in Texas continues to be weighed against the needs of the capitalist process, which includes the home pictured in the beginning of this chapter (figure 5.1). With so much of the town already destroyed, the integrity of the remnants of the town including the Landragan House are called into question and the perception of poor integrity according to the guidelines of the National Register of Historic Places becomes the excuse for a lack of effort. Without strong incentives for preservation or enough political will, the needs of capitalist development will outweigh considerations of the value to be gained by preservation. Through the existing paradigm of value, the homes of people who in the past were deemed to be inferior are not worthy of preservation. This notion is compounded when the neglect is seemingly justified by their inability to contribute to the accumulation of capital. By extension, the buildings are seen as worth less and as barriers to new spatial forms that maximize accumulation.

Conclusion

The archaeological record of Texas, Maryland, demonstrates the process of perpetuating the devaluation of people in order to maximize the accumulation capital during the second half of the nineteenth century and the first half of the twentieth century. This record will be lost when the landscape and its archaeological remains are destroyed. Since historical documents often do not include data on marginalized groups and often accept this capitalist process, the spatial record embodied in the landscape and material culture constitute the most potent evidence of this process and these structural relationships. This record details the complex effects of a hierarchy of value on the everyday lives of the marginalized, who are frequently reshuffled and removed. Unfortunately, further research in Texas has been limited by lack of access and the lack of remaining archaeological deposits, including the material record of workspaces and the homes of quarry owners and operators.

Archaeologists have a responsibility to challenge accepted perspectives about whose experience is valuable in history and to work to understand the processes behind removals of people in the past (Little 2007). Without an effective strategy to contest the logic of this process, future research will remain heavily influenced by the capitalist process and efforts to preserve the diversity of human experience will continue to be stymied. Historical archaeologists need to take a radical stance to partner with others to preserve, control, and use space and the material record in ways that can visibly speak to this process and its devastating logic of hierarchical value based on an exploitative process. In taking such a position, historical archaeologists can challenge and redefine whose history and experiences are deemed to be worth less and contest rather than passively support segregation and removal.

Notes

1. Since the writing of this chapter, the Landragan home has been sold and is listed as a commercial property. However, the property still has no legal protection.

2. James C. Bertram, "Street Signs: Texas," *The Baltimore Sun*, August 8, 1954, SM14.

3. "Baltimore Co. Lime," *American Farmer* 6, no. 11 (1851): 422.

4. "Production of Agricultural Lime in Texas, Baltimore County, MD," 9–10, student paper on file at the Maryland Historical Trust, Crownsville, Maryland, 1980s.

5. "Maryland Marble," *The Baltimore Sun*, August 14, 1872.

6. "Maryland Marble."

7. "Assaulted," *Baltimore County Advocate*, January 7, 1854.

8. The Archaeology of Labor and Immigration Project initiated and operated the research program and archaeological field schools under the direction of Stephen Brighton at the University of Maryland, College Park.

9. "His Indian Blood Tamed," *The Baltimore Sun*, September 18, 1911.

10. "Towson Slum Betterment Promised," *Baltimore Sun*, June 3, 1943, 30.

References Cited

Agamben, Giorgio. 1998. *Homo Sacer: Sovereign Power and Bare Life*. Stanford, CA: Stanford University Press.

Allen, Theodore W. 1994. *The Invention of the White Race*. Vol. 1, *Racial Oppression and Social Control*. London: Verso.

Brighton, Stephen A. 2008. Degrees of Alienation: The Material Evidence of the Irish and Irish American Experience, 1850–1910. *Historical Archaeology* 42(4):132–153.

———. 2009. *Historical Archaeology of the Irish Diaspora: A Transnational Approach*. Knoxville: University of Tennessee Press.

Catholic Editing Company. 1914. *The Catholic Church in the United States of America*. Vol. III. New York: Catholic Editing Company.

Cunnington, Phillis. 1964. *Costume in Pictures*. London: Studio Vista Limited.

Deboalt, Katherine Drew. 1993. Company Town with Stone Foundation. *Sunday Sun Magazine*, February 13.

Dolan, Jay P. 2008. *The Irish Americans: A History*. New York: Bloomsbury Press.

EA Associates. 1986. Section 4(f) Assessment: Beaver Dam Road Widening and Extension from Beaver Court to Padonia Road, Baltimore County, Maryland: Draft Environmental Impact Statement. On file at the Baltimore County Department of Planning, Towson, Maryland.

Entwistle, Joanne. 2000. *The Fashioned Body: Fashion, Dress and Modern Social Theory*. Cambridge: Polity.

Fitts, Robert K. 1999. The Archaeology of Middle-Class Domesticity and Gentility in Victorian Brooklyn. *Historical Archaeology* 33(1):39–62.

Folkmar, Daniel, and Elnora C. Folkmar. 1911. *Dictionary of Races or Peoples.* Reports of the Immigration Commission, Vol. 5. Washington, DC: Government Printing Office.

Foner, Eric. 1978. Class, Ethnicity, and Radicalism in the Gilded Age: The Land League and Irish-America. *Marxist Perspectives* 1(2):6–55.

Foster, James. 1985. The Western Dilemma: Miners, Silicosis, and Compensation. *Labor History* 26(2):268–287.

Fracchia, Adam D. 2014. Laboring in Stone: The Urbanization of Capital in the Quarry Town of Texas, Maryland, and Its Effects, 1840 to 1940. PhD diss., University of Maryland, College Park.

Fracchia, Adam D., and Stephen A. Brighton. 2015. Limestone and Ironstone: Capitalism, Value, and Destruction in a Nineteenth and Twentieth-Century Quarry Town. In *Historical Archaeologies of Capitalism*, edited by Mark P. Leone and Jocelyn E. Knauf, 127–146. Cham: Springer International.

Gonzalez-Ruibal, Alfredo. 2008. A Time to Destroy: An Archaeology of Supermodernity. *Cultural Anthropology* 49(2):247–279.

Harry T. Campbell Sons' Corporation. 1967. *The Campbell Story—75 Years of Growth.* Towson, MD: Harry T. Campbell Sons' Corporation.

Harvey, David. 1985. *The Urbanization of Capital.* Oxford: Basil Blackwell.

———. 1989. *The Urban Experience.* Baltimore, MD: Johns Hopkins University Press.

Jones, Jacqueline. 1999. *A Social History of the Laboring Classes: From Colonial Times to the Present.* Malden, MA: Blackwell.

Kinealy, Christine. 2014. *Charity and the Great Hunger in Ireland: The Kindness of Strangers.* London: Bloomsbury.

Leone, Mark P. 2005. *The Archaeology of Liberty in an American Capital.* Berkeley: University of California Press.

Little, Barbara J. 2007. *Historical Archaeology: Why the Past Matters.* Walnut Creek, CA: Left Coast Press.

Lucas, Michael T. 1994. A la Russe, a la Pell-Mell, or a la Practical: Ideology and Compromise at the Late Nineteenth-Century Dinner Table. *Historical Archaeology* 28(4):80–93.

McCracken, Grant. 1988. *Culture and Consumption: New Approaches to the Symbolic Character of Consumer Goods and Activities.* Bloomington: Indiana University Press.

McGrain, John. 1971. Headstone Inscriptions from St. Joseph's Cemetery, Texas, MD. On file at the Baltimore County Historical Society, Texas, Maryland.

Mrozowski, Stephen A. 2006. *The Archaeology of Class in Urban America.* Cambridge: Cambridge University.

National Park Service. 2017. Technical Preservation Services: Preservation as Treatment. National Park Service. Accessed August 20, 2017. https://www.nps.gov/tps/standards/four-treatments/treatment-preservation.htm.

O'Donnell, L. A. 1997. *Irish Voice and Organized Labor in America: A Biographical Study.* Westport, CT: Greenwood Press.

Olson, Sherry H. 1997. *Baltimore: The Building of an American City*. Baltimore, MD: Johns Hopkins University Press.

Orser, Charles E., Jr. 2007. *The Archaeology of Race and Racialization in Historic America*. Gainesville: University Press of Florida.

Reckner, Paul E. 2004. Home Rulers, Red Hands, and Radical Journalists: Clay Pipes and the Negotiation of Working-Class Irish/Irish American Identity in Late-Nineteenth-Century Paterson, New Jersey. In *Smoking and Culture*, edited by Sean Rafferty and Rob Mann, 241–271. Knoxville: University of Tennessee Press.

Ripley, William Z. 1899. *The Races of Europe: A Sociological Study*. New York: D. Appleton and Co.

Rockman, Seth. 2009. *Scraping By: Wage Labor, Slavery, and Survival in Early Baltimore*. Baltimore, MD: The Johns Hopkins University Press.

Rodgers, Daniel T. 1978. *The Work Ethic in Industrial America 1850–1920*. Chicago: University of Chicago Press.

Rotman, Deborah L. 2010. The Fighting Irish: Historical Archaeology of Nineteenth-Century Catholic Immigrant Experiences in South Bend, Indiana. *Historical Archaeology* 44(2):113–131.

Saitta, Dean J. 2007. *The Archaeology of Collective Action*. Gainesville: University Press of Florida.

Shackel, Paul A. 2009. *The Archaeology of American Labor and Working-Class Life*. Gainesville: University Press of Florida.

Siskind, Janet. 1988. An Axe to Grind: Class Relations and Silicosis in a 19th-Century Factory. *Medical Anthropology Quarterly* 2(3):199–214.

Tropman, John E. 1986. *Conflict in Culture: Permissions Versus Controls and Alcohol Use in American Society*. Lanham, MD: University Press of America.

Wall, Diana diZerega. 1994. *The Archaeology of Gender: Separating the Spheres in Urban America*. New York: Plenum Press.

———. 2000. Family Meals and Evening Parties: Constructing Domesticity in Nineteenth-Century Middle-Class New York. In *Lines that Divide: Historical Archaeologies of Race, Class, and Gender*, edited by James A. Delle, Stephen A. Mrozowski, and Robert Paynter, 109–141. Knoxville: University of Tennessee Press.

Weeks, Thomas C. 1886. *First Biennial Report of the Bureau of Industrial Statistics and Information of Maryland. 1884–84*. Baltimore: Bureau of Industrial Statistics and Information, Baltimore.

White, Carolyn L. 2008. Personal Adornment and Interlaced Identities at the Sherburne Site, Portsmouth, New Hampshire. *Historical Archaeology* 42(2):17–37.

Williams, George H. 1893. Mines and Minerals. In *Maryland, Its Resources, Industries and Institutions*, 89–153. Baltimore, MD: The Sun Job Printing Office.

Wurst, LouAnn. 1999. Internalizing Class in Historical Archaeology. *Historical Archaeology* 33(1):7–21.

———. 2006. A Class All Its Own: Explorations of Class Formation and Conflict. In *Historical Archaeology*, edited by Martin Hall and Stephen W. Silliman, 190–208. Oxford: Blackwell.

Wurst, LouAnn, and Randall H. McGuire. 1999. Immaculate Consumption: A Critique of the "Shop Till You Drop" School of Human Behavior. *International Journal of Historical Archaeology* 3(3):191–199.

Yamin, Rebecca. 2001. Becoming New York: The Five Points Neighborhood. *Historical Archaeology* 35(3):1–5.

6

Removal and Remembering

Archaeology and the Legacies of Displacement in Southern Appalachia

AUDREY HORNING

"Can the year 1650 be fitted into the year 1936?" mused journalist Thomas Henry, pondering the fate of the soon-to-be displaced residents of the Shenandoah National Park region in Virginia's northern Blue Ridge. "Back in the deep, dark pockets of the Blue Ridge Mountains," Henry recalled, "hikers used to stumble on ragged, hungry families housed in windowless, tumble-down shanties and representing about the limit of destitution at which human life could be sustained."[1] When the 190,000-acre park was established in 1936 as the second national park in the eastern United States, much of the land had recently been under cultivation. The park, which was designed to fulfill the recreational needs of 40,000,000 Americans living less than a day's drive away, was pieced together from over 4,000 individual land tracts the Commonwealth of Virginia had purchased or condemned and presented to the federal government. In the process, at least 500 families were displaced in what some considered to be a humanitarian act. To restore, or rather create a "natural" landscape out of the patchwork of recently abandoned settlements, Civilian Conservation Corps volunteers dismantled buildings and endeavored to obscure the detritus of human habitation with imported vegetation.

Such large-scale removals were not unusual in the early part of the twentieth century, as the US government compulsorily acquired vast swathes of land for conversion into military bases or to facilitate infrastructure construction such as the Tennessee Valley Authority's projects. But in considering the character and legacy of removals, the Shenandoah case emerges as different because of the justifications that were employed to support displacement, justifications that still impact on the daily lives of the descendant communities. Removal in this case study adheres to the simple dictionary definition of removal as the act of getting rid of something unwanted: people cast as inferior and understood as being in the wrong place. What determines who and what is unwanted is inevitably bound up in discourses of power, violence, and broader processes of othering, whether it be on the basis of race, ethnicity, economics, or other factors. For the Virginia Blue Ridge, public opinion in favor of removal was strongly influenced by nineteenth- and early twentieth-century local color literature that emphasized the isolation and otherness of communities in southern Appalachia (Batteau 1991; Shapiro 1986). Journalists such as Henry mobilized such literary tropes in reporting on the park movement. In an era of racist eugenics, academics also saw potential in exploiting the park cause and the apparently degenerate nature of the Blue Ridge inhabitants. Most notably, University of Chicago psychologist Mandel Sherman teamed up with Henry to write a study entitled *Hollow Folk* that set forth a theory of social development based on a ranking of five communities in the Shenandoah region (Sherman and Henry 1933). These communities included three mountain hollows, Nicholson, Corbin, and Weakley Hollows (figure 6.1), which were the subjects of the Survey of Rural Mountain Settlement, an intensive historical archaeological study funded by the National Park Service and carried out through a cooperative agreement with the Colonial Williamsburg Foundation (Horning 1999, 2000a, 2000b, 2001, 2004).

According to Sherman and Henry, "within a radius of twenty miles they were able to keep company with the human race on its long journey from primitive ways of living to a modern social order." They argued that since the eighteenth century, the hollows had existed "without contact with law or government" (Sherman and Henry 1933, 214). Sherman and Henry discovered "families of unlettered folk, of almost pure Anglo-Saxon stock, sheltered in tiny, mud-plastered log cabins and supported by a primitive agriculture." Residents had "no community government, no organized religion, little social organization wider than that of the family and clan, and only traces of organized industry." They were "not of the 20th century" (Sherman and

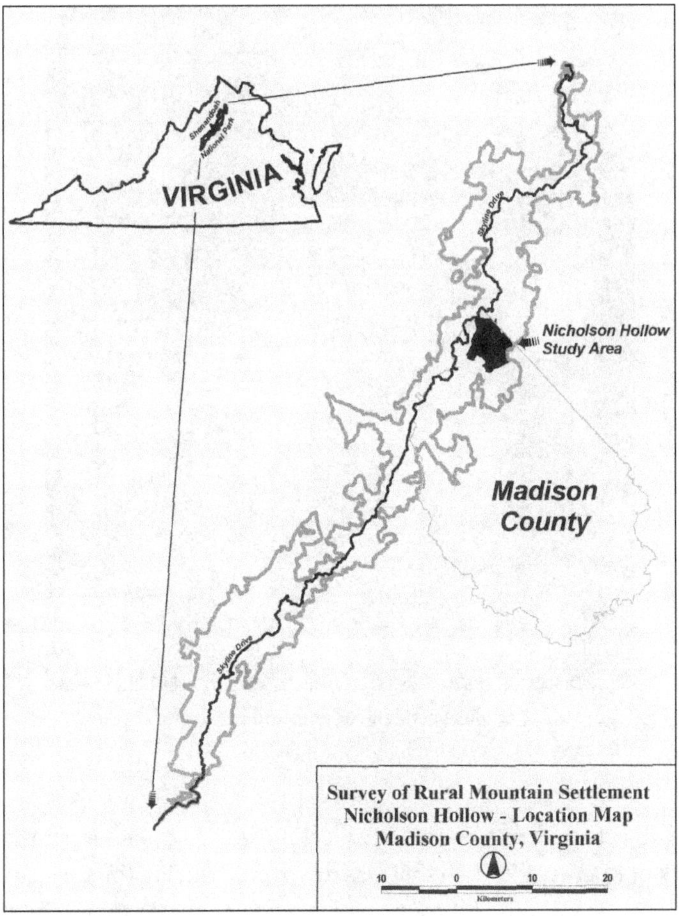

Figure 6.1. Map of Shenandoah National Park study location. Courtesy of Colonial Williamsburg Foundation.

Henry 1933, 1–2). In the introduction to the volume, Fay Cooper Cole of the University of Chicago asserted that the isolated Blue Ridge hollows contained "a wealth of material for science and laymen who are interested in the growth and decline of human culture" (quoted in Sherman and Henry 1933, v). Such a portrayal enabled park promoters and government officials to celebrate the fact that "these people will be moved to more civilized regions of agriculture and industry" (Sherman and Henry 1933, 5).

Archaeological, documentary, and oral historical evidence pertaining to sixty-one historic sites in Nicholson, Corbin, and Weakley Hollows readily and conclusively contradict these 1930s portrayals (Horning 2004).

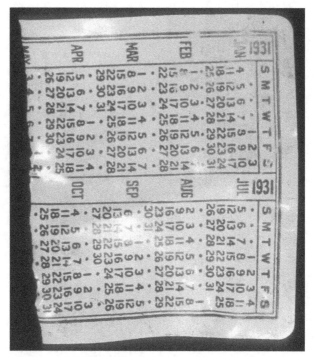

Figure 6.2. Cellulose card calendar found in Corbin Hollow.
Courtesy of Colonial Williamsburg Foundation.

Simple objects such as a battered 1931 cellulose card calendar featuring the artwork of Maxfield Parrish that was discovered during the surface collection of a site in Corbin Hollow provide an obvious and visual refutation of romantic notions about the medieval nature of the inhabitants, just as the finding of automotive parts put the lie to statements about the isolation of mountaineers (figure 6.2). Contrary to the imagery park promoters peddled, Blue Ridge residents did, in fact, wear shoes, cured their sore throats not only with cherry tree bark but also with patent medicines, were as likely to purchase bonded liquor as they were to consume home-grown products, ate their meals from a variety of imported and domestic ceramics and enameled tinwares, listened to popular records on their phonographs, slept in fancy brass beds as well as on cheap metal cots, and served beverages in containers ranging from chipped ironstone mugs and pressed-glass tumblers to porcelain teacups and stemmed wine glasses. In short, the "hollow folk" of the period just before the park owned the same types of goods that are routinely found on archaeological sites of the same era throughout the United States, many of which no doubt originated from the Sears, Roebuck and Company catalog. Hollow residents clearly participated in that milieu according to their own needs and constraints and on their own terms, which were dictated not so much by environment or regional identity as by disparate local and household economies. So how was it possible that entire communities of predominantly white farming families could be forcibly disenfranchised and removed from their homes, some with little to no financial compensation?

The answer lies in a perfect storm that brought together the disparate interests of the eugenics movement, the conservation movement, and the New Deal programs that not only employed the photographers who immortalized mountain poverty through their constructed images but also the laborers who tore down houses, planted trees, and built the Skyline Drive to "restore" nature and bring it safely into the reach of the driving public. The lasting legacy of the removals is considered below through incorporation of descendant perspectives, and contextualized through reference to the archaeology of removal and displacement elsewhere in the American South.

Background: Establishing Shenandoah National Park

The movement to establish Shenandoah National Park can be traced back to 1900, when discussions in Washington focused on the need for a national park in the east. It was not until the 1920s, however, that any serious effort was made to further this plan. In 1924, the Southern Appalachian National Park Committee was formed to select a location in the mountain region (Engle 1998). A charismatic but financially struggling local resort owner, George Freeman Pollock, was quick to see the potential business value of a national park centered on his Skyland resort, which he had founded in 1888, not coincidentally situated in the heart of the region that Sherman and Henry later examined. Pollock (1936) soon emerged as a principal booster for the Blue Ridge as a location for the new national park. One year later, plans were well under way to acquire up to 400,000 acres in the Blue Ridge that the Commonwealth of Virginia, via the Virginia State Commission on Conservation and Development, agreed to subsequently donate to the federal government for Shenandoah National Park. The centerpiece of this new park was to be the ridgetop Skyline Drive, designed to cater to proponents of the new craze for automobile touring. The most appealing element of the new park would be the scenery that could be viewed from the drive, which by and large lay outside the relatively narrow boundaries of the park. As Engle (2006) has chronicled, one of the oddities of the drive is that it was constructed before Shenandoah National Park was officially dedicated. Work began in 1931 and capitalized on New Deal work relief programs to provide the necessary labor.

While it was recognized that any proposed park in the east would have to contend with the reality of dense Euroamerican settlement, there was little agreement throughout much of the park creation process about the appropriate fate of the mountain residents. As Engle (1998, 8–9) has described, "the historian will search in vain in public and private archives in an attempt to find an indication that there was an official master plan, an overriding philosophy, behind the development of Shenandoah in the years 1926–1936." The lack of a master plan also meant lack of agreement over the issue of removal. Many families who either willingly sold their land or were compelled to sell under condemnation proceedings expected to be able to remain as tenants in the national park. It was not until 1934 that Arno Cammerer, director of the National Park Service, announced that all park inhabitants would have to move out of the park. Amid public outcry and a media campaign instigated by Senator Harry Byrd opposing the removal of residents, the administration compromised by authorizing the Resettlement Administration to purchase land outside the park and establish homestead communities for a selection of displaced park families.

The Resettlement Administration built on work already begun by the Division of Subsistence Homesteads, which, according to Jane Becker (1998, 96–97), "worked to relieve rural poverty by building new communities whose economies relied on both domestic production and industry." A New Deal creation, the Division of Subsistence Homesteads has by and large been viewed by scholars in a generally positive light. However, while the New Deal ideologies that supported the work of the Resettlement Administration may have been well intentioned, their impact on individuals and families was not uniformly positive. In the estimation of Wurst and Ridarsky (2014, 234), much historical scholarship on the Resettlement Administration "judges the programs based on intentions as expressed in the rhetoric and fails to examine the outcomes and results of the programs on the people who were affected by them." In the case of the Shenandoah Homesteads project, the results were certainly mixed. Seven communities were constructed, but at such a huge cost that Virginia senator Harry Byrd, who had originally advocated for fair treatment of park residents, was provoked enough to describe the project as "a permanent monument to waste and extravagance" (quoted in Heinemann 1996, 182) Byrd's outrage at the amount being spent on mountaineers was equivalent to, if not exceeded by, the anger white families in the Tidewater directed at two other New Deal–era rehousing efforts designated for black families in the communities of Newport News, Virginia, and Elizabeth City, North Carolina (Carroll 2014). In both cases, rhetoric focused on the degree to which those who would benefit were truly deserving. While the African American community of Aberdeen Gardens in Hampton, Virginia, provided a vehicle for empowerment and, in the estimation of historian Fred Carroll (2014, 529), fostered "a tight-knit community where neighbors looked out for one another and shared responsibility for the maintenance of their neighborhood," the Shenandoah resettlement communities were arguably less successful. The nucleated, suburban nature of the settlements was unfamiliar to mountain residents, many of whom chose to move on.

The uncertainty about the issue of removal of Blue Ridge residents and the disarray it caused was echoed in the other Appalachian national park that resulted from the work of the Southern Appalachian National Park Committee: Great Smoky Mountains National Park in Tennessee and North Carolina. Analogous to the pronouncements made by Virginia's senator Harry Byrd opposing the relocation of Blue Ridge residents, a 1926 statement by US senator L. D. Tyson insisted that the Great Smoky residents would also not be moved: "The bill which has been introduced for this proposed park in the senate and house carries no authority to move anyone" (quoted in Dunn 1988, 244). By 1932, that policy had changed. While leases were granted to a few families, the majority were compelled to leave their homes and farms. In fact, it was the confusion the partial lease system in Great Smoky Mountains National Park caused that led Secretary of the Interior Harold Ickes to insist on a policy of total removal for Shenandoah National Park (Engle 1998).

The notion that the mountain residents would have to leave the park area seems to have been accepted and assumed, at least by outsiders, well in advance of the 1934 decision. In fact, Pollock had long used the living conditions of his nearest neighbors (and employees) in Corbin Hollow to convince members of the selection committee that the presence of hundreds of families should not stand in the way of Shenandoah National Park. Pollock paraded visitors through poverty-stricken parts of Corbin Hollow, where residents relied on income from Skyland. He said, "I knew that without actually visiting these people in their homes one could never conceive of their poverty and wretchedness, and for most of the five miles, I rode next to the Governor telling him tales of the Hollow folk" (Pollock 1960, 247). In Pollock's view, the park was a positive development for his neighbors; he claimed in a 1925 letter to the *Page News and Courier* (based in Luray) that mountain residents "are going to have a great deal provided for you by Uncle Sam."[2] Pollock, of course, expected Uncle Sam to also provide him with a great deal in the form of the opportunity to capture the coins of the tourists who were expected to flock to the new national park.

While Pollock and others focused on the advantages of emptying the mountains of their inhabitants, the mechanism for achieving this end and the agreement of the residents was unclear at best. Confusion surrounded the entirety of the process. Mountain residents were alternately promised that they could remain or that they would be given new homes and land free of charge. Even after the policy of removal had been formalized and land-owning residents had been paid for their land, years went by before families were required to leave. Those with a limited ability to move (principally tenant farmers or those whose age or health precluded ready mobility) were given special use permits. For many, this meant that whatever payments they received were spent on daily necessities in the intervening years, leaving them with little to fund a new life outside the park. As former Corbin Hollow resident Estelle Nicholson Dodson said, "We were glad when the Park taken over it. Cause they made such a promise to us! We thought it was the finest thing ever happened. . . . . But that wasn't true."[3] The tract that Estelle Nicholson Dodson lived on was less than two acres in extent and was assessed at $30; the log house on the property was assessed as worth only $50. The family received a total compensation of $185.00.[4]

Consideration of the use of condemnation and removal in the cases of Shenandoah National Park and Great Smoky Mountains National Park must be recognized as part of an accepted pattern. Such federal actions were readily justified as a necessary sacrifice for the greater good of the nation. For example, the Tennessee Valley Authority, a public corporation that was authorized in 1933, was given the power of eminent domain. This enabled it to acquire property and displace residents so it could tame the Tennessee River and create hydroelectric power (Drake 2001; Hargrove 1994). During the 1930s and 1940s, vast tracts of privately owned land were condemned throughout the country so the government could create military reserves for storage, weapons manufacture, and the training and housing of troops. For example, in 1940, families who owned land in a more than 75,000-acre swath in Caroline County in eastern Virginia had less than a year to surrender and vacate their property to make way for an army installation, Fort A. P. Hill, which opened one year later. Other national parks in Virginia also displaced individual landowners. The federal government's acquisition of Jamestown Island in 1934 required it to condemn the island in order to acquire the property from its private owners, the Barney family, while as late as the 1970s, during the bicentennial-era expansion of Colonial National Historic Park in Yorktown, the government used legal means to seize portions of a historic African American neighborhood (Deetz 2002).

Removal as the Remedy? Evaluating Mountain Life

In the case of both Shenandoah National Park and Great Smoky Mountains National Park, prevailing understandings of mountain culture ultimately provided a ready framework for justifying the acquisition of lands and ultimately, the removal of residents. Influenced by photographs from deprived areas of the park, by the writing of Mandel Sherman and Thomas Henry, and by the generalized popular understanding of upland society rooted in the local color movement, park planners and many outside the park region agreed that the best solution to the removal dilemma was to send "these illiterate persons to the Valleys where they will be absorbed in an educated progressive group [which will] enable the mountaineers to make contacts with a growing industrial society" (McLendon 1930, 70). Widespread media coverage reinforced the belief that mountain people would be best served by removal. The title of one article in the *New York Times* stated the case rather bluntly: "'Lost' Communities in Blue Ridge Hills: Centers Where Intelligence Practically Is Missing Reported by Psychologists."[5] A year later, another journalist visiting the proposed park region reportedly "made the journey, in one day, from 1931 to 1831, or earlier: back to an era and a mode of living only slightly changed from that of Colonial days."[6]

The most influential study produced at the time of park creation was Sherman and Henry's 1933 study *Hollow Folk*. Purportedly a scientific examination of five mountain communities in the park region, the work was based in part on fieldwork conducted by Orange County, Virginia, schoolteacher and self-styled social worker, Miriam Sizer. Sizer was a close associate of George Freeman Pollock. Employed by Pollock in 1929, Sizer taught in the Thorofare Mountain school, which served Corbin Hollow families, and invited researchers under the direction of Mandel Sherman from the University of Chicago and Cora Key from the Washington, DC, Child Research Center to study her Corbin Hollow pupils (see Sherman and Key 1932). The work of Sizer and the researchers from the Washington Child Research Center was reported on in a May 1932 Associated Press newspaper article: "An investigation has been made by a Washington physician and social worker of the condition of the people, and shocking are the results . . . There are six families living in the hollow, all named Corbin or Nicholson. All the adults are cousins. The ancestors of these two families settled there at the close of the Revolution and their descendants have intermarried and had very little to do with the outside world since."[7] Ray Lyman Wilbur, secretary of the interior, visited Corbin Hollow in May of 1932 and heartily approved of the plan to move the Corbin and Nicholson families: "They will be out of the national park then, and better located."[8] Tellingly, this assertion was made before the policy of removal had been officially formulated, agreed upon, and announced.

In the same year, Sizer was awarded a short-term government contract to assess the condition of mountain homes and residents to aid in determining the fate of park-land residents. For two months (May and June), Sizer traveled through Nicholson, Corbin, Weakley, Dark, and Richards Hollows, recording her observations of the inhabitants and her impressions of their material conditions. Sizer's work should be understood in the context of the national racial politics that informed much reform activity in the early twentieth century. In contrast to impoverished African Americans, poor mountain whites were considered to be the deserving poor, fitting subjects for upper-middle-class paternalistic ministrations. As Nina Silber (2001, 247) notes, "In keeping with the conciliatory trend of uniting the whites and isolating the blacks, northern culture celebrated the southern poor white precisely because he was not black. Northern reformers, often with the encouragement of southern whites, consciously cultivated an interest in the crackers as a way to replace earlier philanthropic efforts for the freedmen." Like other reformers, Miriam Sizer was displeased with what she observed and was convinced that not only did she know what was best for the mountain people but also that she was justified in imposing her ideas. Not surprisingly, Sizer earned few friends among the families she patronized, although she did leave behind a valuable, if undeniably biased, description of Depression-era life in the five hollows.

Psychologist Mandel Sherman was less interested in the future of hollow residents than in using the Shenandoah case to support his theory of social development. Sherman ranked the mountain communities along a gross evolutionary scale. At the bottom was Corbin Hollow, which existed "at the lowest level of social development." Next was Nicholson Hollow, "a trifle bewildered by the sudden influx of new ideas." Then came Weakley Hollow, whose inhabitants Sherman and Henry described as "continually running away from reality." More civilized than Weakley Hollow was Richards Hollow, which Sherman and Henry interpreted as "a more compact, socialized community near the foot of the mountains." Sherman and Henry then contrasted these park communities with the nearby village of Criglersville ("they do not wish to be thought of as mountaineers which they generally dislike"), which was at the top of the developmental sequence Sherman and Henry constructed (Sherman and Henry 1933, 5, 7, 8, 17). The pinnacle of social development, according to *Hollow Folk*, was the modern city, not surprisingly the home of both authors.

The pages of *Hollow Folk* are filled with statements about the private lives of mountain residents that in another time and place would clearly be actionable. Although the authors used pseudonyms for the hollows and their inhabitants, actual identities are only thinly disguised; for example, Corbin Hollow becomes Colvin Hollow. Following the long tradition of southern local color writing, Sherman and Henry described their subjects as lawless squatters who had been mentally lulled to sleep by the "deep silence and the drowsiness of the mountains" (Sherman and Henry 1933, 9). The opening paragraph of the book most clearly reveals the influence of local colorists (Sherman and Henry 1933, 1): "The dark interior valleys of the Blue Ridge are realms of enchantment. . . . The ragged children, until 1928, never had seen the flag, or heard of the Lord's Prayer. They speak a peculiar language which retains many Elizabethan expressions."

The authors concluded their study by celebrating the fact that the mountaineers would be removed from the stultifying influence of their hollow homes: "For a century the hollow folk have lived almost without contact with law or government, but soon the strong arm of the government will fall on them, for the land upon which they are 'squatting' is included in the area of a projected national park. Once the federal government takes over this land the mountaineers must abandon their cabins" (Sherman and Henry 1933, 215). Miriam Sizer enthusiastically agreed with their conclusions, as is evident in a letter she sent to the Potomac Appalachian Trail Club urging its members to purchase the book, which she described as "a sociological study of native dwellers in the regions contiguous to Skyland, the heart of Shenandoah National Park. . . . Though written in a popular style and with the customary fictitious names used in such studies to prevent identification, the book is based upon reliable sociological data, in accordance with outlines, suggestions, and conferences provided by the Department of Sociology of the University of Virginia" (Sizer 1933, 36).

It is difficult to gauge the influence of *Hollow Folk* on the decision to compel all families to leave the park area. However, it is clear that Pollock warmly received the book's authors and contributors and it is likely that the study was brought to the attention of Skyland guests and other park boosters. Certainly the initial 1932 study garnered significant media attention. By the time Cammerer announced the decision that all families would have to leave except for a list of elderly residents who would be granted special permission to live out their days in the park, *Hollow Folk* had been available for a year.

Comparative examination of the economic condition of park-area residents in the Old Rag area suggests that Blue Ridge families were actually not worse off than their contemporaries elsewhere in the South, contradicting the claims of Pollock, Sizer, and *Hollow Folk*. Although the average farm size in the South in the 1930s South was seventy-one acres, one-quarter of all southern farms had only twenty acres (National Emergency Council 1938, 10). Using evidence gathered during the Survey of Rural Mountain Settlement, one can clearly argue that even in the most densely populated hollows in the park area and those that received the most outside attention for their presumed degeneracy, conditions were equivalent to if not better than conditions found elsewhere in the rural South. Park tract records indicate that the average farm size in Nicholson Hollow was

60 acres while Weakley Hollow farms averaged 49.5 acres, not far off the regional average of 71 acres.

Corbin Hollow farms were much smaller, averaging only twelve acres. This figure reflects the reliance of Corbin Hollow families on wage labor at the Skyland resort. In 1932, a total of forty individuals in six households lived in Corbin Hollow, twenty-nine of whom were children and grandchildren of the elderly Finnell Corbin, who had purchased land in the hollow in 1894 near a road leading to the nearby Skyland resort. According to Pollock, "those of Corbin Hollow depended altogether on us for their livelihood. We gave them a market for their baskets, fruit and berries; gave them employment working in the garden and cutting wood; and all of the trails for miles around Skyland . . . were built by mountain people" (Pollock 1960, 153). Reliant on the resort, Corbin's offspring occupied properties without title close to the road leading to Skyland.[9] The uncertainties of squatter life are reflected in part by the ephemeral traces of their homes, which were perched on steep, uncleared slopes.

Because they eschewed more traditional agriculture in favor of wage labor and craft sales at Skyland, Corbin Hollow inhabitants had little to fall back on when the Depression hit and the already rocky financial fortunes of the resort plummeted. The resultant poverty in the hollow made it a convenient photographic subject for park promoters and, as noted above, Pollock paraded potential park supporters through the hollow. With the exception of the anomalous land-holding patterns of Corbin Hollow, where ownership of land was traced back to an unfiled transaction in the 1830s (Horning 2002, 2004), Blue Ridge families exhibited a high degree of land ownership in contrast to the rest of the South, where 53 percent of all farm families owned no land at all (National Emergency Council 1938, 21). Of twenty-eight households in Nicholson Hollow, eight (28.5 percent) rented their farms at the time of Miriam Sizer's survey in 1932. However, in all but three cases, the tenants were renting property owned by other family members (Horning 2001, 2004). One of those tenant families, Roosevelt and Maxie Nicholson, actually owned a farm along Indian Run in Nicholson Hollow that they rented to Maxie's brother Woodie while they rented Maxie's father's farm (Horning 2004, 102). Furthermore, park-area farmers, whether tenants or owners, did not rely on monocrop production (e.g., tobacco or cotton), as was the case in many parts of the South. As landowners engaging in mixed agriculture, residents of the hollows enjoyed certain economic and, arguably, psychological advantages over many of their rural compatriots in the Depression-era South who experienced higher levels of anxiety related to the uncertainties of tenancy and sharecropping.

Data from the 1930 census also allows for a consideration of the relative quality of Blue Ridge homes. In that year, nearly one-fifth of all southern farm houses did not have an indoor or outdoor toilet, more than half were unpainted, more than a third had no screens, and only 5.7 percent had any water piped to the house. For southern farm families earning less than $500 per year, fewer than 1 percent had indoor water, only 1 percent had indoor toilets, and fewer than 2 percent had electric light in their houses. Given these statistics, it is clear that the conditions that Miriam Sizer found so appalling in Nicholson, Corbin, Weakley, Dark, and Richards Hollows (such as a lack of indoor plumbing), were—for better or worse—the norm for small farm households throughout the South and were not particular to upland communities. Furthermore, statistics on the monetary value of farm homes across the South suggest that some park surveyors undervalued park-area homes. The average southern farmhouse in 1930 was worth about $650 while the average farm renter's house was worth only $350 (National Emergency Council 1938, 35). By contrast, the average valuation for dwellings in Nicholson and Weakley Hollows totaled only $300, even though many of the homes were above the standards of homes that were valued at $650 or more in a government report on southern housing. Although Blue Ridge homes appear to have been valued at lower values than comparable homes in the rural South, they were on average larger than those found elsewhere in the region, boasting an average of four rooms apiece against a norm of three rooms for the South as a whole in the 1930s.

Additional government statistics also suggest that the lifestyle of Blue Ridge residents was the norm for Madison County, including the Piedmont and lowland zones. In 1948, 38 percent of homes in Madison County occupied by white families were valued at under $700, while 98 percent of households did not cook with electricity, gas, gasoline, or kerosene. Thus, the wood stoves of the Blue Ridge homes were the standard for the county. As late as 1945, 84 percent of Madison County homes lacked running water, 45 percent of families owned no automobiles, and 55 percent of households did not possess radios (Garnett 1948). Archaeological evidence from the Survey of Rural Mountain Settlement such as abandoned cars, car parts, license plates, and an array of dry cell batteries indicate that automobiles and radios had already made their way into the hollows when they were still considered unusual for the county as a whole. Certainly the county-wide figures for the 1940s contradict the expectations of park planners that mountain families would be moving into areas with a significantly higher standard of living.

Capitalizing on the Mountain Folk Image

The attention paid to the supposedly isolated mountain folk cultures of the proposed Shenandoah National Park region also attracted a number of individuals who hoped to find or to encourage native handcraft production. The first handicraft revivalist to concentrate on park communities was Elizabeth Winn, an amateur folklorist and arts and crafts teacher from Baltimore. Winn established the Mountain Neighbors Industrial Crafts Center in Weakley Hollow in 1931 in a bid to "revive handwork in this isolated section in order to afford better social and financial opportunities for its inhabitants" (Eaton 1937, 88). Journalist Joan Hampton captured Winn's efforts to impose industrial standards on mountain craftwork as a form of moral and economic reform in a 1932 feature article in the *Baltimore Sun* entitled "The Primitive Life in Modern Virginia: A Crisis for Hill Folk." Hampton described how Winn was endeavoring to "give the sturdy people in their isolated cabins a method of bettering themselves financially without sacrificing their independence and individuality."[10] Winn's efforts were short lived, as the center went out of business shortly after it moved to Page County in 1935.

The second woman who sought to encourage craftwork in the park was none other than Miriam Sizer. However, when Sizer proposed establishing a community handicrafts center in another building in the Old Rag village in Weakley Hollow, she met fierce local resistance, as evidenced by several items of correspondence in the Shenandoah National Park Archives. One of Sizer's original sponsors, a Mr. H. R. Fulton from the Bureau of Plant Industry in Washington, DC, wrote to Shenandoah National Park superintendent Lassiter in August 1936 opposing Sizer's plans.

On a recent visit to the Corbin Hollow section I find that families there are very much against Miss Sizer's working in that community. This is based on their idea that she is responsible for the things written about them in Sherman and Henry's "Hollow Folk." They have only recently heard about this book, and may not have correct in-formation about it, but it has set them very much against Miss Sizer, which is most unfortunate. In my judgment this situation would make it inadvisable for Miss Sizer to try to carry on any work with the Corbin Hollow group at this time.[11]

More to the point is a letter Weakley Hollow resident Herbert Dyer wrote to Superintendent Lassiter. Dyer was concerned that Sizer had falsi-fied his and his family's signature on a petition for the community center.

We never signed because I dont believe she would help us any. We are not so ignorant as she would make it appear. I dont know of anyone who is starving I will admit we are Poor but I feel confident that we would stay just as Poor as we are if look to Miss Sizer for help. . . . I heard the Park was going to give some woman the job of looking after us as were so unlearned and ignorant, uncivilized. If you give the job to any; I dont believe we would be helped under care of Miss Sizer.[12]

The Voices of the Displaced

As evidenced by Herbert Dyer's letter, Blue Ridge residents did not si-lently accept their fate. Dyer and his other letter-writing neighbors no doubt would also have been incensed to read Miriam Sizer's statement that "the population is unlettered, and mental training is practically un-known to them." Miriam Sizer did admit in her 1932 survey that most residents in the Old Rag vicinity had actually "received the same educa-tional advantages as other rural Virginia sections."[13] Several folders in the Shenandoah National Park Archives are filled with letters residents wrote to park officials, mainly during the years between the dedication of the park in 1936 and the final removal of residents in 1938. In a few cases it is clear that some correspondents had others write their letters for them, but the variety of handwriting and writing styles indicates a higher rate of literacy than the work of Sizer and Sherman and Henry would sug-gest. As literary scholar Katrina Powell (2009, 12) has observed, park-area letter writers "were forced to respond to discussions about them from which they were largely excluded. As residents came into contact with more and more written documents, such as writs of eviction, from various government representatives, they shaped their own responses to remedy their immediate needs and certainly to remedy how officials perceived them." Blue Ridge inhabitants wrote nearly 300 letters to park officials that provide rich insight into both the trauma of displacement and the often-innovative strategies residents used to gain some advantage in a situation over which they had little control. As exemplified by Herbert Dyer's letter, inhabitants of the hollows were clearly aware of how they were being presented to the rest of the nation and were frustrated by the liminality of their existence in the hollows after the park was dedicated.

One of the most accomplished and savvy letter writers was John T. Nicholson of Nicholson Hollow, who carefully cultivated good relations with park staff to ensure that he and his father, John Russ Nicholson, could continue to remain within the park on a special use permit. After he was rebuked for removing windows from a vacated Nicholson Hollow dwelling in January of 1937, Nicholson wrote to Hoskins to apologize:

> Dear Chief Ranger, . . . I humbly beg of your honor to say that I certainly do regret that I took those windows. . . . I needed the windows bad in my house, . . . I simply took them because I heard that nothing was to be taken out of the park, but that we could take from one house and repair another. . . . Dear Chief, since I learned that this displeased you, I have been hurt and troubled over it for more than you may imagine and I have been on my knees before the Lord Jesus Christ—My Saviour, Judged and confessed to Him and has received pardon. . . . Now dear Chief, in closing this feeble letter, let me congratulate you Park Officials with many heart felt thanks for granting me another year's stay in the Park, I greatly appreciate this more than my vocabulary can express. I am writing a book on the Bible, and hope that I can remain here in my quiet home until I have the manuscript ready.[14]

Two years earlier, Nicholson had relied on "repeated use of flattery and religious conviction" to effectively convince Park Superintendent Lassiter to issue the special use permit in the first place (Powell 2007, 73).

While Nicholson relied on his rhetorical skills, others made effective use of their self-awareness of the mountain folk image. Just as Skyland proprietor George Freeman Pollock exploited the labor of the hollow dwellers, they exploited his guests. John T. Nicholson's cousin and neighbor, George Corbin, routinely presented himself as the very epitome of a mountaineer to Skyland guests when he walked or rode his mule up to the resort to sell his homemade whiskey and brandy and rattlesnake skins.[15] However, he left the mule in the pasture when he settled into his Model T Ford to haul his widely celebrated hooch to Washington, DC, and to drive to work in West Virginia. As Skyland guests absorbed local color in the form of moonshine, true mountaineers, judging from routine finds of embossed liquor bottles in all three hollows, chose to also pour measures of bonded commercial liquors. As his son Virgil recalled, George Corbin saved his earnings, whether from moonshine or railroad work, to buy his children Christmas stockings full of toys from the Sears catalog.[16]

George Corbin was not alone in capitalizing on Skyland guests. The practice of traditional basketmaking rapidly expanded in Corbin Hollow owing to the proximity of a ready tourist market eager to own a piece of authentic mountain culture (Martin-Perdue 1983; Suter 1996). By selling their wares directly to guests or setting up alongside Skyline Drive, basket makers endeavored to circumvent the commercial monopoly of the Virginia Sky-Line Company, which the park had employed to run concessions. The park shop at Big Meadows only sold the mountain crafts produced via the Southern Highland Handicraft Guild. To the dismay of Allen Eaton, the guild's founder, the most popular sales items at Big Meadows were "small turkeys made of native materials, leaf and shuck mats, party table favors such as tiny baskets, and pottery buttons" (Becker 1998, 205). Other efforts to target Skyland guests were more direct. One former Corbin Hollow resident recalled how as a child she would deliberately put on her oldest clothes, gather flowers and berries to sell, and "go up on Skyline Drive with our little notes a telling the guest how poor we were. . . . But the rangers wouldn't let us . . if they catch us at it they'd drive us off the mountainside."[17]

Corbin Hollow resident Eddie Nicholson's daughter Estelle recalled that he fed his family from his basketmaking income.[18] Although park officials chided Eddie Nicholson and his brother Charley Nicholson for allowing the children to beg from Skyline guests and travelers on the new Skyline Drive, it seems likely that the entire family was aware of the mountain folk image and played on it to their advantage. Certainly the material record from the site of their former home speaks to a keen awareness of 1930s trends and styles.[19] While many of the objects may have been acquired unconventionally, by means of begging and subsequent donations, the material culture nonetheless was used and discarded by the family. Notable objects include the clasp from a women's purse, ink bottles, patent medicine bottles and cosmetic jars, table glass, and even a porcelain soap dish. Eddie Nicholson appears to have been a savvy, outgoing individual, and his letters to park officials during the "limbo" period between the establishment of the park and 1938, when all occupants had to leave the land, attest to his efforts. For example, by describing his own much-photographed house as "not fit for a dog" in 1935, he managed to attain temporary housing for his family in a more spacious home that had been vacated in nearby Weakley Hollow.

Families of more substantial means than those of Corbin Hollow sought recourse through the legal system. The most substantive challenge to the creation of the park was a lawsuit filed by Rockingham County landowner Robert Via, who owned a sizable apple orchard within the boundaries of the park. Via's case against the Commonwealth of Virginia hinged on the constitutionality of condemning an individual's property. When the US District Court for Western Virginia rejected the case, it was subsequently referred to the US Supreme Court. In the interim, the Via case effectively stalled the entire transfer of lands from the Commonwealth of Virginia to the federal government. Until the US Supreme Court declined to hear Via's case in 1935, the federal government could not accept any of the land the Commonwealth of Virginia had acquired (Engle 2006, 24). Some residents simply refused to move, forcing park officials to physically evict them from their homes. A photograph of Mrs. Walker Jenkins being carried away from her home on Tanner's Ridge with an abandoned horse-drawn wagon in the background captures the trauma of removal. One outspoken opponent of the park, Page County landowner and businessman Melanchthon Cliser, was also forcibly removed from his home alongside the main road across the Blue Ridge at Thornton Gap.

Other forms of resistance to removal took a more damaging approach. Fully aware that the attraction of the new park was its flora, fauna, and vistas, some used fire as a means of expressing their anger. As environmental historian Sara Gregg (2010, 135–136) has noted, fire statistics make it clear how widespread this reaction was. In the same year that the park was dedicated, over 1,000 acres were burned. At least fifteen of the twenty-two individual fires were deliberately set. Gregg has identified a similar pattern for two other new southern national parks where removal was employed: Great Smoky Mountains National Park and Mammoth Cave National Park.

By the end of 1938, all but a handful of elderly mountain residents and their immediate families and, of course, the debt-ridden George Freeman Pollock and his wife Addie Nairn had left the park. Some families purchased farms outside the park or in surrounding counties; other families moved to one of the seven resettlement communities established by the Resettlement Administration of the Department of Agriculture. The exact number of individuals living in the park area when the park movement began will never be known for sure. A 1934 survey of the park lands found 465 families, accounting for 2,317 individuals, still residing within the new boundaries of Shenandoah National Park.[20] An untold number of families had already made other arrangements and left.

Ongoing Legacies of Displacement

In the 1990s, a new focus on cultural resources in Shenandoah National Park coincided with agitation from a descendants' organization known as the Children of Shenandoah that resulted in the removal of questionable interpretive displays. Results of the Survey of Mountain Settlement contributed to a revision of park interpretation in which the complexity of pre-park life and the traumatic experience of displacement were central. The revised portrayal of twentieth-century life in Nicholson and Weakley Hollows, where residents owned farms and businesses, went to church and school, listened to the radio, visited with neighbors, and journeyed afield in their own automobiles, provides an indisputable refutation of the claims of the 1930s scholars.

While this version of Blue Ridge life has been well received by descendants and park staff, weaving tales about the archaeology of the region remains a challenging exercise. Research pinpointed aspects of the past that are considered less palatable in the present; namely the displacement of indigenous peoples and the integral involvement of Blue Ridge settlers in the slave economy of the antebellum South and the racism of the postbellum period. The survey recorded thousands of years of Native American activity that left an enduring mark on the landscape. Although the three hollows under study were no longer occupied by any indigenous communities when the early Euroamerican settlers moved into the region, it is hardly a coincidence that the archaeological traces of early Euroamerican settlement are found alongside extensive evidence for Native American occupation through the Late Woodland period. Native American activity in the lands that are now part of Shenandoah National Park appears to have declined in the seventeenth century when the wider Shenandoah region became a zone of contestation between Native American groups and between Native Americans and Europeans. In the first half of the seventeenth century, the Susquehannocks entered the lower Shenandoah Valley from the north and actively participated in the fur trade until the mid-seventeenth century, when the Iroquois expanded their involvement and power (Gardner 1986). The French subsequently extended their influence through negotiated treaties and trade relations with a number of Native American societies. Conflict between tribal polities and the complexities of relations with colonial powers contributed to the depopulation of many portions of the Valley of Virginia in the opening years of the eighteenth century.

The abandonment of fields and settlements undoubtedly added to the region's attraction for colonists. By 1706, when traveler Louis Michel recorded his observations of the Blue Ridge and the valley beyond, he noted a lack of settlements in the area, documenting that the Shawnee, the Iroquois, and the Susquehannock used the region only as hunting territory (Egloff and Woodward 1992). Shenandoah Valley historian Samuel Kercheval noted the evidence of the preexisting cultural landscape : "The Shenandoah Valley, then, as the first white men found it, had evidence of earlier occupation—Indian fields, Indian burial mounds and village sites, and Indian trails" (Kercheval [1833] 1925, 13). As elsewhere (for example as discussed by Flick and King, this volume), such colonial descriptions conspired to obscure or deny the presence and persistence of Native Americans. Notwithstanding the upheavals of the seventeenth century, Native American communities still live in the wider Blue Ridge region. In January 2018, the Siouan Monacan peoples of Amherst County (just south of Shenandoah National Park) finally attained federal recognition through an act of Congress.

Early white settlers in the Blue Ridge clearly benefited from a preexisting Native American landscape of fields and trails, a reality that sits uneasily next to narratives of taming a wild landscape. Even more challenging is evidence for the existence of slavery and by extension communities of

African Americans in the Blue Ridge. Such evidence is at odds with the constructed pasts of the Blue Ridge, be it local color literature, sociological studies, or the family histories of the white hollow residents. A persistent aspect of understandings of the wider Appalachian experience is that slavery was absent, despite the existence of considerable evidence to the contrary. In addition to the seldom-acknowledged contributions of African Americans to the mountain past, evidence for considerable economic inequality throughout the three hollows is abundant (for extended consideration, see Dunaway 1996 and contributions in Inscoe 2001; for an archaeological perspective on African American communities in the Blue Ridge, see Barnes 2011; for a regional comparison, see Woehlke and Reeves, this volume). While such disparities are not surprising in terms of southern rural history, they do not support romantic notions of the communalism presumed to be the essence of kin-based subsistence economies. The tales woven from the archaeological study exist in an uneasy space, clearly at odds with the accepted history of the region but only conditionally welcomed by the descendant community, the members of which have a vested interest in contemporary presentations of the Blue Ridge past—their past.

Now unified in promoting a positive view of pre-park life, one that celebrates the qualities of independence, morality, and egalitarianism ascribed to the mountain lifestyle, descendants are less interested in evidence of slavery, discord, and economic inequality in the hollows and can be equally uncomfortable with evidence that park residents manipulated stereotypes. Some former residents and their descendants have focused on distancing themselves from the communities at the heart of the *Hollow Folk* study in the interest of a reconstructed Blue Ridge history; some blame their old neighbors for the displacement of all park people. According to one former Weakley Hollow resident, Corbin Hollow families "just lived in little huts and didn't try to do anything for themselves. And those were the people you heard about all the time and that's why they wanted to get them out of the park. Well, you didn't hear anything about the people that worked and made a good living and took care of themselves, and helped each other" (Shenandoah National Park archives 1999 interview tapes).[21] Other informants reiterate the need to distance themselves from Corbin Hollow. One Weakley Hollow man insisted: "Corbin Holler . . . they were good people but they were the poorest class of people that was up in there. . . . It was very seldom that they got out anywhere or if any marriages taken place it was among, you know, in the families and all."[22]

While upholding the negative image of the hollow, former neighbors were not blind to George Freeman Pollock's blatant manipulation of Corbin Hollow. Two women who grew up nearby continue to blame Pollock for his role in the creation of the park. "It was a good life up in there . . . and I feel terribly bitter at the people who did this." One woman felt "especially betrayed by George Pollock . . . [for] pushing the people out. And, you know, coming up with all the stories of the areas that were just, really poor. They didn't ever say anything about the people who worked, and made a good living and, and lived there peacefully and nicely."[23]

Significantly, sites in Corbin Hollow exhibit a range of goods that were not encountered on the sites in Weakley and Nicholson Hollows (Horning 2004). In addition to reflecting differences in subsistence strategies—for example, far higher percentages of tin cans and commercial food jars are found in Corbin Hollow than in the neighboring hollows—other items reflect connections with Skyland and hint at the material impact of the visiting tourists, journalists, and social scientists. While decorated and undecorated whitewares predominate on twentieth-century sites in Weakley and Nicholson Hollows, the ceramics in Corbin Hollow assemblages are primarily bulk-produced hotel wares of vitrified porcelain that closely match varieties unearthed in a dump at Skyland. These wares may have been acquired by the hollow residents surreptitiously. However, Pollock routinely took legal action against his employees for incidents as minor as cursing, and any thefts—even of discards—would not have passed unnoticed. More likely, the materials were either purchased from Pollock or, even more likely, the notoriously cash-impaired resort owner may have paid his employees with cheap tablewares that he purchased in bulk.

Corbin Hollow sites also yielded the highest percentages of costume jewelry and toys (figure 6.3) found in the project area, including toy trucks, porcelain doll fragments, a baseball, a harmonica, and even a portion of a 33 Repeater pop ray gun made in Wyandotte, Michigan. This ample archaeological evidence contrasts sharply with the claim of Mandel Sherman and Cora Key that "the children have . . . no toys nor do they know the meaning of the term toys."[24] The plethora of toys and leisure items (including 78 rpm records) reflects two possible scenarios: one, the availability of cash generated by wage labor allowed for the purchase of

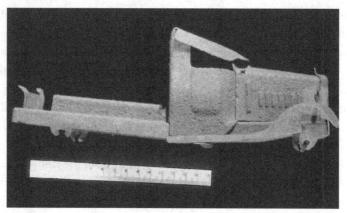

Figure 6.3. Toy truck recovered from Corbin Hollow. Courtesy of Colonial Williamsburg Foundation.

such items, even if it was to the detriment of subsistence; or two, a percentage of the toys and records were donations (figure 6.3). The truth likely lies somewhere in between.

Some items encountered on Corbin Hollow sites clearly were acquired by way of charity. For example, the second-largest class of surface artifacts encountered on the Finnell Corbin site was footwear, totaling 178 individual artifacts or 24 percent of the overall assemblage. Significantly concentrated an arm's throw downslope of the front porch, the assemblage consists of a minimum of thirty-eight pairs of shoes that range from men's boots and dress wingtips to ladies' heels to girls' Mary Jane buckled loafers. Only one example shows any evidence of wear, suggesting that the discarded shoes simply did not fit or otherwise suit anyone in the household. While Finnell Corbin's daughter and granddaughters may have enjoyed owning dress pumps, heels were hardly practical for everyday wear. Such donations may have assuaged the consciences of their contributors, but they were hardly useful to the Corbin family, as evidenced by their inauspicious deposition.

Whether or not objects found on Corbin Hollow sites were acquired unconventionally, by means of charity, or by barter, the materials were used and discarded by residents in much the same way as items that were purchased at local stores, from itinerant peddlers, or via mail-order catalogs. Showcasing her misunderstanding of the self-aware nature of such means of material acquisition, Miriam Sizer complained bitterly about one Corbin Hollow family that "often sells or trades supplies they are given." She expressed disbelief about one man who was "an inveterate trader, keeping practically nothing he buys or has given to him, [he] traded an overcoat for a puppy, . . . his wife trades off everything she gets, often for milk. Giving to these people is like pouring water through a sieve."[25] The recipients made choices based on their needs and desires, not according to Sizer's perspective on their requirements. Trading for milk is suggestive of a genuine household need, while one can imagine that the puppy that was preferred over an (ill-fitting?) overcoat may have assisted in hunting and provided companionship for the family. The material record from Corbin Hollow also reflects most clearly the challenges of the actual processes of removal. Because the hollow was not readily accessible by automobile, in contrast to the neighboring communities of Nicholson and Weakley Hollows, residents appear to have had little choice but to abandon the iron bedframes that still lie scattered around the home sites, accompanied by cast-iron stove parts and fragments of iron cookware. The archaeological evidence speaks very clearly of the last days of the residents in their mountain homes.

Conclusion

The experience of displacement and forced relocation in the Virginia Blue Ridge Mountains was not a singular event for the time period and the locality, and in scope and scale it differs significantly from the traumatic experiences addressed elsewhere in this volume. Most hollow residents received some form of compensation, and no one was separated from their family or forced to move thousands of miles from home. And of course, for most of the people who were displaced from the park, whiteness ensured certain advantages in the Jim Crow South. But comparing and contrasting degrees of trauma serves no useful purpose, as it denigrates individual lives and destabilizes senses of place and identity. The pain the people of the Blue Ridge Mountains who lost their homes experienced may have been somewhat ameliorated by an ability to maintain community and kin ties through relocation within the same region. But at the same time, being confronted on a daily basis by a view of what was lost, seeing their homeplace on the skyline, watching hard-won fields slowly taken over by vegetation, and perhaps also reliving memories of seeing their ancestral homes dismantled, rendered the loss ever present. For those who have been taken far away from their homeland, landscapes of home can live on in memory and one can imagine that nothing has changed. This was not an option for the people of the Blue Ridge. The sense of loss and bitterness still felt in the region, now primarily by the children and grandchildren of those who were displaced who see themselves as having been denied their own life on the mountain, continues to be fueled by anger over the one-sided portrayals of mountain life that were peddled by park advocates in the 1920s and 1930s. The settlements exist most strongly today in the minds of descendants and even in the perceptions of modern park visitors.

In essence, the establishment of the national park imposed the boundaries and the physical isolation that subsequently created both a unity among those who were displaced and a bounded, and now unpopulated, homeland. Archaeological work has played an important role in challenging the stereotypes that gave support to removal and that still exercise descendants. But at the same time, the archaeological work also runs the risk of undermining this present-day sense of a unified community identity among descendants by exposing the complexities of the past. As ever, a balance has to be struck. Empirical honesty demands that the data, and by extension the voices of the ancestors, should be heard. Doing so in a manner that is empowering rather than destabilizing demands inclusive practices.

Author's note: The archaeological work described in this chapter took place in the 1990s and was funded by the US National Park Service via a cooperative agreement with the Colonial Williamsburg Foundation. I remain indebted to those who made the project happen, especially David Orr, Marley Brown, Reed Engle, and Dan Hurlbert, and to all the individuals who shared their family experiences with me and with others. While it has been nearly fifteen years since I conducted any Blue Ridge fieldwork, I continue to receive correspondence from descendants of those displaced from Shenandoah National Park who have encountered the archaeological project through a book I wrote for the Shenandoah National Park Association. That so many are moved to track me down and write to me to express gratitude suggests just how deeply the trauma of displacement is still felt. I am humbled and honored by their words. The work I was privileged to do in Shenandoah National Park leaves me convinced that archaeology does indeed have a powerful and positive role to play in society. I am very grateful to Terrance Weik for allowing me the opportunity to again reflect on this role, on life on the mountain, and on the enduring legacy of its loss.

Notes

1. Thomas Henry, "200 Years of Calm in Blue Ridge Hollow Broken as Resettlement Workmen Erect New Village," *Washington Post*, 1936, clipping on file in Shenandoah National Park Archives, Luray, VA (hereafter SNPA).

2. Newspaper clipping, *Page News and Courier*, 1925, L. Ferdinand Zerkel Papers, SNPA.

3. "Estelle Nicholson Dodson Interviewed by Dorothy Noble Smith, Transcribed by Sharon G. Marston," November 23, 1977, Shenandoah National Park Oral History Collection, JMU Scholarly Commons, James Madison University, https://commons.lib.jmu.edu/cgi/viewcontent.cgi?article=1031&context=snp.

4. Tract and Land Acquisition Records in the State Commission on Conservation and Development Land Records, 1869–1995, SNPA.

5. Elsie Weil, "'Lost' Communities in Blue Ridge Hills: Centers Where Intelligence Practically Is Missing Reported by Psychologists," *New York Times*, October 19, 1930, clipping on file at SNPA.

6. Joan Hampton, "The Primitive Life in Modern Virginia: A Crisis for Hill Folk," *Baltimore Sun*, May 1, 1932, magazine section, clipping on file at SNPA.

7. Hampton, "The Primitive Life in Modern Virginia."

8. Associated Press article, *Journal Courier* (New Haven, CT), May 6, 1932, clipping on file at SNPA.

9. Tract and Land Acquisition Records.

10. Hampton, "The Primitive Life in Modern Virginia."

11. H. R. Fulton to James Lassiter, August 12, 1936, Box 99, Folder 4, L. Ferdinand Zerkel Papers, SNPA.

12. Herbert Dyer to James Lassiter, January 1, 1938, Box 99, Folder 4, State Commission on Conservation and Development Land Records, 1869–1995, SNPA.

13. Miriam Sizer, "Tabulations: Five Mountain Hollows," p. 4, 1932, Record Group 79, Central Files, Shenandoah National Park File 204, National Archives and Records Administration, College Park, MD.

14. R. Taylor Hoskins, "Compilation of Park Area Families, 1937," Box 100, Folder 3, State Commission on Conservation and Development Land Records, 1869–1995, SNPA.

15. George Corbin, interview with Charles Petersen, January 9, 1966; George Corbin, interview with Dorothy Noble Smith, June 24, 1977. Both manuscripts on file at SNPA.

16. George Corbin, interview with Charles Petersen; "Virgil Corbin, Interviewed by Dorothy Noble Smith, Transcribed by Sharon G. Marston," January 3, 1979, SNP036, manuscript on file, SNAPA.

17. "Estelle Nicholson Dodson Interviewed by Dorothy Noble Smith," p. 10.

18. "Estelle Nicholson Dodson Interviewed by Dorothy Noble Smith," pp. 2–4, 7–8, 18.

19. Shenandoah National Park superintendent James R. Lassiter to Charley and Maizie Nicholson, November 1936, Shenandoah National Park Resource Management Records, 1880–1996, SNPA.

20. Ferdinand Zerkel, "Virginia CWA Project, Shenandoah National Park Evacuation and Subsistence Homesteads Survey," 1934, Box 101, L. Ferdinand Zerkel Papers, SNPA.

21. Dorothy Dyer Trahos and Myrdell Dyer Clatterbuck, interview by Reed Engle, 1999, transcript on file, SNPA.

22. LeRoy Nicholson, interview with Dorothy Noble Smith, 1978, p. 44, recording and transcript on file, James Madison University Library.

23. Trahos and Clatterbuck interview.

24. Mandel Sherman and Cora Key, "Report of a Preliminary Psychological and Sociological Survey of Corbin Hollow, Va.," October 11, 1929, 2, 4, Misc. Correspondence 1929, Lou Henry Hoover Papers, White House General Files, Herbert Hoover Presidential Library.

25. Sizer, "Tabulations: Five Mountain Hollows," 15.

References

Barnes, Jodi. 2011. An Archaeology of Community Life: Appalachia, 1865–1920. *International Journal of Historical Archaeology* 15(4):669–706.

Batteau, Allen. 1991. *The Invention of Appalachia*. Tucson: University of Arizona Press.

Becker, Jane S. 1998. *Selling Tradition: Appalachia and the Construction of an American Folk 1930–1940*. Chapel Hill: University of North Carolina Press.

Carroll, Fred. 2014. The Racial Politics of Place: Jim Crow, the New Deal, and Suburban Housing on the Virginia Peninsula. *Journal of Urban History* 40(3):514–535.

Deetz, Kelley. 2002. Slabtown: Yorktown's African American Community, 1863–1970s. Undergraduate honors thesis, Swem Special Collections Research Center Archives, William & Mary Libraries, College of William and Mary, Williamsburg, VA.

Drake, Richard B. 2001. *A History of Appalachia*. Lexington, University of Kentucky Press.

Dunaway, Wilma A. 1996. *The First American Frontier: Transition to Capitalism in Southern Appalachia, 1700–1860*. Chapel Hill: University of North Carolina Press.

Dunn, Durwood. 1988. Cades Cove: The Life and Death of a Southern Appalachian Community 1818–1937. Knoxville: University of Tennessee Press.

Eaton, Allen H. 1937. *Handicrafts of the Southern Highlands*. New York, Russell Sage Foundation.

Egloff, Keith, and Deborah Woodward. 1999. *First People: The Early Indians of Virginia*. Charlottesville: University Press of Virginia.

Engle, Reed. 1998. Shenandoah National Park: A Historical Overview. *Cultural Resource Management* 21(1): 7–10.

———. 2006. *The Greatest Single Feature: A Skyline Drive*. Luray, VA: Shenandoah National Park Association.

Gardner, William M. 1986. *Lost Arrowheads and Broken Pottery: Traces of Indians in the Shenandoah Valley*. Manassas, VA: Thunderbird Museum.

Garnett, W. E. 1948. *Housing of Madison Farm Folk.* Rural Sociology Report no. 50, Blacksburg, VA: Virginia Polytechnic Institute and Virginia Agricultural Experiment Station and Agricultural Extension Service.

Gregg, Sara M. 2010. *Managing the Mountains: Land Use Planning, the New Deal, and the Creation of a Federal Landscape in Appalachia.* New Haven, CT: Yale University Press.

Hargrove, Erwin C. 1994. *Prisoners of Myth: The Leadership of the Tennessee Valley Authority, 1933–1990.* Princeton, NJ: Princeton University Press.

Heinemann, Ronald. 1996. *Harry Byrd of Virginia.* Charlottesville: University of Virginia Press.

Horning, Audrey J. 1999. In Search of a "Hollow Ethnicity": Archaeological Explorations of Rural Mountain Settlement. In *Current Perspectives on Ethnicity in Historical Archaeology,* edited by M. Franklin and G. Fesler, 121–138. Williamsburg, VA: Colonial Williamsburg Foundation.

———. 2000a. Archaeological Considerations of "Appalachian" Identity: Community-Based Archaeology in the Blue Ridge Mountains. In *The Archaeology of Communities: A New World Perspective,* edited by Marcello Canuto and Jason Yaeger, 210–230. Hoboken, NJ: Taylor and Francis.

———. 2000b. Beyond the Valley: Interaction, Image, and Identity in the Virginia Blue Ridge. In *After the Backcountry: Nineteenth-Century Life in the Valley of Virginia,* edited by Kenneth E. Koons and Warren R. Hofstra, 145–168. Knoxville: University of Tennessee Press.

———. 2001. Of Saints and Sinners: Landscapes of the Old and New South. In *Contested Memories and the Making of the American Landscape,* edited by Paul Shackel, 21–46. Gainesville: University Press of Florida.

———. 2002. Myth, Migration and Material Culture: Archaeology and Ulster Influence on Appalachia. *Historical Archaeology* 36(4):129–149.

———. 2004. *In the Shadow of Ragged Mountain: Historical Archaeology of Nicholson, Corbin, and Weakley Hollow.* Luray, VA: Shenandoah National Park Association.

Inscoe, John C., ed. 2001. *Appalachians and Race: The Mountain South from Slavery to Segregation.* Lexington: University Press of Kentucky.

Kercheval, Samuel. (1933) 1925. *A History of the Valley of Virginia.* Strasburg, VA: Shenandoah Publishing House.

McLendon, William Porter. 1930. Economic Aspects of the Shenandoah National Park Project. MA thesis, University of Virginia.

Martin-Perdue, Nancy. 1983. Case Study—On Eaton's Trail: A Genealogical Study of Virginia Basketmakers. In *Traditional Craftsmanship in America: A Diagnostic Report,* edited by J. Charles Camp, 79–104. Washington, DC: National Council for the Traditional Arts.

National Emergency Council. 1938. *Report on Economic Conditions of the South.* Washington, DC: US Government Printing Office.

Perdue, Charles, and Nancy Martin-Perdue. 1979–1980. Appalachian Fables and Facts: A Case Study of the Shenandoah National Park Removals. *Appalachian Journal* 7(1/2):84–103.

Pollock, George Freeman. 1936. Why Skyland? *Potomac Appalachian Trail Club Bulletin* 5.

———. 1960. *Skyland, the Heart of the Shenandoah National Park*. N.p.: Virginia Book Company.

Powell, Katrina. 2007. *The Anguish of Displacement: The Politics of Literacy in the Letters of Mountain Families in Shenandoah National Park*. Charlottesville: University Press of Virginia.

———, ed. 2009. *"Answer at Once": Letters of Mountain Families in Shenandoah National Park, 1934–1938*. Charlottesville: University Press of Virginia.

Shapiro, Henry. 1986. *Appalachia on Our Mind. The Southern Mountains and Mountaineers in the American Consciousness, 1870–1920*. Chapel Hill: University of North Carolina Press.

Sherman, Mandel, and Thomas Henry. 1933. *Hollow Folk*. New York: Thomas Crowell and Son.

Sherman, Mandel, and Cora B. Key. 1932. The Intelligence of Isolated Mountain Children. *Child Development Magazine* 3(4):279–290.

Silber, Nina. 2001. "What Does America Need So Much as Americans?": Race and Northern Reconciliation with the Southern Appalachians, 1870–1900. In *Appalachians and Race: The Mountain South from Slavery to Segregation*, edited by John C. Inscoe, 245–258. Lexington: University of Kentucky Press.

Sizer, Miriam. 1933. Recent Study of Mountain Folk. *Potomac Appalachian Trail Club Bulletin* 2(2):36.

Suter, Scott Hamilton. 1999. *Shenandoah Valley Folklife*. Jackson: University Press of Mississippi.

Wurst, LouAnn and Christine Ridarsky. 2014. The Second Time as Farce: Archaeological Reflections on the New New Deal. *International Journal of Historical Archaeology* 18(2):224–241.

7

Creating a Community in Confinement

The Development of Neighborhoods in Amache, a World War II Japanese American Internment Camp

APRIL KAMP-WHITTAKER AND BONNIE J. CLARK

In one of the largest mass relocations of the twentieth century, Japanese Americans were forcibly removed from the West Coast of the United States in 1942 and transferred to ten government-run incarceration centers. While not all Japanese Americans were removed into internal exile (see Starzmann, this volume), internment impacted the vast majority, those living along the West Coast. The process of removal ruptured many social ties, dividing families and communities. Residents of smaller communities were frequently sent to the same relocation centers, although the populations of larger, more urban areas were sent to multiple centers. Families who lived in the same community often were relocated together; however, families spread across greater geographical distances often became separated during removal. During the four years that the internment centers were in operation, residents were sometimes moved from one center to another, further disrupting social ties. The complicated processes of relocation into Japanese internment camps provides an opportunity to see how communities navigate and work to mitigate the effects of forced removal even in a situation of confinement.

Research from four years of fieldwork at the Granada Relocation Center National Historic Landmark (better known as Amache) in Colorado can be used to examine how Japanese Americans negotiated removal and incarceration. This chapter examines how relocated communities re-form and individuals negotiate change even in less-than-ideal settings. Data from six residential areas in the Amache internment camp show how these processes can be visible in the archaeological record.

This research links to larger studies on displacement and removal that use the neighborhood as a unit of study. Racial or economic motives are common threads in many studies of removal (Sanchez 2010). However, our focus here is not so much on the process of removal or on what was left behind but on the locale where one population was forced to live and how that population responded to forced relocation (e.g. Casella 2007; Ryzewski 2015).

To understand how internees re-created social ties and ideas of community, we have focused on the development of neighborhoods as social units with distinct identities and sets of interactions. Internment camps can be studied as cities with communities that extended across the urban setting and were organized at a district level or at the neighborhood scale. As in contemporary cities, participation in both close-knit local networks of interaction and more widely established networks facilitated the establishment of social groups. Some archaeologists suggest that a focus on the middle, or "mesoscale" is particularly appropriate when studying marginalized groups. At the suprahousehold level is where "social collectives were able to act meaningfully within and against structural forces such as institutionalized racism" (Voss 2008, 47). Through an examination of Amache's neighborhood, or suprahousehold, level networks, we can understand the social organization of internment. The short time frame and rapid development of internment centers make them strong case studies for understanding the formation of community among relocated populations. In this chapter, we use archaeological, archival, and oral historical data to recover evidence for social organization and identify neighborhoods as nexuses of community.

We draw upon three other bodies of evidence to highlight the role of neighborhoods in the social organization of Amache and demonstrate their role as a coping mechanism. Historical directories document the hometowns of internees and their address at Amache, providing data on the presence of social, economic, or geographic clustering among residents. We also use material culture to define social neighborhoods that were bounded by commonalities of behavior or consumption practices. We examine four artifact classes found at Amache to see if their prevalence can be used to identify neighborhoods. Finally, we examine landscape features as examples of social interaction in the forms of organized planning, social mimicry, or resource sharing. Each line of evidence contributes information about aspects of the social organization of neighborhoods in the camps and how their formation mitigated the effects of forced removal by fostering the development of new communities. The data also reveal how maintaining individual and communal identities can intertwine with strategies for coping with a situation of upheaval.

History of Japanese American Internment

In 1942, approximately 120,000 individuals of Japanese descent were forcibly relocated from the West Coast to incarceration camps located across the interior of the country. Internment was a direct reaction to the bombing of Pearl Harbor and was the culmination of years of racial discrimination. President Franklin D. Roosevelt signed Executive Order 9066 on February 19, 1942, allowing the exclusion of any and all persons from designated areas for the purpose of ensuring national security (Burton et al. 1999; Ng 2002).

Originally intended to spur voluntary relocation, the exclusion order soon became enforced through mandatory removal of all individuals of Japanese descent in an area that extended from the state of Washington through parts of Arizona. Systematic mandatory evacuation began on March 29, 1942, with the posting of instructions on where to assemble and what to bring (Burton et al. 1999). Families were forced to make rapid arrangements for their homes, businesses, and pets, and many sold possessions or entrusted them to friends. The United States Army oversaw transfer of evacuees to temporary assembly centers to await permanent relocation (Ng 2002, 31). Evacuees were generally moved to temporary detention centers located near their homes, so most residents from one neighborhood were transferred to the same center. Detention centers were established in public facilities that were quickly converted for residential occupation. The most well known is the Santa Anita Racetrack, where many families lived in converted horse stalls (Commission on the Wartime Relocation and Internment of Civilians 1997, 137). Despite the difficult conditions, internees established social and public services and worked toward a semblance of normal life. Internees could live in these temporary detention centers for up to four months before they were transferred to a euphemistically named "relocation center" (Linke 2014).

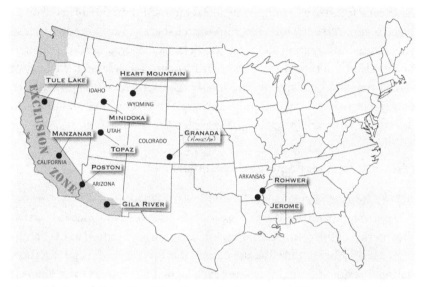

Figure 7.1. Map of all ten War Relocation Authority camps and the zone from which Japanese Americans were removed during World War II. Created by Anne Amati.

The War Relocation Authority (WRA), a civilian agency, was formed to manage the relocation and coordinate the construction and management of relocation centers. The WRA established ten relocation centers across the country, most in remote areas (figure 7.1). Internees were transferred from military custody in the assembly centers and were moved by train or bus to one of the relocation centers, where they entered the custody of the WRA. (Relocation centers are still referred to by a variety of terms, including internment camp and concentration camp [Himel 2015].) Amache, located in Prowers County, Colorado, was the smallest of the ten camps and housed around 10,000 individuals during its three years of operation. While Amache remained in operation for the duration of internment, its population was not stagnant. In 1943, several new groups of internees were relocated to Amache. For example, when the Jerome Relocation Center in Arkansas was closed, some internees there were moved to Amache. In one of the most controversial acts in the management of internment, internees were asked to fill out a loyalty questionnaire. Those who failed to answer the questions correctly were deemed disloyal to the United States and were sent to Tule Lake in California. Following this internal change, a large number of internees from Tule Lake were moved to Amache. This continued forced removal between internment centers along with the ability of internees to leave the centers for employment in the Midwest and on the East Coast meant that the camp always had a dynamic population.

The camp officially closed in October 1945, although internees had been leaving both temporarily and permanently for the interior of the United States since it opened (Commission on the Wartime Relocation and Internment of Civilians 1997). Most left in the summer of 1945, by which time the surrender of Germany made the end of the war appear imminent and the children of the camp had completed their school year. A lucky few were able to return to their homes and farms in California, but many restarted their lives in yet another new locale.

Camp Layout and Function

The ten camps, including Amache, were all built based on specifications provided by the War Department and were constructed by the Army Corps of Engineers. At Amache, internees began arriving before the camp was completed, so internee labor was used to construct some areas. Each camp had an administrative area for the WRA offices, a hospital, a motor pool, and homes for military police, administrators, and WRA personnel. The second section of the camp contained residential barracks and primary services for the internees. The central areas of each camp were enclosed by barbed wire punctuated by guard towers. The towers, which were manned by armed military police, also had searchlights.

At Amache, the central fenced area was divided into thirty-four blocks separated by a system of streets that were given a letter or a number designation, depending on their direction. Blocks were then assigned a name based on the north and west cross streets (for example, Block 6G was located at the intersection of streets 6 and G) (Simmons and Simmons 2004). The internee area contained twenty-nine residential blocks, a block for the elementary school, two blocks for the high school, an empty block, and a block that served as a commercial and public area.

Each residential block contained twelve barracks, a recreation hall, a mess hall, and a bathhouse. Residential barracks were divided into six living units. Each unit was furnished only with cots, a central light fixture, and a small coal-burning stove. Barracks were placed in two north-south-running rows. The entryways faced each other, separated by a twelve-meter open area. Except for the recreation center, all communal facilities

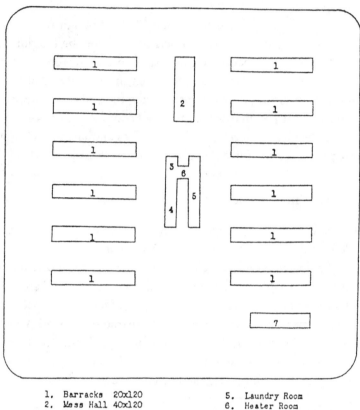

TYPICAL HOUSING BLOCK
WAR RELOCATION CENTER

1. Barracks   20x120
2. Mess Hall 40x120
3. Women's Latrine
4. Men's Latrine

5. Laundry Room
6. Heater Room
7. Recreation Hall

Figure 7.2. Layout of a typical residential block with centrally located facilities and housing along the sides. Source: J. L. DeWitt, *Final Report: Japanese Evacuation for the West Coast* (Washington DC: Government Printing Office, 1943).

were placed in the center of the block (figure 7.2; DeWitt 1943). These facilities included a mess hall that provided meals for the block's residents and a bathhouse and laundry facility. Recreation centers, located at one end of a row of barracks, provided a range of community services that varied across the blocks. Some served as preschools, churches, a town hall, or a Boy Scout headquarters (Simmons and Simmons 2004). Each residential block was designed to contain the essential services needed for residents' daily activities.

Definition of Neighborhoods

Neighborhoods have long been both a unit of analysis and a topic of study in the social sciences. The general consensus is that they are an almost universal attribute of urban settlement (Smith 2010). Definitions of neighborhoods range widely, but most include both a social and a spatial element and some include networks of relationships, associations, and patterns of use (Chaskin 1998). Generally a neighborhood is a subsection of a larger population that can be spatially defined but is also influenced by culture, ecology, or politics (Sampson 2003). Neighborhoods are frequently described as developing through frequent face-to-face interactions among a limited number of people and as natural communities. Smith (2010, 139) defines a neighborhood as a "residential zone that has considerable face-to-face interaction and is distinctive on the basis of physical and/or social characteristics." These bodies of research have also identified two broad categories of neighborhoods—administrative and social. Administrative neighborhoods are determined by boundaries established by nonresident organizations such as local municipal governments or planning agencies. These units are established for the purposes of organization, control, and administration. The locations of service facilities such as schools, open areas, or water resources contribute to definitions of administrative neighborhoods. Social neighborhoods are self-defined and may not have firm or visible boundaries; rather, they are identified through patterns of interaction, shared activities, and social behaviors. These two types of neighborhoods are not mutually exclusive and most neighborhoods are defined by both administrative and social boundaries.

In this chapter, we define communities as individuals who share a group identity and often a mutual concept of place. Within communities, neighborhoods provide a physical location for smaller communities to emerge. They also serve as venues for interactions that allow for the development of mutual identities.

Mumford defines neighbors as "people united primarily not by common origins or common purposes but by the proximity of their dwellings in space" (Mumford 1954, 257). Such a definition might seem well suited to the study of places such as internment camps, where residents are forcibly relocated from their communities of origin and are seemingly randomly dispersed into new neighborhoods that are strongly defined administrative units. The use of this understanding of neighborhoods limits the potential agency of residents and in the case of Amache does not seem refined enough to reflect the continuities in neighborhood activities and residents that we found. A more nuanced definition that retains this concept of spatial association but includes more social or cultural components is needed. In their analysis of neighborhood formation processes in semi-urban settlements, Smith and colleagues (2014) note the joint importance of administrative features, surveillance, and control in the initial construction and design of residential blocks in internment camps. They also recognize the role of sociality, defined as social interaction and peer monitoring, as a factor in maintaining successful neighborhoods later in the camps' use. We will use a definition that recognizes the importance of interaction in the formation of new communities and the continuation of existing behaviors within the boundaries of the camp's residential blocks.

Methods for Identifying Neighborhoods

For most archaeological studies of neighborhoods, analysis begins with the isolation of spatial zones (Smith 2010). Defining a neighborhood as a spatial or social unit can be challenging, especially in the archaeological record. The definitions of spatial units vary based on the data available but often rely on the presence of visible boundaries, such as the existence of major cross streets, the physical separation of a group of houses, or the presence of administrative units used by local governments or authorities, as seen in the location of service facilities. Once spatial units are determined, the social characteristics that define neighborhood groups can be identified.

It is important to identify the existence of group behaviors that may indicate the existence of a social neighborhood, defined by interaction or shared traits among residents. Archaeologically this is often done by identifying groups of artifacts that indicate group behaviors or interactions. Similarities in household consumption have been used as an indicator of social cohesion and the presence of neighborhoods (Cheek and Seifert 1994). This is based on the assumption that groups with similar ethnic, economic, or social backgrounds are frequently clustered and that households with similar lifestyles will consume the same types of material goods and engage in similar behaviors (Mazrim 2013; Slaughter 2006). Identifying trends in the presence of material objects should enable an archaeologist to differentiate social groups or neighborhoods. At Amache, an extensive pool of archival and oral historical data and archaeological material enabled us to test for the existence of neighborhoods using several lines of evidence.

During four seasons of fieldwork, seventeen residential blocks have been recorded using intensive pedestrian surveys. The goal of these surveys was to locate artifacts that are potentially diagnostic for specific behaviors, activities, or groups of residents and to document the existence of landscape features (Clark 2017b). For the purposes of this chapter, we examined six residential blocks to look for the existence of neighborhoods, as indicated by similar behaviors (figure 7.3). We chose these blocks because they had high physical integrity and were the residences of both rural and urban people. They also vary in the diversity and intensity of visible evidence for social interaction among residents. Our initial step was to use archival residential directories to understand the regional composition of the blocks. We then measured four artifact types that are affiliated with specific consumption patterns and social activities for each of the blocks. Comparing the frequency of the artifacts across the blocks helped us assess differences in behaviors related to the consumption of these classes of artifacts. Landscape features, which were found almost universally throughout Amache, are the final line of evidence. Variations in the materials used, the locations of these features in the blocks, and the level of community organization required for construction are indicators of interaction among internees and evidence for the development of community in the internment center. A common element of removal of any population is separation from other residents of the same community. We posited that residential blocks with more residents from the same regional areas or cities would have more evidence of social interaction among residents and potentially a greater sense of community.

Spatially Defined Neighborhoods

The first step in analyzing neighborhoods at Amache is defining their spatial extent. The series of regular blocks and linear arrangement of apartments in the WRA camps simplified the task of identifying spatial zones. Each block can be easily thought of as a neighborhood and the WRA probably conceptualized each as such. This is indicated by the labeling of each residential unit by a number and letter designation, which created administrative groupings of residents. The central placement of

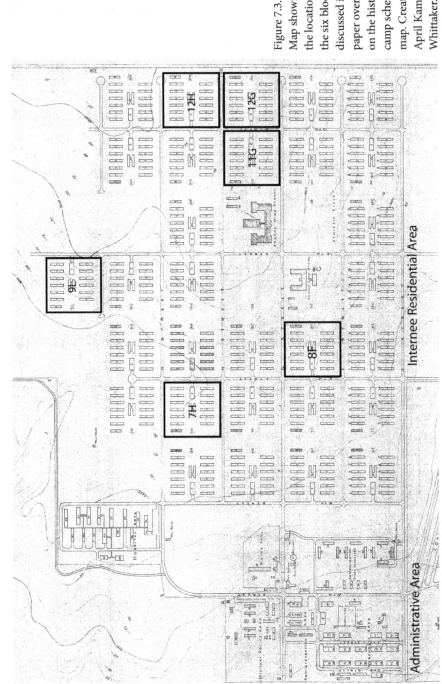

Figure 7.3. Map showing the location of the six blocks discussed in the paper overlaid on the historic camp schematic map. Created by April Kamp-Whittaker.

communal services, such as mess halls and bathhouses, reinforced both the WRA's and residents' understanding of neighborhood spatial units. Each resident was assigned to eat at the mess hall in their block and, with a few exceptions, they seem to have generally done so. While residents could access bathhouses on other blocks, the distance would have been twice as far and oral histories do not suggest that this was a common practice. Each residential block is an administrative neighborhood—residents were united by access to common facilities and by administrative control. The question remains whether these were also social neighborhoods that developed through a bottom-up process of daily interaction.

Socially Defined Neighborhoods

Socially defined neighborhoods developed as soon as internees began to arrive at Amache. Internees were transferred in large groups, and individuals and families moved together from assembly centers to relocation centers. This meant that social units could be transferred to relocation centers intact, a potential that was increased by the way barracks were assigned at Amache. It was essentially a first-come, first-served system, one that people who wanted to live together seem to have used to their advantage.

Camp directories and our discussions with former internees suggest that certain blocks were associated with specific populations that had formed before relocation, such as the three farming colonies of Cressey, Livingston, and Cortez. Many of the residents whom WRA records indicate as residents of Los Angeles were in fact from Seinan, a neighborhood with a high population of Japanese Americans and other ethnic minorities.[1] Even residents of more dispersed rural areas maintained what connections they could. This was true for some of the residents of one of our study blocks, 8F, as suggested in one resident's memoir: "When leaving, we three families stood together in the same spot and were pushed as a group with our baggage onto the open truck which had come to take us to the station. . . . All three families were to be placed in the 8F Block" (Hirano 1983, 11). Thus, communities that had formed before relocation or those that developed in the assembly centers might have been reestablished in Amache and other internment camps. This runs counter to many narratives that portray internment as a complete rupture of these networks. At least at Amache, evidence suggests that, while their lives were heavily disrupted, for some internees community and family ties might have remained intact or have been reestablished.

To determine if the settlement of families, friendship groups, or regionally defined social networks as units was common at Amache, we examined the residential data from two directories. In 1943 and again in 1945, residents of Amache organized the publication of a "city" directory that included the name of the head of each household, the name of each resident, the block name and apartment of where each household was located at Amache. In 1945, the directory included information critical for this project—each person's community of origin. This data allows us to see residential patterns and trace the movement of individuals and changes in block composition between the two dates.[2] We focused on three tasks: identifying regional groupings of residents, determining if a single community of origin dominated the block, and determining whether home communities were urban or rural in nature. We used 1940 population census data to determine if a community was urban or rural and relied on the Census Bureau's definition of rural communities as those with populations of less than 2,500.

An examination of the spatial patterning of residents at Amache exhibited a series of trends. Many blocks demonstrate at least some level of regional grouping. Households from one city tended to dominate a block, as in block 12H, where 95 percent of the residents in 1943 and 79 percent in 1945 were from Los Angeles. Some blocks included households from a roughly similar geographical area, such as the households from northern California in block 8F, or households from predominantly urban or rural areas of the state, as in block 7H, which was heavily rural (table 7.1). The development of these spatial patterns was neither random nor intentionally orchestrated by the WRA. It is probably the result of several factors: movement of internees from regionally established relocation centers in large groups, which made it possible for people to remain with friends or family, and people's intentional selection of residential areas where other households with similar social, economic, or geographic backgrounds were already residing.

The first groups of internees who arrived at Amache were able to select from the available completed residential units, which enabled them to settle in familiar social groups. As residential units at Amache began to fill, newer arrivals had fewer options about where to live, which presumably increased the diversity of residential blocks between 1943 and 1945.

Table 7.1. Composition of residential blocks included in this study showing the demographic composition based on the source communities of residents

Blocks	Year	Number of source communities	Dominant place of origin	Percent from dominant place	Percent urban	Percent rural
7H	1943	15	Walnut Grove/ Woodland	46	50	50
	1945	21	Walnut Grove	35	50	50
	Change	+6		-11	0	0
8F	1943	24	Colusa/Yuba City	15	48	52
	1945	34	Colusa	15	59	41
	Change	+10		0	11	-11
9L	1943	6	Los Angeles	88	98	2
	1945	11	Los Angeles	75	96	4
	Change	+5		-13	-1	1
11G	1943	4	Los Angeles	94	96	4
	1945	11	Los Angeles	83	98	2
	Change	+7		-11	2	-2
12G	1943	4	Los Angeles	86	100	0
	1945	11	Los Angeles	66	92	8
	Change	+7		-20	-8	8
12H	1943	3	Los Angeles	96	100	0
	1945	10	Los Angeles	85	98	2
	Change	+7		-11	-2	2

Note: The two time periods represent data captured by a residential directory created during the occupation of Amache and show changes in the compositions of the blocks over time.

This change is visible in the increased number of communities of origin represented in all the blocks we sampled. However, this pattern does not fully explain the geographic patterns we see in the data. Two large influxes of internees, first from Jerome in Arkansas and then from Tule Lake in California occurred in the period 1943–1945. These two influxes are partially responsible for some of the shifts in population in some residential blocks. It appears that latter arrivals at Amache were able to remain in family groups and in many cases to retain their geographical affiliations. A comparison of block composition in the 1943 and 1945 directories

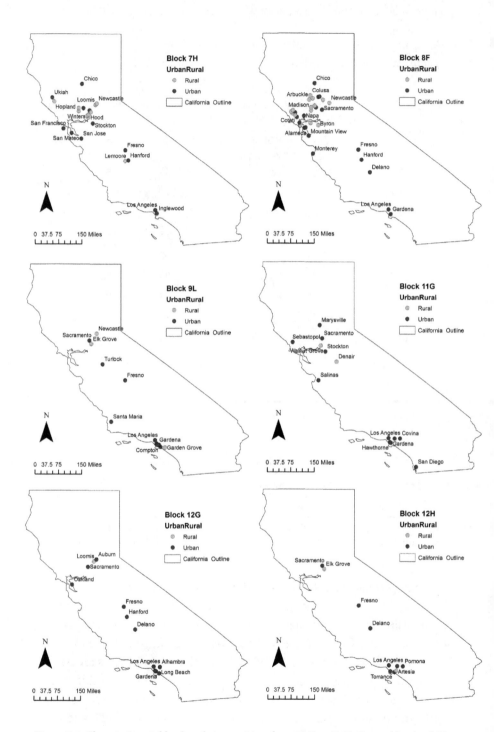

Figure 7.4. Changes in neighborhood composition from 1943 to 1945. Created by April Kamp-Whittaker.

shows that the geographic origin and overall urban or rural nature of the blocks did not vary greatly. Household groupings remain consistent in the 1943 and 1945 residential surveys, and the overall composition of blocks experienced little change (figure 7.4). Growth in the population of residents from a particular community seems to be the most common change that occurred during these years. The second change is the development of a new geographical grouping as seen in the case of blocks 11G, 9L, and 12G. In these blocks, which were predominantly populated by residents from the Los Angeles area in 1943, a second group had developed from northern California by 1945, potentially due to clustering from internees who arrived after 1943.

Studies have shown that migrants often form groups with residents from their home region or with people who share their ethnicity (Cohen 2011; MacDonald and MacDonald 1964; Pamuk 2004). At Amache, it appears that new arrivals had at least some ability to choose their residential area and these patterns in internee residential choice indicate that they were trying to select residential blocks where the social composition might be familiar or where there were some existing social networks. The choice to settle in blocks that contained individuals from similar regions of California or from familiar urban areas probably relates to economic similarities, differing levels of cultural assimilation, and a social divide between residents from urban and rural communities.[3] Individuals in urban residential areas frequently form groups based on economic, social, and geographical factors, and scholars use such groups to differentiate and define neighborhoods. Greater homogeneity in neighborhoods is also associated with greater interaction, community longevity, and overall social cohesion (Hipp and Perrin 2009; Letki 2008; Cheung and Leung 2011).

The presence of some level of social homogeneity or existing networks of interaction may help explain the rapid development of social services at Amache (Sampson, Raudenbush, and Earls 1997; Cassiers and Kesteloot 2012). The social services established shortly after Amache opened included camp-wide organizations such as Buddhist and Christian churches, nursery schools in several blocks, three community libraries, and branches of service organizations such as the Boy Scouts and the Blue Star Mothers of America. Classes were held in recreation halls and public buildings on traditional flower arranging, wood carving, Japanese language, jujitsu, sumo wrestling, painting, typing, sewing and garment construction, and any other topic where both an audience and instructor could be found. Celebrations for major holidays were held in the civic and commercial blocks and were attended by many residents. These activities, employment in the camp, and participation in religious organizations were part of the broader patterns of social interaction that extended beyond the block level and helped create a sense of community beyond the boundaries of neighborhoods. Social interactions that occurred across the center were central to the lives of many residents. We explore how those relate to neighborhood-level integration elsewhere (Kamp-Whittaker and Clark in press).

The broader social community that formed at Amache is important for understanding the impact of social interaction in the camp, but it is difficult to see at an archaeological level. Social neighborhoods, which may or may not conform to the spatially defined boundaries of administrative neighborhoods, are easier to identify by locating spatially discreet practices. Individuals draw neighborhood boundaries as they negotiate relationships and activities in a spatial setting. These boundaries do not necessarily conform to those defined for administrative purposes. At Amache it appears that the blocks the WRA designed served as a basis for how many residents conceptualized their neighborhood unit. While residents engaged in social interactions or social activities outside their immediate neighborhood, our research suggests that block-level social interactions were of greater import for a sense of community. Within each block there was a general sense of community. Oral histories from former residents and archival documents such as the *Granada Pioneer*, the newspaper at Amache published from 1942 to 1945, document the existence of block-based clubs, social groups, and in some cases nicknames.

While large celebrations and classes were organized on a camp-wide scale, some residential blocks organized their own social events such as sports games, movies, and dances. As one camp resident recalled, "The youth of 8F got together under a good leader and formed a band and rehearsed whenever they had free time. . . . By Christmas they had become quite accomplished so that dance parties were held" (Hirano 1983, 15). Such events required a high degree of coordination among block residents, an indication that individual blocks had social networks that were well enough developed to coordinate larger-scale activities. Archaeological evidence for neighborhood-level social activities includes the construction of *usu* (large mortars for producing the traditional pounded-rice dish *mochi*), sumo rings, baseball diamonds, and *ofuros* (traditional

Japanese baths). Block residents constructed these facilities for at least some communal use. Both *ofuros* identified through site survey were located near the central bathhouse in public spaces, and from oral histories we know that a range of the block's inhabitants used them and that they even drew residents from other blocks. Distinctive cultural features such as *mochi* pounders or *ofuros* appear to have been more common in blocks with high numbers of residents from rural areas and may have contributed to the creation of distinct block identities and unique sets of activities. The development of these additional shared facilities and the increase in social interaction between residents that organized activities fostered served to increase neighborhood identity.

As distinctive neighborhood activities and facilities developed, block identities were created as residents began to develop a sense of membership and belonging. While many internees viewed the centrally located communal facilities in each block negatively because of their institutional flavor, they served as social arenas and helped foster neighborhood interaction. Social arenas can be defined as places where segments of a community gather for an event or an activity (Ferman and Kaylor 2001). In Amache and other camps, daily activities such as communal dining would have facilitated social interaction among block residents, increased the likelihood that a neighborhood would create an identity, and fostered collective organization among residents.

The presence of block-wide recreation facilities shows the development of social arenas outside the regular camp infrastructure. One baseball diamond has been identified archaeologically and archival evidence indicates that a number of blocks constructed fields for playing baseball and basketball and recreation areas such as playgrounds. These would have been social gathering places for block residents and would have functioned the way neighborhood parks and sports fields do in modern urban settings. One former internee, George Hirano, remembered that his residential block had one of the best baseball teams in the camp (personal communication, 2014). Memories such as this and mementos from the camp indicate the development of identification with a block-based group that created a sense of neighborhood pride and unity.

Oral histories from the camp also document the development of block identities through the existence of slang names for some blocks. Block 9L was commonly referred to as "Chinatown," in reference to the more liberal behaviors of the block's inhabitants such as playing of music late at night.[4]

Fieldwork in the central area of this block uncovered a large communal garden that was perhaps lighted at night. A survey of the block identified further evidence of communal activities such as a fragment of a record album and even a few frames of commercially produced film. Based on these archival and oral historical sources, which identified unique block identities and sets of activities, we used survey data to see if they could be found in the archaeological material.

Artifact Patterns

Groupings or increased frequencies of certain artifact types are another indicator of the character of individual neighborhoods. Comparing survey data from four seasons showed that the artifact distributions among the blocks varied greatly. We selected four classes of artifacts for comparison: fragments of clear or aqua glass jugs, modified metal, marbles, and porcelain.

The production and consumption of alcohol was prohibited in camp, but sake appears to have been quite common (Slaughter 2006; Driver 2015). Commercially produced sake was available for purchase (at least for a time) from a drugstore in nearby Granada and internees could obtain passes to travel there (Harvey 2004). Vessels discovered at Amache with maker's marks of sake breweries are typically large aqua glass jugs with a lug handle, although a few clear glass examples exist as well. Oral histories indicate that some people brewed sake on site, and concentrations of artifacts that may have been used in brewing operations have been recovered in several areas. Such items include homemade strainers, bleach for cleaning equipment, and hoops from large barrels. While aqua jugs were definitely reused for this purpose, clear glass one-gallon jugs similar to the aqua sake jugs were likely also used. The presence of either clear or aqua glass lug-handled jug fragments may be an indicator of sake consumption or manufacture in a block.

A wide variety of modified metal objects have been recovered at Amache. The most common are tin cans modified by adding a handle or a puncture on the bottom or sides. Other objects such as homemade rug beaters made of wire, fishing nets made of window screen, and planters made of wash basins have also been found. Reusing and modifying metal may have been a response to the limited materials available in camp, to the economic hardship internees experienced, and to the need for objects to facilitate everyday activities (Swader 2015).

Marbles are one of the most ubiquities object categories and were a popular toy remembered by most former internees. Younger residents played marble games and such games were a social activity that gathered groups of children together (Kamp-Whittaker 2010). Greater frequencies of marbles in a residential block may serve as an indicator of greater sociality among the children who lived in the block. Families with young children are often more attached to their neighborhoods in part because of the adult social interactions fostered by children's friendship groups (Comstock et al. 2010; Hunter 1979).

Porcelain, especially if imported from Japan, would have been an expensive commodity even before the war. It would have been impossible to purchase Japanese porcelains (which make up the vast majority of porcelain sherds discovered at Amache) during the war (Skiles and Clark 2010). However, if residents had the resources to have personal goods shipped to them, they could supplement what they carried to the assembly centers. Oral histories suggest that internees transported porcelain to Amache when they were relocated. Unsure of the living conditions at assembly and relocation centers, families packed many basics, including dishes. Porcelain rice and tea bowls were recovered in many areas of the camp. These were important objects related to consuming food in culturally appropriate and familiar ways. Fragments of rice bowls are the most common porcelain artifacts found and are likely linked to rice consumption as a daily practice with spiritual overtones.

Each of the artifact categories we selected can be used to determine if an activity is present and for comparison across residential blocks (Table 7.2). Such distributions have been used in other urban contexts to demonstrate the existence of ethnic enclaves or distinct neighborhoods differentiated by access to materials, activities, or economics (Cheek and Friedlander 1990; Cheek and Seifert 1994; Mazrim 2013). Both blocks 7H and 8F demonstrated a disproportionally high percentage of modified tin cans (10.94 and 10.53 percent, respectively). Most residents of these blocks also came from more rural areas of northern California that were dominated by the farming industry. The intensive reuse of materials in these cases may be associated with the lower economic status of the residents in these blocks and a pre-camp history of reusing objects in farming activities.

Table 7.2. Counts of artifacts recovered in each residential block during pedestrian survey

	Marbles		Modified metal		Glass jugs		Porcelain		Other artifact		Total	
Block	N	%	N	%	N	%	N	%	N	%	N	%
7H	16	8.33	21	10.94	7	3.65	2	1.04	146	76.04	192	100.00
8F	7	7.4	10	10.5	8	8.4	2	2.1	68	71.6	95	100.0
9L	2	2.3	3	3.45	5	5.75	3	3.45	74	85.05	87	100.00
11G	2	3.6	3	5.5	0	0	5	9.1	45	81.8	55	100.0
12G	3	10.7	1	3.6	1	3.6	7	25.0	16	57.1	28	100.0
12H	2	6.3	3	9.4	2	6.3	8	25.0	17	53.0	32	100.0

Note: The category "other artifact" captures all other artifact classes that were not singled out for analysis.

Block 12H is a bit of an anomaly. Although its population largely derived from Los Angeles, it also has a relatively high percentage of modified cans (9.4 percent), although the overall number is actually quite low (3 artifacts). Because pierced cans often held plants, the higher percentage may relate to the large number of trees located in the block. Like block 12H, most residents of block 12G were from Los Angeles. Both blocks yielded an abnormal number of porcelain fragments. Twenty-five percent of all individually documented artifacts in these two blocks were porcelain, compared to between 1 and 4 percent for the other blocks we analyzed. The residents of these blocks brought substantially more porcelain with them to Amache, they had the resources to have porcelain objects shipped to them, or they used these ceramics in a different manner. These quantities of porcelain are most likely indicative of the greater financial resources of the residents of blocks 12H and 12G before they were relocated and show that the residential grouping that occurred may have been based in part on social differences created by pre-camp economic status.

Distributions of glass jugs likely related to sake consumption are approximately even across a majority of the blocks, making up from 3.45 to 6.25 percent of total artifacts recorded. The exceptions are found in block 11G, which contained no evidence of sake production or consumption, and block 8F, which had a higher-than-average number of jugs. These blocks probably represent the extreme ends of the spectrum. Residents of block 8F may have been actively producing sake. Alcohol can be simultaneously socially disruptive and integrative. Amache fits the models seen in other communities under pressure, where solitary drinking can be problematic but social drinking taps into tradition and religion (Smith 2008). At Amache, sake consumption was associated with communal events such as weddings and the celebration of New Year's Day (Chang 1999). Because of the physical and administrative restrictions of camp facilities and the requirements for brewing sake, it is very likely that producing sake was an activity that brought residents of a block together (Driver 2015).

Marbles at Amache are often recovered in areas that children likely frequented (Kamp-Whittaker 2010). Four of the blocks we surveyed had roughly similar percentages of marbles (ranging from 6.25 to 10.71 percent of total artifacts recorded) (table 7.2). Only blocks 9L and 11G had lower-than-average percentages of marbles. This indicates that children may not have been gathering socially in public areas as frequently in these blocks, potentially because of the number or ages of children living in the block. Reductions in children's sociality may also reflect decreased social interaction at a wider block level. Although the material evidence from Amache is not overwhelming, there are differences in the material composition of the blocks analyzed here. Such variation is indicative of distinct neighborhood identities.

Landscaping

While Amache was a landscape of confinement, camp administrators and military police did not monitor most daily activities or compel internees to work at jobs in the camp. (Many chose to work, however, including those who populated the camp's police force, who reported to a white chief.) This situation provided internees with the time and opportunity to develop their own activities and their own social structure and to create landscape modifications to support and enhance daily life.

Anthropological explorations of place (e.g., Basso 1996; Low 2000) suggest that attachment to place is one of our most strikingly human behaviors. We are among those scholars who see sites of institutional confinement as particularly appropriate locales for testing the powers and limits of place making as a social strategy (Casella 2007; Helphand 2006). Although Japanese Americans imprisoned at Amache were living in a place they did not choose for an unknown length of time, they radically transformed their carceral landscape (Clark 2017a). Thus, some of the

Figure 7.5. View of the same block at Amache when internees first arrived (*top*) and after internee landscaping efforts (*bottom*). Photographs courtesy of the Amache Preservation Society.

most striking archaeological evidence for block-level social organization is the landscape features internees constructed.

During the construction of Amache, the native vegetation of the high plains of Colorado (sage brush, short grasses, and some cacti) was cleared, leaving an open and sandy plain. After the internees arrived, they began constructing landscape features in private areas, around their barracks, and in public spaces. These features included household vegetable gardens, shade trees, entryway gardens, and larger formal gardens (Clark

Table 7.3. Number of landscaping features identified
during pedestrian survey in each residential block

Block	Number of Landscaping Features
7H	19
8F	22
9L	22
11G	4
12G	5
12H	5

Note: All landscaping features included here were created
by internees and represent both household and communal
landscape features.

2011). Before the war, over 60 percent of Japanese Americans were employed in agriculture, as gardeners, or in agriculture-related businesses (Helphand 2006, 158). They used their skills and expertise at Amache to construct complex and successful gardens. Such features had a transformative effect on the camp, as can be seen in historic photographs that show the rapid alteration of the landscape (figure 7.5).

While all residential blocks had landscape features, the extent and coordination of these varied widely. During four seasons of survey, we recovered 160 landscaping features. In the residential blocks that we completely surveyed, we recorded an average of 9.4 landscaping features. Table 7.3 presents the number of landscaping features in the six focus blocks. Three types of neighborhood or block-level organization can be seen in these features: neighborhood-wide coordination of garden construction, sharing of resources, and imitation of styles and design. Each can be seen as an indication of social interaction and cohesion in the block.

Block 7H provides the most concrete example of coordinated block-wide design and implementation of garden features. It also had double the average number of landscaping features in the blocks we surveyed. Most barracks in block 7H had front-yard gardens planted with a regular arrangement of trees placed approximately two meters from the front of the barrack and located at regular intervals along the front of the barrack. This arrangement is so regular and systematic through twelve barracks that it had to have been intentionally planned and implemented. Such patterns indicate that block residents coordinated their labor. The presence of community landscape features in several blocks supports the hypothesis of neighborhood-level organization. Here landscape features were constructed in public areas for use by multiple residents.

It is useful to compare the systematic scheme of block 7H with the landscaping of blocks 11G and 12G, where mostly residents from Los Angeles lived. Although both blocks had trees planted around the communal buildings, only block 12G also had quite a few trees planted in barrack entryways. Although such trees were common in block 12G, the placement was not nearly as consistent as in 7H. Oral history with a former resident of 12G whose family owned a nursery before the war reveals that landscaping in his block was both individual and communal.[5] Mr. Shigekuni's older brother visited a local nursery to buy plants for the residents of the block. Although he purchased all the trees and a bale of peat moss (to increase the success of transplanting), each resident paid for, planted, and watered their own trees.

Areas around the co-op building, which was located in a public block in the center of camp, appear to have been landscaped with an arrangement of trees, planting beds, and a system of raised limestone walkways that provided access to buildings. This may have been a communal effort of the internees who worked at the co-op and the police headquarters. Residents of the neighboring block, 8F, coordinated the continuation of this walkway along the east-facing edge of their block, a major construction endeavor. The walkway is consistent with the overall commitment to communal facilities by the residents of block 8F, reflected both in the *usu* discussed earlier and their astonishing twenty-two recorded landscaping features. Centrally located landscape features have been found in several other locations. These range from gazebo-like structures with accompanying gardens in block 9L (another block with twenty-two landscaping features) to a large Japanese-style hill-and-pond garden in block 6H near the town hall. Public landscape features would have required coordination or agreement among residents and the effort of gathering or paying for materials. Once constructed, such features provided common gathering places and acted as social arenas that facilitated neighborhood social networks and group identities (figure 7.6).

Communal gardens and individual landscape features in some blocks show heavy usage of and access to materials that would have been limited and available only to a few internees. Several blocks show increased access to building supplies such as concrete and cinder blocks. These materials

Figure 7.6. This page from a former internee's scrapbook captures both an identification with the other residents of her block (the 6H gang) and the amenities found in it. The hill and pond garden in block 6H provide the background for the group photograph and are also depicted in the hand-drawn sketch on the left. Courtesy of the family of Joy Takeyama Hashimoto.

would, at least initially, not have been easily accessible in large quantities and would primarily have been available to internees working on construction crews, where small amounts could be removed for personal use. In block 9L, a distinctive gray cinder block was used to construct the large central garden, which featured two oval garden beds encircled with cinder blocks that had been carefully split to resemble basalt (figure 7.7) The same cinder block was used in seven other landscaping features, some associated with specific barracks but others in public areas of the block. Only in block 9L was cinder block used this extensively, suggesting that a resident or group of residents had differential access to the material and shared the excess with their neighbors.

In other blocks, we have evidence of the sharing of resources, but in ways that led to landscape variability. In block 12H, test excavations revealed two very different entryway gardens that faced one another across the pathway between barracks buildings. The garden in front of the Okumura's barrack followed traditional Japanese garden design. It was a *karesansui*, or dry garden, that was built using an asymmetrical arrangement made of concrete "islands" surrounded by a sea of gravel. The garden of their neighbors, the Hirotas, looked much more like an American-style front yard; it had planters set in the ground at right angles to the doorway. Although these gardens did not share much in aesthetics, they reveal similar strategies in terms of materials.

Figure 7.7. Oval garden bed in 9L as exposed during excavations, including split cinder-block wall and remains of tree planted in the center of the garden. Photograph by Bonnie J. Clark, 2008.

Although the Okumuras were in their 70s, they made extensive use of gravel from the Arkansas River, located three miles north of the camp, in their garden. The labor of procuring that gravel may have fallen to the Okumura's daughter or son-in-law, who lived in the barrack building to the north (the same one as the Hirotas). In their garden, the Hirotas ingeniously used broken water pipes buried with the collar up to mimic plant pots. These broken construction materials should have been disposed of outside of the camp but instead were used in 12H. Given that Mr. Hirota was in his mid-50s when he was in the camp, it is unlikely he had the kind of manual labor job that would have provided direct access to the pipes.

It was likely a neighbor or friend who provided these materials to the Hirotas.

Other blocks demonstrate the repeated use of innovative or unique materials in landscape design. In block 7H, unburned coal was found around the bases of a number of trees in both public and residential garden contexts. Coal would have been a readily available resource, since the WRA provided it for the barrack stoves, the mess hall, and the bathhouses. However, it is not commonly used as a landscape material. Repetitious use of coal by a number of residents in a block suggests that in some blocks neighbors imitated each other or shared design ideas and material uses.

Conclusion

Our focus on the development of community structures and neighborhoods at Amache is not intended to imply that residents considered this a home, which many did not (Arensberg 1942). Rather, we are interested in exploring how internees were able to negotiate the system in a way that retained some previously existing community networks or develop new ones centered on Amache's residential blocks, thus potentially mitigating some of the effects of removal. The impetus for this focus came from several seasons of survey, excavation, and oral history collection, during which we began to understand the importance of block-based community identity for many residents at Amache.

Narratives about communities and neighborhoods portray them as fragile and often in the process of forming and breaking apart (Garrioch and Peel 2006). While this may be true of interactions between individuals, our research on neighborhoods at Amache seems to show that larger networks of regional affiliation or cultural behavior are more difficult to fully disrupt and easier to resurrect in new settings. Relocation first to assembly centers and then internment camps fragmented the interpersonal networks of many internees because they were removed from their home communities. Residents of primarily non–Japanese American communities might have arrived with few friends or relatives, a more complete disruption of the neighborhood and communities that were formerly part of their daily activities. Yet significant portions of neighborhoods such as the Seinan in Los Angeles and the farming colonies of the Central Valley were relocated to Amache in groups. This left some networks of interaction intact as neighboring residents were transferred together. This was likely the situation for the residents of blocks 9L, 12G, and 12H, which had high populations of residents from Los Angeles. Residents of other blocks worked hard to create ties among what were more dispersed formerly rural populations, as in blocks 7H and 8F. The archaeological remains in these blocks are evidence of significant physical investment in socially integrative practices. At Amache, residents mobilized larger-scale bonds of cultural behavior, geographic location, and urban or rural lifestyles after they were forcibly removed to foster the rapid development of social communities. The activities former internees discussed and that are represented by artifactual remains and landscaping features reveal numerous strategies for recreating human bonds in an inhumane place. The actions of internees at Amache suggest that when studying sites of removal we should consider the ways that communities actively worked to re-form and potentially contest the destabilizing effects of forced relocation.

Acknowledgments

This chapter is dedicated to all who have been part of the Denver University (DU) Amache Project, especially former Amacheans and their descendants. Their participation has given life to our work. The Center for Community Engagement to Advance Scholarship and Learning at the University of Denver has provided support for volunteer and intern participation in the field school. History Colorado's State Historical Fund and the Japanese American Association of Colorado have provided generous funding for the field school for many years. Hearty thanks to them and to our individual donors for their support.

Notes

1. Notes from an Amache Community Meeting, 2011, DU Amache Project, on file at the Department of Anthropology, University of Denver.

2. Data from the residential directories was compiled using heads of household data to identify family units. Any household lacking a community of origin was removed from the data set. Since information from the 1943 directory is less complete this created small disparities in the apparent number of block residents between 1943 and 1945.

3. Group interviews with former internees at Amache Reunion, 2009, DU Amache Project, notes on file at the Department of Anthropology, University of Denver.

4. Group interviews with former internees at Amache Reunion, 2009, DU Amache Project, notes on file at the Department of Anthropology, University of Denver.

5. Thomas Shigekuni, interview with DU Amache personnel, 2011, on file at the Department of Anthropology, University of Denver.

References Cited

Arensberg, Conrad M. 1942. Report on a Developing Community, Poston, Arizona. *Human Organization* 2(1):1–21.

Basso, Keith H. 1996. *Wisdom Sits in Places: Landscape and Language among the Western Apache*. Santa Fe: University of New Mexico Press.

Burton, Jeffery F., Mary M. Farrell, Florence B. Lord, and Richard W. Lord. 1999. *Confinement and Ethnicity: An Overview of World War II Japanese American Relocation Sites*. Seattle: University of Washington Press.

Casella, Eleanor Conlin. 2007. *The Archaeology of Institutional Confinement*. Gainesville: University Press of Florida.

Cassiers, Tim, and Christian Kesteloot. 2012. Socio-Spatial Inequalities and Social Cohesion in European Cities. *Urban Studies* 49(9):1909–1924.

Chang, Gordon H. 1999. *Morning Glory, Evening Shadow: Yamato Ichihashi and His Internment Writings, 1942–1945*. Stanford, CA: Stanford University Press.

Chaskin, Robert J. 1998. Neighborhood as a Unit of Planning and Action: A Heuristic Approach. *Journal of Planning Literature* 13(1):11–30.

Cheek, Charles D., and Amy Friedlander. 1990. Pottery and Pig's Feet: Space, Ethnicity, and Neighborhood in Washington, DC, 1880–1940. *Historical Archaeology* 24(1):34–60.

Cheek, Charles D., and Donna J Seifert. 1994. Neighborhoods and Household Types in Nineteenth-Century Washington, DC: Fannie Hill and Mary McNamara in Hooker's Division. In *The Historical Archaeology of the Chesapeake*, edited by P. A. Shackel and B. J. Little, 267–281. Washington, DC: Smithsonian Institution Press.

Cheung, Chau-kiu, and Kwan-kwok Leung. 2011. Neighborhood Homogeneity and Cohesion in Sustainable Community Development. *Habitat International* 35(4):564–572.

Clark, Bonnie J. 2011. *The Archaeology of Gardening at Amache, Summary Report—Summer 2010*. Washington, DC: Dumbarton Oaks.

———. 2017a. Cultivating Community: The Archaeology of Japanese American Confinement at Amache. In *Legacies of Space and Intangible Heritage: Archaeology, Ethnohistory, and the Politics of Cultural Continuity in the Americas*, edited by Fernando Armstrong-Fumero and Julio Hoil Gutierrez, 79–96. Boulder: University Press of Colorado.

———. 2017b. Digging Yesterday: The Archaeology of Living Memory at Amache. In *Historical Archaeology through a Western Lens*, edited by Mark Warner and Margaret Purser, 210–232. Lincoln: University of Nebraska Press.

Cohen, Erik H. 2011. Impact of the Group of Co-Migrants on Strategies of Acculturation: Towards an Expansion of the Berry Model. *International Migration* 49(4):1–22.

Commission on the Wartime Relocation and Internment of Civilians. 1997. *Personal Justice Denied: The Civil Liberties Public Education Fund.* Vancouver: University of Washington Press.

Comstock, Nicole, L. Miriam Dickinson, Julie A. Marshall, Mah-J. Soobader, Mark S. Turbin, Michael Buchenau, and Jill S. Litt. 2010. Neighborhood Attachment and Its Correlates: Exploring Neighborhood Conditions, Collective Efficacy, and Gardening. *Journal of Environmental Psychology* 30(4):435–442.

Desmond, Matthew, and Tracey Shollenberger. 2015. Forced Displacement from Rental Housing: Prevalence and Neighborhood Consequences. *Demography* 52(5):1751–1772.

DeWitt, J. L. 1943. *Final Report: Japanese Evacuation from the West Coast.* Washington, DC Government Printing Office.

Driver, Christian. 2015. Brewing behind Barbed Wire: An Archaeology of Saké at Amache. MA thesis, University of Denver.

Ferman, Barbara, and Patrick Kaylor. 2001. Building the Spatial Community: A Case Study of Neighborhood Institutions. *Review of Policy Research* 18(4):53–70.

Garrioch, David, and Mark Peel. 2006. Introduction: The Social History of Urban Neighborhoods. *Journal of Urban History* 32(5):663–676.

Harvey, Robert. 2004. *Amache: The Story of Japanese Internment in Colorado during World War II.* Boulder, CO: Taylor Trade Publishing.

Helphand, Kenneth I. 2006. *Defiant Gardens: Making Gardens in Wartime.* San Antonio: Trinity University Press.

Himel, Yoshinori H. T. 2015. Americans' Misuse of Internment. *Seattle Journal of Social Justice* 14(3):797.

Hipp, John R., and Andrew J. Perrin. 2009. The Simultaneous Effect of Social Distance and Physical Distance on the Formation of Neighborhood Ties. *City & Community* 8(1):5–25.

Hirano, Kiyo. 1983. *Enemy Alien.* Los Angeles: JAM Publications.

Hunter, Albert. 1979. The Urban Neighborhood: Its Analytical and Social Contexts. *Urban Affairs Review* 14(3):267–288.

Kamp-Whittaker, April. 2010. Through the Eyes of a Child: The Archaeology of WWII Japanese American Internment. MA thesis, University of Denver.

Kamp-Whittaker, April, and Bonnie J. Clark. In press. Social Networks and the Development of Neighborhood Identities in Amache, a WWII Japanese American Internment Camp. In *Excavating Neighborhoods: A Cross Cultural Exploration.* Archaeological Papers of the American Anthropological Association, Number 30, edited by David Pacifico and Lise Truex. Hoboken, NJ: Wiley Press.

Letki, Natalia. 2008. Does Diversity Erode Social Cohesion? Social Capital and Race in British Neighbourhoods. *Political Studies* 56(1):99–126.

Linke, Konrad. 2014. Assembly Centers. Densho Encyclopedia. http://encyclopedia.densho.org/Assembly%20centers/.

Low, Setha M. 2000. *On the Plaza: The Politics of Public Space and Culture*. Austin: University of Texas Press.

MacDonald, John S., and Leatrice D. MacDonald. 1964. Chain Migration: Ethnic Neighborhood Formation and Social Networks. *Milbank Memorial Fund Quarterly* 42(1):82–97.

Mazrim, Robert. 2013. Consumer Practices and the Visibility of Identity in Antebellum St. Louis: A 1,200-Vessel Archaeological Sample from an Irish and German Neighborhood, 1845–65. *International Journal of Historical Archaeology* 17(4):684–712.

Mumford, Lewis. 1954. The Neighborhood and the Neighborhood Unit. *Town Planning Review* 24(4):256.

Ng, Wendy. 2002. *Japanese-American Internment during World War II*. Westport, CT: Greenwood Press.

Pamuk, Ayse. 2004. Geography of Immigrant Clusters in Global Cities: A Case Study of San Francisco. *International Journal of Urban and Regional Research* 28(2):287–307.

Ryzewski, K. 2015. No Home for the "Ordinary Gamut": A Historical Archaeology of Community Displacement and the Creation of Detroit, City Beautiful. *Journal of Social Archaeology* 15(3):408–431.

Sampson, Robert J. 2003. Neighborhoods. In *Encyclopedia of Community: From Village to the Virtual World*, edited by K. Christensen and D. Levinson, 973–977. Thousand Oaks, CA: Sage.

Sampson, Robert J., Stephen W. Raudenbush, and Felton Earls. 1997. Neighborhoods and Violent Crime: A Multilevel Study of Collective Efficacy. *Science* 277(5328):918–924.

Sanchez, George J. 2010. Disposable People, Expendable Neighborhoods. In *A Companion to Los Angeles*, edited by William Deverell and Greg Hise, 131–144. Malden, MA: Wiley-Blackwell.

Simmons, Thomas H., and Laurie Simmons. 2004. National Historic Landmark Nomination Form, Granada Relocation Center (Amache), edited by National Park Service, United States Department of the Interior. Accessed January 5, 2011. https://npgallery. nps.gov/NRHP/GetAsset/NHLS/94000425_text.

Skiles, Stephanie A., and Bonnie J. Clark. 2010. When the Foreign Is Not Exotic: Ceramics at Colorado's WWII Japanese Internment Camp. In *Trade and Exchange: Archaeological Studies from History and Prehistory*, edited by Carolyn Dillian and Carolyn White, 179–192. New York: Springer Press.

Slaughter, Michelle A. 2006. An Archaeological and Ethnographic Examination of the Presence, Acquisition, and Consumption of Sake at Camp Amache, a World War II Japanese Internment Camp. MA thesis, University of Denver.

Smith, Frederick H. 2008. *The Archaeology of Alcohol and Drinking*. The American Experience in Archaeological Perspective. Gainesville: University Press of Florida.

Smith, Michael E. 2010. The Archaeological Study of Neighborhoods and Districts in Ancient Cities. *Journal of Anthropological Archaeology* 29(2):137–154.

Smith, Michael E., Ashley Engquist, Cinthia Carvajal, Katrina Johnston-Zimmerman, Monica Algara, Bridgette Gilliland, Yui Kuznetsov, and Amanda Young. 2014. Neighborhood Formation in Semi-Urban Settlements. *Journal of Urbanism: International Research on Placemaking and Urban Sustainability* 8(2):1–26.

Swader, Paul. 2015. An Analysis of Modified Material Culture from Amache: Investigating the Landscape of Japanese American Internment. MA thesis, University of Denver.

Voss, Barbara L. 2008. Between the Household and the World System: Social Collectivity and Community Agency in Overseas Chinese Archaeology. *Historical Archaeology* 42(3):37–52.

8

Topographies of Removal

Rethinking the Archaeology of Prisons

MARIA THERESIA STARZMANN

When you're serving a life-without-parole sentence it's as if you're experiencing the broken heart of knowing you'll never love or be loved again in any normal sense of the word, while simultaneously mourning the death of the man you could have and should have been.

The only difference is that you never recover, and can move on from neither the heart break nor the death because the pain is renewed each morning you wake up to realize that you're still here, sentenced to life-without-parole. It's a fresh day of utter despair, lived over and over for an entire lifetime.

Joseph Dole, *Prison Diary*

Incarceration produces scars in the lives of individuals and communities. Those who have passed through the US prison system, who have endured its deprivations and humiliations, leave it in a permanently altered state. What this state is remains a matter of debate among scholars, who disagree about whether the objective of the prison is to reform, to deter, or to punish. While they quarrel with the purpose of the penal system, my concern is its underlying logic: the anatomy of punishment in US society and its development over time.

With 1 out of every 143 citizens imprisoned, the incarceration rates in the contemporary United States are historically unprecedented (Ferguson 2014). The punitive impulse of the US justice system has produced soaring numbers of prisoners through systematic forms of social exclusion. Those who are imprisoned are overwhelmingly the poor and the racialized. In

2010, black Americans were incarcerated at rates five times higher than whites, while Hispanics were incarcerated at double the rate of whites (Sakala 2014), and the number of prisoners of color continues to grow. State-by-state analyses also show that Native Americans, who constitute 1 percent of the US population, are overrepresented in the criminal justice system: 4 percent of Native Americans are under correctional supervision, including those on parole (Sakala 2014). In addition, dramatic gaps exist between the incomes of non-incarcerated people and those of incarcerated people prior to their imprisonment. The latter typically make 41 percent less than non-incarcerated people of similar ages. The median annual pre-incarceration income for incarcerated people is lower than $20,000 (Rabuy and Kopf 2015). The "warehousing" of prisoners is a means of controlling communities; it removes those considered to be economically unproductive and socially undesirable from mainstream society (Wacquant 2000, 2010; see also Horning, this volume).

Archaeologists who study institutional life approach prisons through a double lens. They examine "how power was materially exerted over those confined" (Casella 2007, 3) and they study the material culture that has resulted from imprisonment. The physical world of prisons allows processes of corrective discipline to take hold. At the same time, strategies of subversion can challenge existing power structures (Myers 2009; Myers and Moshenska 2011). Architectural remains, for instance, define practices of surveillance and oppression, while individual artifacts may be used as tools of resistance (e.g., Beisaw and Gibb 2009; Casella 2007).

However, the focus of archaeologists on material traces often eclipses the fact that absences can be essential to the workings of power. As strategic sites of removal, prisons create both social and spatial absences. By seizing people from familiar environments, incarceration creates social absences that disrupt the cohesion of communities (but see also Kamp-Whittaker and Clark, this volume). Prisons translate these social absences into spatial ones. Prisons are distributed across vast landscapes that give shape to "topographies of removal." Here, forms of social exclusion go hand in hand with powerful spatial processes. What this means is that prisons do not simply restrict personal freedom. By rendering human bodies immobile, they create an "internal exile" (Simon 2007, 175) that prevents people from participating in civil society and politically incapacitates social subjects (but see O'Hearn and Grubačić 2016).

Concentrating on several historical moments in the organization of carceral space in North America, I consider removal as a lasting historical process rather than the result of isolated policy decisions. When the earliest prison-like institutions, such as almshouses and poorhouses, were set up in the seventeenth century, agricultural land was transformed into carceral space. The farmland had been wrested from the hands of Native American nations (Taylor 2002). The dispossession of indigenous people, alongside practices that removed, resettled, and institutionalized them, ties the history of penalty to a colonial past (see Burich 2007; Peña 2001; Flick and King, this volume; Weik, this volume). In addition, the issue of human captivity in the United States cannot be separated from the history of capitalism, given its extension of individualized land use and its valuation of land and labor as property (see also Woehlke and Reeves, this volume).

Removal is not simply a temporal act constituted by successive stages of exclusion or expulsion. Taking over entire landscapes, it is also an expanding spatial practice (Hicks 2016). From an archaeological perspective, carceral landscapes are best understood as simultaneously physical and cultural spaces (Hicks, McAtackney, and Fairclough 2009; Ingold 2000; Ucko and Layton 1999). Shaped by human activity over time, they provide a setting for human action (Branton 2009; Low and Lawrence-Zúñiga 2003). Since the early nineteenth century, remote areas in upstate New York have been favored as sites for prisons precisely because they appear to be relatively "empty." In such a landscape, the "morally and physically repugnant practices" (Pachirat 2011, 14) of incarceration can easily be concealed, and prisons and prisoners become a political afterthought (see also Martin and Mitchelson 2008; Smith and Gazin-Schwartz 2008).

Incarceration is a far-reaching practice, both historically and spatially. This is why a rigorous study of topographies of removal needs to take into account the unfolding relationship between penal politics and changes in cultural landscapes over time. Focusing on New York State, this chapter identifies points of contact between moments of penal "reform" and larger political-economic processes—such as the dispossession of land, the growth of emergent capitalist enterprises, and disinvestment in the course of deindustrialization. The aftershocks of these processes can still be felt today. They have significantly impacted agricultural and manufacturing economies across the state, where the deterioration of rural communities goes hand in hand with the proliferation of the prison industry (Huling 2002; Mah 2012).

Historical aftershocks do not always come with a clatter, however. Their reverberations may make themselves felt quietly, in the form of decaying infrastructure and abandoned homes. In subtle ways, they illuminate how the past is part of the present, and in doing so they remind us to think about what is at stake and for whom. Removal is not just a past experience, and archaeologists in particular have to be vigilant to recognize it as an active process that affects living communities. In the context of the growth and increasing privatization of the prison-industrial complex and mounting levels of vigilante and state-sponsored violence against migrant populations (Grabowska and Doering-White 2016), practices of detention, incarceration, forced eviction, and deportation harm the lives of countless people around the globe (Peutz 2006; Sassen 1999; Walters 2002).

Although I have relied on the tools and methods available to me as an archaeologist, this chapter is written first and foremost from a place of concern for the captivity of human life in an era of neoliberal disinvestment and postindustrial decline. By addressing these issues from a historical perspective, my hope is to counter discourses that frame incarceration as "normal" or "necessary." Exposing prisons as contested, even tenuous, sites is not merely about increasing the material visibility of prisons. While physical obstacles and cultural limits to what we can see need to be addressed (see, e.g., Campana and Piro 2008), it is just as crucial that we sharpen our political perception. Once we refuse to take the prison's existence for granted, its power—which has become "less and less juridical" (Foucault 2003, 28)—can no longer easily be defended but needs to be reckoned with.

An Anatomical Approach

Most archaeological studies of prisons examine how practices of confinement are organized materially. In other words, they analyze how the "material world of the institution" (Casella 2007, 28) creates immobility so that confinement emerges as "*the* primary mode of management for noncitizen populations" (Casella 2011, 286, Casella's emphasis). Yet these studies often overlook the issue of how institutions get hold of the populations they have in lockdown. Prisons not only configure immobility, they also prescribe movement by seizing undesirable populations and ejecting them from mainstream society to sequestered spaces. As the state acts out its right to punish, this practice is as much a form of governance as it is a way of constructing the position of the presumably delinquent citizen—of a subject that needs to be reigned in, removed, controlled.

The Directionality of Power

The focus in archaeological studies of prisons on immobility is linked to a number of theoretical and methodological problems. On the theoretical level, most archaeologists conceptualize prisons as "total institutions" (Goffman 1961) that expose those who are incarcerated to constant surveillance. Drawing on Michel Foucault's (1977) historical exploration of punishment, they argue that prisoners internalize the institution's disciplinary regime (Casella 2007). This view offers valuable insights into how disciplinary power is exerted in an institution, but it also necessitates several interventions regarding the directionality of power.

First, while social control is a crucial function of prisons, some archaeological accounts misread Foucault's work by undervaluing resistance. The point on which *Discipline and Punish* (1977) ends and that *The History of Sexuality* (1978) specifies is that power is neither absolute nor unidirectional. There are always moments when prisoners resist, subvert, or seize power. From Long Kesh Prison in Northern Ireland, for instance, we know of a series of highly politicized uprisings. Best known among them is maybe the Dirty Protest, during which IRA prisoners held in isolation units demanded better treatment by the authorities (Aretxaga 1995). Because the material world always figures into struggles over power, as archaeologists we are able to discern the traces that resistance leaves behind. In Long Kesh, the protesters engaged in destructive actions, such as breaking prison-issued items or damaging prison infrastructure (especially by smashing windows), but they also carried out creative acts, including painting graffiti and murals in cells (McAtackney 2014).

It is significant that what played out inside the prison had an impact beyond the walls of Long Kesh. In 1981, the Dirty Protest culminated in a hunger strike led by Bobby Sands. During his imprisonment, Sands was nominated for Parliament. When he died after sixty-six days of hunger strike on May 5, 1981, his example inspired political movements around the world (O'Hearn 2006). The fact that prisoners launch protests and build solidarity movements is proof that power is not totalizing but "operates as moments of opportunity" (Casella 2007, 77).

Second, when archaeologists explain prisons as sites of total control, they suggest that because power is dispersed, all are similarly subjected to it. This is a misleading argument, however. The power of prisons runs through the individual just as much as through the social body. The compulsory compartmentalization of the prison, which is aided by its architectural design of "a cellular system of individualization" (McAtackney 2014, 155), produces a diversity of experiences. It makes little sense therefore to wedge explanatory models regarding the power of prisons into binary frameworks of domination/resistance or oppressor/oppressed. Doing so invariably constructs the identities of those engaged in struggles over power—such as inmates and guards—as stable. It also eclipses the reality that institutions undergo organizational shifts that lead to the reconstitution of identities.

Third, we have to consider that penal power is not meted out indiscriminately in society. While it is true that state violence has become "a constant, regular, and normal feature" (Parenti 2015) of everyday life in the United States, this violence disproportionately targets marginalized populations. In light of the renewed increase in the size of the US prison and jail population, Ruth Gilmore (2015) points out that the categories under which individuals are imprisoned, "such as 'serious' or 'violent' felonies are not natural or self-evident, and more important, that their use is part of a racial apparatus for determining 'dangerousness.'"

The main flaw in existing archaeological studies lies in their somewhat vague and abstracted use of the term "power," which obscures rather than reveals the impact of prisons in some—but not all—people's lives. The central questions are not how power operates and what tools, techniques, or regiments it relies on but how power is distributed in society and whom it targets. While incarceration is a technique of state power to manage populations, this power is neither absolute nor evenly allocated; it is strategic and directed.

The Culture of Punishment

The theoretical problems I just identified are related to two methodological concerns. The first centers on the fact that most archaeological investigations of prisons are small-scale in focus. The analyses concentrate on individual bounded sites and their development over time, including phases of rebuilding and repurposing an institution. Although these studies might survey the surrounding areas of an "institution-specific site" (Beisaw 2009), such as yards and outbuildings, they do not always investigate the larger landscapes prisons are situated in (but see Casella 2001; McAtackney 2014).

Of course, studies of individual prison sites usually take into account historical context, as the work of James Garman demonstrates. Garman investigated the first Rhode Island state prison, focusing on the prison's place in nineteenth-century capitalism and industrialization. However, his main objective remained interpreting "the contestation of power *within* the walls of the institution" (Garman 1999, 6, my emphasis). This focus on the inside reinforces the idea that prisons—with their walls, locks, and fences—produce immobility. The broader implications of the question "Who becomes subjected to confinement, and under what sort of circumstances?" are sidestepped (Casella 2011, 285).

A second methodological concern emerges from studies that investigate not a single site but a *type* of institution. These comparative studies examine how life on the inside is controlled, regimented, and isolated. Although they are helpful in detailing the deprivations of institutional life and in particular what it means to "not have freedom to come and go" (Baugher 2009, 6), these studies examine the purpose of prisons rather than their anatomy (De Cunzo 2006). Their goal is to show that all total institutions, whether they be almshouses, poorhouses, reformatories, residential schools, asylums, or prisons, produce "docile bodies" (Foucault 1978, 135). Prisons are primarily seen as places that limit the mobility of incarcerated populations because they are extremely isolated and isolating.

A concern with the workings of power "on the inside" is, of course, absolutely important—especially if we want to confront how state violence goes unchecked in these institutions. Prisons do not exist in isolation, however. They are embedded in a physical and cultural landscape through which people and things move and are moved. Goods for consumption by prisoners, for example, such as food, clothing, hygiene products, laundry items, and stamps, enter the prison economy on a regular basis.[1]

At the same time, US prisons also function as sites of corporate capitalism that sell the commodities that marginalized workers produce. The corporation Federal Prison Industries (UNICOR) alone employs 22,560

Figure 8.1. Cameron Rowland, *Attica Series Desk*, 2016. Steel, powder coating, laminated particleboard, distributed by Corcraft 60 × 71½ × 28¾ inches. Rental at cost. The Attica Series Desk is manufactured by prisoners in Attica Correctional Facility. Prisoners seized control of the D Yard in Attica from September 9th to 13th, 1971. Following the inmates' immediate demands for amnesty, the first in their list of practical proposals was to extend the enforcement of "the New York State minimum wage law to prison industries." Inmates working in New York State prisons are currently paid $0.10 to $1.14 an hour. Inmates in Attica produce furniture for government offices throughout the state. This component of government administration depends on inmate labor. Rental at cost: Artworks indicated as "Rental at cost" are not sold. Each of these artworks may be rented for 5 years for the total cost of the Corcraft products that constitute it. Image by permission of artist.

prisoner-workers, whose wages range from $0.23 to $1.15 per hour. The products that leave prison-owned factories include anything from regular household items to law enforcement gear and apparel to government furniture and university stationery. As the work of artist Cameron Rowland points out, the state relies heavily on this labor. In his piece *Attica Series Desk* (2016), Rowland displays government office furniture produced by prisoners at the Attica Correctional Facility in upstate New York (figure 8.1). Items like an office desk highlight the seeming paradox that state bureaucracy is dependent on inmate labor while reproducing itself through it.

Of particular significance for the argument I am advancing is that prisons serve as nodes in a network of movement spanning entire landscapes. The labor force that is housed inside prisons has been pulled out of familiar environments and forcefully relocated to remote places where "punishment is its own lonely problem" (Ferguson 2014, 3). As such, incarceration emulates other forms of population transfer, such as deportation or expulsion (Walters 2002). Additionally, incarcerated individuals are frequently moved between institutions, so that friendships, communal experiences, organized solidarity among prisoners, and access to support networks on the outside are easily disrupted (but see Christian 2005; Christian et al. 2015).

This shows that prisons do not function in segregation from larger society but are part and parcel of the society that hosts them. We cannot ignore the various tendons that link us, more or less intimately, to this institution. Even if prisons occupy liminal spaces in our political consciousness, they are still embedded in a wider social web and are impacted by it. As politically concerned scholars, we need to pay attention to the various points of contact that exist between an institution and its physical, cultural, and historical environment. This is why instead of analyzing the form and interior power structure of carceral sites, I examine the anatomy of the modern prison in its cultural context. Given that "how a culture punishes is part of its very meaning" (Ferguson 2014, 5), my goal is to dissect the connective tissue that defines the location of the prison in a given culture and to situate it relative to other social institutions.

Topography of Removal

Relying on the practice of transferring people from freedom to confinement, prisons function as strategic sites of governance within a larger topography of removal. They establish the line between different categories of citizens—or, more precisely, between legitimate and illegitimate subjects—and thereby generate social distance. Like any slanted "civilizing process" (Elias 2000) that produces the full citizenship status of some by denying it to others, incarceration disenfranchises second-class citizens. Yet in mainstream public discourse, it is the very fact that an individual is imprisoned that serves as validation of the categorical distinction between "legal" and "illegal" subjects.

Political Marginalization

The practice of removal highlights a critical contradiction in liberal democracies. While freedom of movement is considered to be one of the most valuable rights granted to the liberal subject (Kotef 2015), states increasingly limit mobility of people, both between and within national spaces. Unlike the unimpeded flow of goods, services, and finances that characterizes the globalized neoliberal economy, the failure of states to regulate movement of people is seen as a threat to the political-economic order. In response, tactics such as stop-and-frisk legislation and checkpoints in borderland areas and occupied territories are used to prevent evasion, flight, and migration.

In light of the extreme restrictions placed on free movement, the practice of enforcing movement through evictions, deportations, renditions, and so forth serves governments by ejecting undesirable populations from a given political space (Walters 2002). The upsurge in antiziganist practices in Western Europe in recent years is a case in point. The French government, for example, has long been chasing Roma communities from *campements illicites* ("unauthorized settlements") under the guise of "integrating" them into the nation-state. Despite attempts to regulate state-governed evictions since spring 2012, Roma families continue to be forcibly removed from their homes. While such practices supposedly create stability for "uprooted" or "displaced" populations, they are really aimed at "taming mobility" (Kotef 2015, 11). At the same time, French authorities continuously fail to provide social assistance and adequate opportunities for rehousing (see, e.g., Astier 2014; Fekete 2014), so that enforced movement marginalizes already-vulnerable populations.

This demonstrates how the practice of strictly governing and administering movement can lead to political-economic disenfranchisement. Through their monopoly on ordering and regulating movement, states delineate who is or is not a legitimate subject, who is or is not worthy of full citizenship status, and, ultimately, who "is disposable and who is not" (Mbembe 2003, 217). It is in this sense that the "free movement of some, limits, hides, even denies the existence of others" (Kotef 2015, 54).

As a form of removal, incarceration effectively draws the line between those who are granted the benefits of full citizenship and those who are deprived of them. Tom Wicker has identified this as the double function of the prison—"to keep *us* out as well as *them* in" (quoted in Rhodes 2001,

68, Rhodes's emphasis). By excluding undesirable subjects from civil society and referring them to a realm in the nation-state that is, *legibus solutus*, outside the law, prisons create a category of nonpersons. Constricted to a space that is defined by law but not accountable to it (Agamben 1998), the rights of prisoners are, like those of refugees or colonial subjects, extremely tenuous (see also Sassen 1999).

Incarcerated existence has been likened to "social death" (Gordon 2011, 10) because it so frequently results in the violation of the prisoners' physical and mental integrity. This resonates with Joseph Dole's account from the beginning of this chapter. Serving a sentence of life without parole after being wrongfully convicted of a double murder and having spent almost ten years of his life in solitary confinement at the now-decommissioned Tamms Correctional Center, a supermax prison in Illinois, Dole (2013) mourns "the death of the man you could have and should have been."

Imprisonment can also result in "political death" (Foucault 2003, 256). As the contemporary practice of prison-based gerrymandering illustrates, prisoners in the United States are largely divested of their political status. A political phenomenon otherwise known as a modern-day version of the Three-Fifths Compromise of 1878—which determined that the enslaved population of the southern United States counted as three-fifths of their total number for legislative and taxing purposes—prison-based gerrymandering implies that inmate populations are listed in the census. As a result, prisoners, who are not allowed to vote, are considered to be residents of the legislative district in which they are incarcerated instead of their home district. This increases the political power of districts that house large numbers of prisons. The forty-fifth Senate District of New York State, for instance, which includes Franklin, Clinton, Essex, Hamilton, Warren, and Washington Counties, listed a census population of 299,603 in 2007. This number included not only its actual resident population of 285,442 but also the 14,161 individuals who were locked up in the district's thirteen prisons (Prison Policy Initiative 2010).

This shows not only that incarceration results in political disenfranchisement but also that it relies on it. The census numbers are hard proof that prison-based gerrymandering is characterized by "a distinct veneer of racial discrimination" (Wagner and Kopf 2015). While people of color account for the highest percentage of prisoners in the United States, many prisons are located in majority-white areas such as upstate New York. The disproportionately high incarceration rates among people of color reveal that removal is a strategy aimed at second-class citizens. Otherwise put, while penalty in the United States adheres "to no normative theory save that more is always better" (Ferguson 2014, 102), punishment is not meted out indiscriminately: Incarceration "absorbs [members of] the poor and working class" (Parenti 2015) whose political status is already precarious.

Producing Invisibility

By reconstituting subject positions from free to captive, incarceration is not a temporary banishment but a long-term form of systematic exclusion (Walters 2002). It does not target individuals; it takes hold of entire communities. Transferring people into prisons en masse is a way of "disappearing" (Rhodes 2001, 67) undesirable segments of the population. Sequestered in land zones specifically set aside for their confinement, prisoners are not only marginalized politically, they are also hidden from sight.

Removal operates on a broad geographical scale and pushes deep into cultural landscapes. This gives shape to a "topography of removal" that spans a vast political-geographic space. Although it is extremely ordered and policed, this space is also highly fragmented. Scattered throughout it are "carceral archipelagos" (Foucault 1977, 297)—jails, state prisons, and federal institutions of various security levels all the way up to supermax facilities—that are reserved for "'securing'—detaining, locking up/away— problematic populations of one kind or another" (Philo 2012, 4).

Historically speaking, topographies of removal have often emerged in remote places. The earliest institutions of confinement in the United States were typically set up just outside city limits. Later, prisons moved into out-of-the-way rural areas, where they took over other forms of land use that were once centered on agriculture or resource extraction (Gilmore 2007). In New York State, correctional facilities began sprawling across rural upstate regions in the nineteenth century. To this day, mostly small, declining rural communities are host to prison facilities (Glasmeier and Farrigan 2007; King et al. 2004).

The fact that I take note of the isolated geographical locations of many carceral institutions in the United States is not to suggest that prisons are not "common, ubiquitous components" (Morin 2013, 7) of everyday life

Figure 8.2. Satellite view of Guantánamo Bay Detention Center using the 3D viewing option in Google Maps. Image by Maria Theresia Starzmann.

in many American communities. Given the extremely high incarceration rates in the United States, prisons are far from marginal to people's lives. In addition, even relatively remote areas are less insulated than they used to be. As a result of infrastructure development and new technologies, prisons are more visible today than ever before, and even the most cordoned-off institutions, such as the Guantánamo Bay detention camp, can easily be discerned through satellite imagery (Myers 2010) (figure 8.2).

Yet it remains true that a discursive and material opaqueness surrounds incarceration in the United States. While we may not be actively discouraged from seeing prisons, the only permitted look is "an ephemeral one" (Schept 2014, 199). Whether a "correctional facility" is visible from a major highway or is announced by road signs, its presence does not invite reflection and engagement. Existing in "relative anonymity" (Augé 1995, 101), prisons are abstract spaces with no apparent history. For those situated on the outside, the prison does not constitute an actual lived and experienced place akin to, say, a pedestrian zone. As is true for other "non-places," the passerby "is absolved of the need to stop or even look" (Augé 1995, 97) at the prison, which is rendered simultaneously familiar and opaque.

An Archaeological Politics of Sight

As a discipline that is forever in search of what is hidden or concealed, archaeology may help expose "what's there in the blind field" (Gordon 2011, 3). By tracing how topographies of removal have emerged over time, archaeology may also enable us to formulate political alternatives to this age of mass incarceration.

From an archaeological point of view, the material presence of prisons, which manifests a troubling tension between visibility and opacity, might best be captured by the phrase "hidden in plain sight." From this vantage point, rethinking an archaeology of prisons (and other institutions of confinement) is not motivated by rendering visible what cannot be seen. Indeed, if we were to shift prisons from our ephemeral to our central field of vision, we would risk succumbing to an uncritical familiarity "with the terms provided by the prison itself" (Rhodes 2001, 68). Popular TV shows, like the MSNBC documentary *Lockup* (2017–) or the Netflix original fiction series *Orange Is the New Black* (2013–), simulate such experience of familiarity for a wide audience by taking an "intimate" look inside the institution. Foregrounding the tenuous, vulnerable lives of incarcerated populations, these accounts leave the viewer suspended between fascination and repulsion.

Because we are not technically denied the right to look at (or into) prisons, the goal of an archaeological "politics of sight" (Pachirat 2011) is to understand how an extremely violent institution can exist largely unexamined in the midst of American society. Because we have acquired a disposition to not see prisons, it is crucial to interrogate how we are simultaneously located at a distance from and in proximity to carceral spaces. In other words, in order to disrupt the perception of prisons as normal, we need to illuminate what can be seen and what remains unseen, how, and why.

To this end, I propose two methodological steps, the first of which aims at capturing the political spatiality of prisons. Instead of opting for a visual analysis that seeks to reveal the material logic of prisons, such as their highly repetitive spatial and architectural arrangements, I assess degrees of in/visibility of prisons based on readings of satellite and street-view imagery available through Google Earth. The second step of my analysis contends with the fact that the growing number of prisons in the United States is not simply a phenomenon of the recent past or the present but a historical process. Tracing the siting of prisons over time, I examine how the layered political topography of New York State is tied to particular institutional histories.

Hidden in Plain Sight

When assessing degrees of in/visibility, we need to consider how prisons are inscribed into contemporary landscapes. Ideally, this would involve discerning the ways these institutions shape the experiences of those who live in carceral landscapes and relate to them through deep historical roots and thick cultural ties.

However, given the largely programmatic nature of this chapter, site visits and interviews are beyond the scope of my inquiry. I limit my discussion to an archaeological landscape analysis that relies on techniques of remote sensing. This is both analytically and methodologically relevant, because gaining access to prisons—including taking photos or producing maps of prison facilities from the outside—can be extremely difficult if not impossible for researchers (Waldram 2009; see also Fine and Torre 2006).

Of course, the use of remote sensing data can also be problematic, because it runs the risk of turning into its own form of panoptic surveillance (Myers 2010). In addition, the conventional technique of reading satellite images, which are highly abstract representations of the world, can produce "flat," or ahistorical, results: They locate researchers at a great distance from the landscape and at an even greater distance from those who are incarcerated.

This is why it is important to consider the perspective of those who travel through or dwell in a given space. Although no "substitute for fieldwork" (Myers 2010, 462), my approach combines satellite and Google Street View imagery in order to approximate an understanding of how we perceive carceral landscapes. My example of Fishkill Correctional Facility (FCF) in New York State is a snapshot of a much larger context that allows me to lay out the basic analytical steps for assessing in/visibility.

Fishkill Correctional Facility, which administratively belongs to both the town of Fishkill and the city of Beacon in Dutchess County, New York, is a medium security prison. As of 1998, it also has a maximum security S-block of isolated confinement cells that has 200 beds (Prison Visiting Project 2012). FCF houses around 1,800 male prisoners in a community

Figure 8.3. Traffic sign on the shoulder of I-84/NY-52 reading "Correctional Facility Area—No Stopping" with Fishkill Correctional Facility in the background. Image by Maria Theresia Starzmann.

of just over 2,100, according to the 2010 census for Fishkill. It is located less than a mile off I-84 (NY-52), and most travelers will encounter it only from a distance. A closer look, however, immediately imparts a sense of "spatial violence" (Morin 2013, 1). On nearing Fishkill, a "No Stopping" sign on the right shoulder of I-84 warns drivers of the existence of a correctional facility in the area (figure 8.3). The architectural structures of FCF emerge on the far right just moments after passing the sign.

It is significant that the view of the prison is relatively unrestricted. A view-shed analysis carried out in Google Earth Pro calculates the location of the prison at a linear distance of approximately 0.7 kilometers from the viewer on I-84 (figure 8.4). While visibility tends to drop significantly at a distance of four kilometers between the viewer and an object, the prison is located within the one-kilometer radius that is considered visual foreground (Ogburn 2006). Seen from the location of the "No Stopping" sign on I-84, FCF is only partially obscured by trees and bushes, and visibility is likely to increase in the winter when most trees have lost their foliage. Even according to the categories of a fuzzy view-shed analysis—that is, "usually visible," "sometimes visible," or "visible only under favorable conditions" (Ogburn 2006, 408)—FCF would be considered "usually visible."

Visibility is, of course, never a matter of visual acuity alone—of what can and cannot be seen. It also pertains to the questions of "how visible is visible" (Ogburn 2006, 407)? When carrying out a view-shed analysis we need to remember that our perception is not just contingent on quantifiable factors, such as eyesight, object size, distance, visual angle, lighting, and weather conditions. It also relies on sensory and cognitive

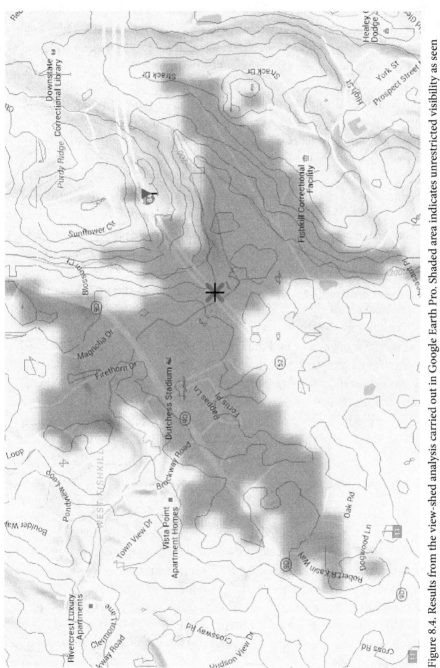

Figure 8.4. Results from the view-shed analysis carried out in Google Earth Pro. Shaded area indicates unrestricted visibility as seen from the location of the viewer (marked by the asterisk) on I-84/NY-52. Map by Maria Theresia Starzmann.

processes. We may, for example, perceive a landscape differently depending on whether we look at it from the window of a car or we walk through it. In addition, our senses are always in touch with our cultural sensibilities. Just like other cultural practices, seeing is subject to social norms and individual expectations (Sturken and Cartwright 2001).

This is not to say that we can readily separate the biological or environmental constraints on our visual perception from cultural obstacles to seeing. In some cases, visual acuity coincides with seemingly self-evident ways of seeing. It is, for example, often true that objects with a high degree of visibility—that is, objects that have "a significant visual presence within the everyday lives of people" (Ogburn 2006, 408)—also matter most in people's experiences of the world. In other instances, however, cultural practices of looking involve moments when abundant visual presences go unseen. For example, while FCF is relatively visible from the road and recognizable as a prison, it is a common cultural practice to crop carceral institutions from our visual experience.

A critical politics of sight is not supposed to come up with a more "complete" picture. Rather, studying the in/visibility of prisons enables us to pay attention to the moments "when things are not in their assigned places, when the cracks and the rigging are exposed, . . . when disturbed feelings won't go away" (Gordon 2011, 2). These are the moments when our personal experiences are no longer compliant with widely shared cultural expectations. If prisons are often considered "repugnant" sites that are best kept out of sight, a politically accountable response refuses to ban the violent practices of mass incarceration from our political consciousness.

Landscape Histories

While training our eyes to look at prisons is a first step toward exposing "carceral logics" (Schept 2014, 203), as archaeologists we need to dig deeper. If we want to resist the presentist view that tacitly accepts prisons as timeless institutions, we have to add historical depth to our analysis. While most archaeological studies are concerned with how the form of the institution has changed over time as techniques of punishment were reorganized, elaborated, and refined, they tend to carry a silent agreement that there is, and always has been, a need for society to punish (see, e.g., Casella 2007).

Figure 8.5. Google Street View from Matteawan Road in Beacon, New York, of the nineteenth-century buildings at Fishkill Correctional Facility. Image by Maria Theresia Starzmann.

With my analysis, I seek to counter tacit assumptions about the "*prison normal*" (Winter 2010, 102, Winter's emphasis). The concept of "topographies of removal" highlights that today's carceral landscapes have resulted from a series of socioeconomic transformations that unfolded over long time periods: the removal of Native Americans to reservations, shifts in farming practices, the reuse of agricultural land for institutional confinement, and, most recently, the decommissioning and repurposing of those institutions. If prisons appear "normal" or "natural," it is because their emergence, which was conditioned on acts of violence, is obscured from official histories. Similarly obscured is the fact that many of the processes that have impacted carceral landscapes in the past continue to take effect in the present. An archaeological politics of sight should therefore not end at the present moment but should also consider the past and the future.

The official history of Fishkill Correctional Facility dates back to 1886, when a New York State legislative commission purchased the 24-acre Dates Farm in the village of Matteawan (today part of the city of Beacon) in the Hudson Valley for $25,000. Six years later, the farmland became the site of the Asylum for Insane Criminals. In 1893, the asylum was renamed Matteawan State Hospital and, from 1896, was run as the Matteawan State Hospital for the Criminally Insane. When the hospital was repurposed as medium security prison for male prisoners in 1977, the original buildings, which remain in use today, became part of FCF (figure 8.5).

In the course of these historical transformations, several acts of dispossession occurred. When land was set aside to build the earliest prisons in the United States, the farmland was taken from Native American groups. The land along the eastern bank of the Hudson River where FCF is located was purchased in 1683 from the Wappinger Indians by Dutch merchant–fur traders Francis Rombout and Gulian Verplanck. The emergence of the US penal system is undeniably entangled with the historical structures of colonialism.

Exploitation of "inmate labor" constitutes another form of dispossession. Spurred by uneven processes of capitalist development, prisons constitute at least in part a "geographical solution" (Morin 2013, 3) to an unfolding economic crisis. Starting in the nineteenth century, labor power drawn from almshouses, asylums, and prisons became part of the solution to challenges "posed by the expansion of a national capitalist economy" (Summerhill 2005, 2). Under the guise of "occupational therapy" (New York Correction History Society n.d.), institutionalized people were forced to do productive labor. At Matteawan State Hospital, for example, the "furiously mad" (New York Correction History Society n.d.) carried out indoor work, such as maintaining the hospital and manufacturing utilitarian items (baskets, rugs, clothing, and bedsheets) or participated in agricultural tasks on the "colony farm" that extended over approximately 700 acres of rural land.

The extraction of prisoner labor is an economic form of control and an act of statecraft. By promoting labor as a form of "moral treatment" (New York Correction History Society n.d.), incarceration produces normative citizenship centered on ideas of industriousness and health. The decision to keep patients locked up was driven by powerful processes of risk assessment of entire populations. In the history of FCF, for example, the category of the "criminally insane" was introduced in 1896 to designate individuals who had become mentally ill while serving a prison sentence. Once diagnosed, they were transferred to Matteawan State Hospital, where they could be kept indefinitely even after they had served their time. This suggests that in the course of the nineteenth century, the practice of locking people away emerged as a measure of economic and social precaution. Because the state was more concerned with the social than the individual body, the evaluation of potentially criminal and/or mad subjects was aimed at "achieving an overall equilibrium that protects the security of the whole from internal dangers" (Foucault 2003, 249).

FCF is just one example of an institution that underwent the transition from state hospital to hospital for the criminally insane to correctional facility. This transition is marked by material continuities between these institutions and by an enduring logic of punishment that articulates disciplinary and biopolitical power. Just like the nineteenth-century hospital, the twentieth-century prison manages the individual body through means of surveillance and it controls populations through a kind of "regulatory disciplinary power" (Foucault 2003, 254). In other words, the management of the "criminally insane" in the nineteenth century haunts the practice of warehousing prisoners in correctional facilities across the United States in the twentieth and twenty-first centuries. Both institutions function as civic security measures of sorts—as means of protection and of predictability—installed to optimize populations in the nation-state.

Conclusion

Contemporary landscapes often appear like palimpsests—layered, complex, yet shot through with erasures and silences (Starzmann 2018). Looking at the history of FCF, we can probe these layers and discern how processes of removal are deeply inscribed in the topography of the United States. The traces of various reorganizations of political and economic power, including colonial dispossession and early capitalist exploitation, that have structured the cultural landscape over time are still visible today.

Often, these trends continue in the present with only slight variations. The prison industry has proliferated tremendously in recent years—at a time when many rural communities in the United States are experiencing dramatic economic decline due to deindustrialization and disinvestment. In addition, the fact that the incarceration regime is extremely racist cannot be delinked from the colonial power matrix that has historically conditioned the US juridical system. Archaeologists who understand these historical processes as continuities cannot exclusively focus on the past but need to also consider ongoing transformations of cultural landscapes.

Illuminating the historical processes that have led us into this age of mass incarceration is not merely about exposing an uncomfortable truth, or "making the repugnant visible" (Pachirat 2011, 247). In fact, forcing prisoners into sight is a risky undertaking. As is so well illustrated in the captivating work of digital media artist Jon Rafman, like all practices of looking, "making visible" carries the risk of voyeurism and objectification.

Figure 8.6. *Unknown Road, Carltonville, Johannesburg, South Africa* (2012) from Jon Rafman's *The Nine Eyes of Google Street View* series (2009–). Image used by permission of artist.

Pulling screenshots from Google Street View images, Rafman highlights the tension between the camera's removed vantage point and the human need for narrative and meaning. In his series *The Nine Eyes of Google Street View* (2009–), the artist has included an image titled *Unknown Road, Carltonville, Johannesburg, South Africa* (2012), which shows a man in an orange jumpsuit—an escaped prisoner?—sprinting down a deserted, dusty road in broad daylight (figure 8.6). The camera disrupts all visual norms by exposing what was never meant to be seen to a global audience. As cyberflâneurs, we "witness but do not act in history" (Rafman 2009), which renders the prisoner eerily distant, strange, not belonging, and potentially dangerous.

Seeing, then, implies more than "looking at." It requires us to actively write and act against the powerful silences that surround penalty in US society. Considering the extremely violent conditions that exist inside contemporary prisons and jails, we cannot limit ourselves to the questions of what was there before a prison was built or how the form of the contemporary prison has emerged. With approximately 300 decommissioned prison sites in the United States today (Morin 2013) and Gov. Andrew Cuomo's recent pledge to reduce overcrowding in prisons and jails in New York State, we need to confront the politically pressing issue of what may come after (Ewing 2016).[2] If we are concerned with the captivity of human life, how will the closing of prisons affect local communities and their economic livelihood? But also, how may the decision to decommission state-run prisons in an era of neoliberal disinvestment impact the business in private facilities? And if there is a need for alternative forms of justice, what would these look like?

Addressing questions regarding the future of the US prison system does not contradict archaeology's concern with the past. Rather, by linking the historical processes that have shaped carceral landscapes over time to our political concerns in the present, we can reconceptualize archaeology as the study of a "future past." In addition to revealing what has been, this archaeology would also examine what could or should have been. It is by leafing through the hauntings of the past that we may see future possibilities emerge—and it is up to us whether we formulate these as the reform of a deeply troubling institution or its abolition (Davis 2005).

Acknowledgments

This chapter has benefited much from a series of conversations about the archaeology of prisons, including a sustained e-mail exchange with Terry Weik, who I would like to thank for his gentle insistence that I submit this chapter for publication. I have recently revisited the issue of mass incarceration through encounters with contemporary artists whose works offer essential new perspectives. Thank you, in particular, to Jon Rafman and Cameron Rowland. The ideas generously shared with me by graduate students at McGill University, whose reading group I briefly joined, were similarly crucial to the development of this chapter. I owe much to the brilliant minds of Federico de Musso, Fern Thompsett, Jonathan Wald, and Rine Vieth.

Notes

1. *The Prison in Twelve Landscapes*, dir. Brett Story (N.p.: Oh Ratface Films, 2016), DVD.

2. Ewing (2016); "Gov. Cuomo's Push on Justice Reform," *New York Times*, January 15, 2016, http://www.nytimes.com/2016/01/16/opinion/gov-cuomos-push-on-justice-reform.html.

References Cited

Agamben, Giorgio. 1998. *Homo Sacer: Sovereign Power and Bare Life*. Stanford, CA: Stanford University Press.

Aretxaga, Begoña. 1995. Dirty Protest: Symbolic Overdetermination and Gender in Northern Ireland Ethnic Violence. *Ethos* 23(2):123–148.

Astier, Henri. 2014. France's Unwanted Roma. *BBC Magazine*, February 13. http://www.bbc.com/news/magazine-25419423.

Augé, Marc. 1995. *Non-Places: Introduction to an Anthropology of Supermodernity*. London: Verso.

Branton, Nicole. 2009. Landscape Approaches in Historical Archaeology: The Archaeology of Places. In *International Handbook of Historic Archaeology*, edited by Teresita Majewski and David Gaimster, 51–65. New York: Springer.

Baugher, Sherene. 2009. Historical Overview of the Archaeology of Institutional Life. In *The Archaeology of Institutional Life*, edited by April M. Beisaw and James G. Gibb, 5–13. Tuscaloosa: University of Alabama Press.

Beisaw, April M. 2009. Constructing Institution-Specific Site Formation Models. In *The Archaeology of Institutional Life*, edited by April M. Beisaw and James G. Gibb, 49–66. Tuscaloosa: University of Alabama Press.

Beisaw, April M., and James G. Gibb, eds. 2009. *The Archaeology of Institutional Life*. Tuscaloosa: University of Alabama Press.

Burich, Keith R. 2007. "No place to go": The Thomas Indian School and the "Forgotten" Indian Children of New York. *Wicazo Sa Review* 22(2):93–110.

Campana, Stefano, and Salvatore Piro. 2009. *Seeing the Unseen: Geophysics and Landscape Archaeology*. Boca Raton: CRC Press.

Casella, Eleanor C. 2001. To Watch or Restrain: Female Convict Prisons in 19th-Century Tasmania. *International Journal of Historical Archaeology* 5(1):45–72.

———. 2007. *The Archaeology of Institutional Confinement*. Gainesville: University Press of Florida.

———. 2011. Lockdown: On the Materiality of Confinement. In *Archaeologies of Internment*, edited by Adrian Myers and Gabriel Moshenska, 285–295. New York: Springer.

Christian, Johnna. 2005. Riding the Bus: Barriers to Prison Visitation and Family Management Strategies. *Journal of Contemporary Criminal Justice* 21(1):31–48.

Christian, Johnna, Damian J. Martinez, and Denisse Martinez. 2015. Beyond the Shadows of the Prison: Agency and Resilience among Prisoners' Family Members. In *And Justice for All: Families & the Criminal Justice System*, edited by Joyce A. Arditti and Tessa le Roux, 59–84. Groves Monographs on Marriage and Family, vol. 4. Ann Arbor: Michigan Publishing.

Davis, Angela Y. 2005. *Abolition Democracy: Beyond Empire, Prisons, and Torture*. New York: Seven Stories Press.

De Cunzo, Lu Ann. 2006. Exploring the Institution: Reform, Confinement, Social Change. In *Historical Archaeology*, edited by Martin Hall and Stephen W. Silliman, 167–189. Malden: Blackwell.

Dole, Joseph. 2013. Prison Diary. PEN America, July 16. https://pen.org/prison-diary/.

Elias, Norbert. 2000. *The Civilizing Process: Sociogenetic and Psychogenetic Investigations.* Oxford: Blackwell Publishers.

Ewing, Maura. 2016. How New York State Plans to Fund Major Criminal-Justice Reforms with Wall Street Money. *The Atlantic,* January 12. http://www.theatlantic.com/politics/archive/2016/01/how-new-york-state-plans-to-fund-major-criminal-justice-reforms-with-wall-street-money/458802/.

Fekete, Liz. 2014. Europe against the Roma. *Race & Class* 55(3):60–70.

Ferguson, Robert A. 2014. *Inferno: An Anatomy of American Punishment.* Cambridge: Harvard University Press.

Fine, Michelle, and María Elena Torre. 2006. Intimate Details: Participatory Action Research in Prison. *Action Research* 4(3):253–269.

Foucault, Michel. 1977. *Discipline and Punish: The Birth of the Prison.* New York: Vintage.

———. 1978. *The History of Sexuality.* New York: Pantheon Books.

———. 2003. *"Society Must Be Defended": Lectures at the Collège de France, 1975–1976.* New York: Picador.

Garman, James C. 1999. "Detention Castles of Stone and Steel": An Historical Archaeology of the First Rhode Island State Prison, 1838–1878. PhD diss., University of Massachusetts at Amherst.

Gilmore, Ruth W. 2007. *Golden Gulag: Prisons, Surplus, Crisis, and Opposition in Globalizing California.* Berkeley: University of California Press.

———. 2015. The Worrying State of the Anti-Prison Movement. *Social Justice: A Journal of Crime, Conflict & World Order,* February 23. http://www.socialjusticejournal.org/the-worrying-state-of-the-anti-prison-movement/.

Glasmeier, Amy K., and Tracey Farrigan. 2007. The Economic Impacts of the Prison Development Boom on Persistently Poor Rural Places. *International Regional Science Review* 30(3):274–299.

Goffman, Erving. 1961. *Asylums: Essays on the Social Situation of Mental Patients and Other Inmates.* Chicago: Aldine.

Gordon, Avery F. 2011. Some Thoughts on Haunting and Futurity. *borderlands* 10(2):1–21.

Grabowska, Sam, and John Doering-White. 2016. Material Memories: (Re)Collecting Clandestine Crossings of the U.S.-Mexico Borderlands. In *Excavating Memory: Sites of Remembering and Forgetting,* edited by Maria Theresia Starzmann and John R. Roby, 199–217. Gainesville: University Press of Florida.

Hicks, Dan. 2016. The Temporality of the Landscape Revisited. *Norwegian Archaeological Review* 49(1):5–22.

Hicks, Dan, Laura McAtackney, and Graham J. Fairclough. 2007. *Envisioning Landscape: Situations and Standpoints in Archaeology and Heritage.* Walnut Creek: Left Coast Press.

Huling, Tracy. 2002. Building a Prison Economy in Rural America. In *From Invisible Punishment: The Collateral Consequences of Mass Imprisonment,* edited by Marc Mauer and Meda Chesney-Lind, 197–213. New York: The New Press.

Ingold, Tim. 2000. *The Perception of the Environment: Essays in Livelihood, Dwelling, and Skill.* London: Routledge.

King, Ryan Scott, Marc Mauer, and Tracy Huling. 2004. An Analysis of the Economics of Prison Siting in Rural Communities. *Criminology and Public Policy* 3(3):453–480.

Kotef, Hagar. 2015. *Movement and the Ordering of Freedom: On Liberal Governances of Mobility.* Durham, NC: Duke University Press.

Low, Setha M., and Denise Lawrence-Zúñiga, eds. 2003. *The Anthropology of Space and Place: Locating Culture.* Malden, MA: Blackwell.

Mah, Alice. 2012. *Industrial Ruination, Community, and Place: Landscapes and Legacies of Urban Decline.* Toronto: University of Toronto Press.

Martin, Lauren L., and Matthew L. Mitchelson. 2008. Geographies of Detention and Imprisonment: Interrogating Spatial Practices of Confinement, Discipline, Law, and State Power. *Geography Compass* 3(1):459–477.

Mbembe, Achille. 2003. Necropolitics. *Public Culture* 15(1):11–40.

McAtackney, Laura. 2014. *An Archaeology of the Troubles: The Dark Heritage of Long Kesh/Maze Prison.* Oxford: Oxford University Press.

Morin, Karen M. 2013. Distinguished Historical Geography Lecture: Carceral Space and the Usable Past. *Historical Geography* 41:1–21.

Myers, Adrian. 2009. Bodies and Things Confined: Archaeological Approaches to Control and Detention. *Anthropology News* 50(1):8–9.

———. 2010. Camp Delta, Google Earth and the Ethics of Remote Sensing in Archaeology. *World Archaeology* 42(3):455–467.

Myers, Adrian, and Gabriel Moshenska, eds. 2011. *Archaeologies of Internment.* New York: Springer.

New York Correction History Society. N.d. "Fishkill Correction Facility." http://www.correctionhistory.org/html/chronicl/docs2day/fishkill.html.

Ogburn, Dennis E. 2006. Assessing the Level of Visibility of Cultural Objects in Past Landscapes. *Journal of Archaeological Science* 33(3):405–413.

O'Hearn, Denis. 2006. *Bobby Sands: Nothing But an Unfinished Song.* London: Pluto Press.

O'Hearn, Denis, and Andrej Grubačić. 2016. Capitalism, Mutual Aid, and Material Life: Understanding Exilic Spaces. *Capital & Class* 40(1):147–165.

Pachirat, Timothy. 2011. *Every Twelve Seconds: Industrialized Slaughter and the Politics of Sight.* New Haven, CT: Yale University Press.

Parenti, Christian. 2015. The Making of the American Police State: How Did We End Up with Millions behind Bars and Police Armed Like Soldiers? *Jacobin Magazine,* July 28. https://www.jacobinmag.com/2015/07/incarceration-capitalism-black-lives-matter/.

Peña, Elizabeth S. 2001. The Role of Wampum Production at the Albany Almshouse. *International Journal of Historical Archaeology* 5(2):155–174.

Peutz, Nathalie. 2006. Embarking on an Anthropology of Removal. *Current Anthropology* 47(1):217–241.

Philo, Chris. 2012. Security of Geography/Geography of Security. *Transactions* 37(1):1–7.

Prison Policy Initiative. 2010. Prison-Based Gerrymandering Profile. Prison Policy Initiative, May 11. http://www.prisonersofthecensus.org/factsheets/ny/district_45_profile.pdf.

Prison Visiting Project. 2012. Fishkill Correctional Facility: 2012. Correctional Association of New York. Accessed August 6, 2017. http://www.correctionalassociation.org/wp-content/uploads/2013/12/Fishkill-C.F.-Final-Report.pdf.

Rabuy, Bernadette, and Daniel Kopf. 2015. Prisons of Poverty: Uncovering the Pre-Incarceration Incomes of the Imprisoned. Prison Policy Initiative, July 9. http://www.prisonpolicy.org/reports/income.html.

Rafman, Jon. 2009. IMG MGMT: The Nine Eyes of Google Street View. Art F City, August 12. http://artfcity.com/2009/08/12/img-mgmt-the-nine-eyes-of-google-street-view/.

Rhodes, Lorna A. 2001. Toward an Anthropology of Prisons. *Annual Review of Anthropology* 30:65–83.

Sakala, Leah. 2014. Breaking Down Mass Incarceration in the 2010 Census: State-by-State Incarceration Rates by Race/Ethnicity. Prison Policy Initiative, May 28. http://www.prisonpolicy.org/reports/rates.html.

Sassen, Saskia. 1999. *Guests and Aliens*. New York: The New Press.

Schept, Judah. 2014. (Un)seeing Like a Prison: Counter-Visual Ethnography of the Carceral State. *Theoretical Criminology* 18(2):198–223.

Simon, Jonathan. 2007. *Governing through Crime: How the War on Crime Transformed American Democracy and Created a Culture of Fear*. Oxford: Oxford University Press.

Smith, Angèle, and Amy Gazin-Schwartz. 2008. *Landscapes of Clearance: Archaeological and Anthropological Perspectives*. London: Routledge.

Starzmann, Maresi. 2018. The Fragment and the Testimony: Reflections on Absence and Time in the Archaeology of Prisons and Camps. *International Journal of Historical Archaeology* 22(3):574–592.

Sturken, Marita, and Lisa Cartwright. 2001. *Practices of Looking: An Introduction to Visual Culture*. Oxford: Oxford University Press.

Summerhill, Thomas. 2005. *Harvest of Dissent: Agrarianism in Nineteenth-Century New York*. Urbana: University of Illinois Press.

Taylor, Alan. 2002. The Divided Ground: Upper Canada, New York, and the Iroquois Six Nations, 1783–1815. *Journal of the Early Republic* 22(1):55–75.

Ucko, Peter J., and Robert Layton, eds. 1999. *The Archaeology and Anthropology of Landscape: Shaping Your Landscape*. London: Routledge.

Wacquant, Loïc. 2000. The New "Peculiar Institution": On the Prison as Surrogate Ghetto. *Theoretical Criminology* 4(3):377–389.

———. 2010. Crafting the Neoliberal State: Workfare, Prisonfare, and Social Insecurity. *Sociological Forum* 25(2):197–220.

Wagner, Peter, and Daniel Kopf. 2015. The Racial Geography of Mass Incarceration. Prison Policy Initiative, July. http://www.prisonpolicy.org/racialgeography/report.html.

Waldram, James B. 2009. Challenges of Prison Ethnography. *Anthropology News* 4/5(50):1.

Walters, William. 2002. Deportation, Expulsion, and the International Police of Aliens. *Citizenship Studies* 6(3):265–292.

Winter, Yves. 2010. San Quentin 94974—The Everyday Prison. *Carceral Notebooks* 6:101–114. http://www.thecarceral.org/cn6_Winter.pdf.

9

The Janus Face of Removal

CHARLES E. ORSER

Removal is despair. On September 14, 1847, at the height of the Great Hunger in Ireland, what many people today call the Irish Potato Famine, landlord Denis Mahon wrote to his estate agent, telling him "I quite agree with you that it will be very advantageous to get rid of the Pauper Tenants in Many instances. . . . It will be very satisfactory to me, now being on the spot (and indeed at all times) if you should submit to me, previous to any final arrangement, the names of those persons . . . [because it] will enable me to give my approval to any plan that may be submitted to me."[1] The "plan" Mahon had in mind was the full-scale removal of the hundreds of tenant farmers on his sprawling estate. Only a year earlier, when his monocropping tenant farmers were just beginning to confront the harsh realities of the potato blight, two tenants with holdings on Mahon's estate petitioned him for relief. The writer of one letter described petitioner James Smyth as "a poor Starving Man" with a family of six, and the author of the second note, possibly the same writer, described tenant James Killian as "starving all this year, has not a Potatoe to eat this day when he goes home."[2] Want was everywhere in rural Ireland in the mid-1840s. A fungus was ravaging the potato crops that rural families depended on for sustenance. So rapid, severe, and horrible was the disease that industrious farmers could turn in at night content with their rich, green fields only to discover withered, blackened plants in the morning.

The death of the potato crop was devastating for the island's rural families. Their suffering far outpaced that experienced by almost any other nineteenth-century people. But landlords like Mahon also curiously found themselves victims of the potato blight. Financially stretched without the flow of his tenants' rents, his social position as a "principal man of standing" in the county was in jeopardy. Position and rank in elite society required him to maintain the grand lifestyle befitting the landed Protestant Ascendancy; he should project grace and manners even as those around him starved. Tenant want meant that Mahon could no longer rely on their toil to maintain his lifestyle. The only recourse available to landless tenants like Smyth and Killian—and there were thousands like them—was to send mournful petitions to the back doors of their landlords' great houses. Smyth's and Killian's pleadings were like many others streaming in from the countryside's thousands of tiny, thatched cabins. Faced with the reality of the ruined condition of the potato crop, Mahon's decision, rendered from his stately Palladian mansion—which was built on land confiscated from the Gaelic Irish in the 1660s—was harsh but personally practical. Having calculated the numbers, his estate agent reasoned that it would be less expensive and decidedly much more expedient for Mahon to fund the removal of his tenants than to wait and hope that they could remit their full rents when the potato blight had run its course and profitable times returned. One feature of the account is that many contemporary commentators viewed Mahon as a good and decent landlord.

The plan Mahon and his agent devised fell under the broad heading of "assisted immigration." These were schemes landed Irish gentry devised who found themselves in financial straits because of the agricultural disease. For others, the famine blight provided a convenient excuse to rid themselves of an often-troublesome tenantry, people they tended to sneer at because of their Catholic "superstitions," their odd-sounding Gaelic language, and their strange traditions. Sheep presented none of these problems. Regardless of each landlord's personal rationale, removal was an option that could appear sensible for the times and conditions, at least as far as the gentry were concerned.

Depending upon one's perspective, the landlords' acts of removal were either bold and inventive or cruel and heartless. Some landlords, and even some tenants, saw the forced migration first to North America and later also to Australia, as a life-saving opportunity for better lives in wealthier, more optimistic environments. With removal, the realities facing evicting landlords improved immediately, but most displaced tenants could begin to envision the benefits of removal only in retrospect. The view backward often took generations to be appreciated. Whether removal was ultimately beneficial, hope for prosperity fueled the imaginations of many Irish immigrants even as their feelings were comingled with thoughts of despair. Many men and women torn from their homelands perceived the entire process as terrorism designed to separate them from their histories, soil, and heritage. In forcing the famine Irish across the Atlantic, removal—whatever the rationale—deposited them in unfamiliar lands among strange people, many of whom did not welcome the influx of Catholic foreigners. The profound despair the Irish who emigrated experienced is kept alive in the many emigration songs men and women of Irish heritage still sing today in pubs around the world. These ballads attest to the depths of feeling aroused by removal.

The despair of removal is deepened by the reality that rebellion as a long-term strategy is usually doomed to failure. The condition of individuals and families deemed "worthy" of removal seldom have the political, social, or economic capital needed to fight and win, either legally or militarily. County Roscommon, the scene of several mass evictions, including those of the Mahon estate, had a long history of rural revolt (Coleman 1999). As with any small, close-knit society, some disturbances were merely the result of jealousy and mistrust between neighbors. But on a much larger scale, the ubiquitous rebellions in Ireland stemmed from the yoke of British rule and from the inequalities inherent in a hierarchical social system unfairly tilted to the advantage of Protestants of Anglo-Irish (or simply Anglo) heritage. The tenants of Ballykilcline—one of Mahon's former estates that was governed by the Crown after 1834—fought a protracted rent strike for twelve years before being evicted. For his role in removal, whether his intentions were good or merely self-serving, Mahon was assassinated as he headed home one evening from a relief meeting (Duffy 2007; Reilly 2014; Vesey 2008). As removal in the county proceeded, men, women, and children were forced out of their homes, down the road, and across the ocean. But the horrors of removal, although mentally suppressed for many years, could not be forever submerged. The descendants of many former residents of Mahon's estate, now living throughout the United States and Canada, formed themselves into a group called The Ballykilcline Society. These assembled families celebrate their heritage, survival, and resilience in the face of removal, famine, and disease (Dunn 2008).

The case of the Irish tenant farmers during the famine is unique in time and place. The chapters in this volume demonstrate the same inherent idiosyncrasies of removal as played out in each case study. Bound by space and time, each account is necessarily exceptional. The historical actors and spatial geographies are wholly distinctive to each account. When viewed strictly at the local scale, commonalities between the cases are difficult to discern. Individuality is clear in each chapter, and each studied group demonstrates special resourcefulness and determination in their ability to survive and even to thrive by adopting situationally sensible tactics and strategies. As was the case with the County Roscommon evictions, it appears in hindsight that some removed individuals eventually benefited from the experience by obtaining more secure livelihoods. Many of the removed families represented in the present chapters were resourceful and determined enough to engage in successful place making. These instances constitute the tangible successes and intellectual resistances enacted against those with the power and authority to demand, encourage, and rationalize removal.

The success stories, as impressive and as hopeful as they indeed are, illuminate the awful truth behind removal when viewed on a broad scale. All cases of forced removal involve racialization and discrimination in some fashion. Japanese internees, Appalachian hill folk, and all the others chronicled here, faced what was essentially the same process despite the disparities of time and place. The reason for the structural similarity arises because at its core, removal is a straightforward process that requires little modification over time. At its most fundamental, removal is a power play. People in authority have the will, for whatever reason, to rid themselves of individuals they have designated "undesirable," also for whatever reason. As is true of the case studies presented in this book, society's elites often perceive removal as a simple process of ethnic cleansing. The second definition of "removal" in the *Oxford English Dictionary* is "the act of 'removing' a person by murder," and although the cleansing process may include actual homicide, it need not do so. The removal process only requires that the unwanted become invisible in their former places of residence. The spatial disjunction caused by such erasure is routine. Chickasaws living on land coveted by land-hungry Americans, African Americans facing gentrification, Piscataways being elbowed out by settlers, and homesteaders chased away by government employees seeking to create national landmarks have endured the same process. It unfolded in rural Ireland as well. Once-vibrant landscapes were ultimately laid bare of human habitation by mass eviction, even if the removals were sequenced and protracted. An eyewitness in Ireland during the height of the famine stated the case plainly: "As each family was dispossessed, their cottage was levelled to the ground—cottages which to them had many endearing associations, as having been the home of their forebears and the place of their own nativity—a place which is ever most dear to the Irish heart" (Doolan 1847, 13). In County Mayo years later, residents still recalled with sadness the horrors of eviction. One elder person remembered that one local landlord "laid waste a large tract of the parish along the way and places are pointed out where entire villages once stood" (Póirtéir 1995, 239). Silence and emptiness prevail.

Paradoxically, however, removal is also opportunity. The violent realities of eviction appear to render this statement insensitive. But archaeologists, unless they are intimately engaged with contemporary cases of erasure, tend to be distant from the psychology of removal. The poignant realities usually stand beyond the archaeologist's reach unless images of some sort have memorialized the events in some fashion. In the Irish case, early nineteenth-century drawings depicted the horrors of displacement as they were occurring. One oft-reprinted and evocative image that first appeared in the *Illustrated London News* on December 16, 1848, makes the trauma of eviction easy to imagine. A woman, undoubtedly the resident of a small, stone dwelling, stands outside the door pleading with folded hands to an unsympathetic bailiff on horseback. The family's possessions lay carelessly strewn about the yard, obviously having been removed by the soldiers idly standing by with fixed bayonets. Men straddle the ridge of the house's roof and tear off the thatch to render the interior unlivable in the wet Irish weather. Concerned bystanders wait at the edges of the image, perhaps pondering whether their homes may be next (see Litton 1994, 96). The truth of this drawing as a snapshot of reality is unimportant. The image proclaims the personal horror of displacement, whether it is apocryphal, a conflation of many eviction scenes, or the actual illustration of a true event. The caption for the drawing in Tóibín's (1999, 41) short history of the famine proves that the image still has the power to evoke: "The evictions were usually ruthless. Families were turned out on to the road by bailiffs supported by the police and army." Later in the century, photographs of evictions replaced drawings. These pictures show how the agents of evicting bailiffs smashed holes in the stone walls of Irish cabins using a battering ram swung on a tripod (see Percival 1995, 102). Clever photographers may have staged some of these events, but again, the veracity of the images is not as important as their evocative character. Perhaps photographs are even more powerful because many people believe them to be more reliable as truth tellers than sketches. Such images retain value for archaeological research despite their veracity as exacting historical accounts (see, e.g., Orser 2001).

So what are the implications of suggesting that removal is opportunity? It is worth noting that one of the hard realities of archaeological research is that removals often offer one-of-a-kind evidence unavailable in other historical sources. Because removals necessarily involve material objects—ranging from landscapes to tiny fragments—the archaeological evidence for these events can remain buried in the soil and possibly undisturbed for generations. In the case of the Mahon estate, excavations at the homes of evicted tenants have provided abundant, otherwise undocumented evidence about past daily life, including information about household economy, the rural farmers' access to the British commercial market, and the settlement dynamics of a nineteenth-century Irish townland. Most of the collected information has derived not from written records or even images but from the material objects owned and used by the cabins' residents. Some of the most important evidence seems so mundane that few contemporary chroniclers would have ever noticed it or appreciated its significance. For example, at the townland of Ballykilcline, a settlement of over 500 people evicted in five groups between September 1846 and October 1848 (Scally 1996), excavators found five unremarkable glass beads. The beads were not special in any readily discernable way. No two beads were alike in color, shape, or size. The most straightforward interpretation was that they were probably once part of a necklace composed of whatever beads happened to be available. Irish folklore, however, suggests a much more profound interpretation that the beads were part of lace making, a little-documented cottage industry. It seems that women living in nineteenth-century rural Ireland often decorated their lace bobbins with different-colored beads. These beads created identifiable individuality, expressed creativity, and had the practical purpose of providing a little weight to the bone and wooden bobbins. When strung on a bobbin, the beads constituted little pieces of functional art. These artifacts suggest that tenant women supplemented their families' agrarian economies by making and selling lace (see Orser 2003).

Evidence for removal forever rests in landscapes. Each of the removals documented in this volume provide ample evidence for the topography of removal. Each geography examined by the chapters' authors illuminate the creation of empty spaces where life had once prospered. Silence replaces life. In the case of rural Ireland, the landscapes that entice multitudes of foreign tourists to the counties of the west—those that witnessed the greatest losses by eviction—truly do present "a terrible beauty" (Yeats [1921] 1989, 180). The dispossession represented in these empty expanses are as tangibly appalling as those documented in this book, whether they exist in seventeenth- or nineteenth-century Maryland, Appalachia, or rural Mississippi. Many of the "discovery points" the Irish Tourist Board recommends to foreign tourists—places green and dramatic but empty and silent—were former sites of daily life. Archaeology is most needed in such vacant, albeit often starkly beautiful, places.

In nineteenth-century Ireland, the process of destruction that accompanied forced eviction, terrible as they were in every respect, have left remains, but usually only under the earth's surface. Old sod houses crumble in the elements and stone structures succumb to the same modernizing pressures exerted upon African Americans facing gentrification in Virginia. What remains is often only there for archaeologists to unearth. The so-called crowbar brigades of nineteenth-century Ireland were extremely proficient in their work of erasure. The homes that once populated Ballykilcline were completely invisible before excavation. After the evictions were finally completed in 1848, the land agent allocated the space to grazing sheep. It remained so until excavation in the 1990s. Without the use of geophysical testing, the houses—which were made of turf or stone—were imperceptible on the surface. As efficient as the house destroyers were, however, they could not remove all traces of human life. Hundreds of tiny artifacts, like the glass beads from the bobbin, remained locked in the earth. An inexpensive thimble, stamped "Forget Me Not," tells of love and friendship; whiteware cups painted with deep blue dragons reference the finery of Chinese export porcelain; and an iron reaping hook speaks to blisters and aching backs. In the stone-built houses, only a thin layer of small rocks from the interior of the large-stone walls lingers. Tenants fortunate enough to remain in the vicinity had assisted in the process of erasure by taking the largest stones for their own buildings. Only a thin layer of burned thatch provided testimony to the former presence of the poorest farmers' turf dwellings (see Orser 2006).

Archaeologists today are overtly and proudly cognizant of the roles memory and forgetting play in history and heritage, and each author in this volume has addressed those subjects in some fashion. One of the elements of forgetting concerns the necessary connection between past and present. The tie is evident in the example from New York State's prisons. Sadly, we learn that removal, like enslavement, belongs not to the past alone. That such frightful processes continue to be enacted around the globe references one of the most important features of archaeological research: interrogating the line between past and present. The connections between past and present are more than philosophical; they also exist in places where the link between them is remarkably palpable.

In 1849, after most of the funds for Irish relief had evaporated, even though the famine still raged, the Choctaw Nation of Oklahoma sent a cash donation to the Irish Relief Fund to aid destitute farmers in County Mayo. The precise amount they donated—either $170 or $710, the sources disagree—is less important than the fact that relief was sent from one heartlessly removed people to another (Kinealy 1995, 163). Uninformed Americans considered the Choctaws, like the Chickasaws present in this book, to constitute one people within a culturally uniform group they designated the Five Civilized Tribes. The lack of cultural distinction in the dominant society was a callous act of racialization, a creative fiction that all Native Americans were essentially the same. The Choctaws' gift, an act of humanity by a people who had known little humanity in nineteenth-century America, forcefully denounced the dominant nation's formulaic racialization. Such selfless charity transcends time. Members of the Choctaw Nation still travel to County Mayo to participate in a walk that commemorates the Irish who died during the famine (Byrne 1997). The Choctaw-Irish connection, as odd as it may appear to the uneducated racialist, links the past, present, and future despite significant cultural, historical, and spatial differences.

The archaeology of removal is not a happy subject. Lives are transformed, psychological images are imprinted, and landscapes are denuded by ejectment. But new histories are created in the ruins left behind. At first look, the winners of the removal process seem obvious. As troublesome, poor, or simply unwanted peoples are made to disappear, landscapes are freed from human habitation. In many cases, the landscapes may revert to what may be perceived as a state of nature; in other situations, the land is consciously transformed to be more "productive." The silences foisted upon the past in such places remain in effect until archaeologists, in their work of unearthing, can give them voice again. Herein, then, lies one of the incredible strengths of archaeological research. As demonstrated in this volume, excavation, study, and interpretation illuminate histories denied to other scholars. The potency of excavation, when united with myriad contributing sources, permits archaeologists to glimpse the past uniquely. Archaeologists see removal in stark and undeniable ways—as the remnants of broken homes and smashed artifacts—but also in retrospect as the tenacity of the human spirit. The archaeologist's gaze never ends with simple backward glances. As demonstrated in this book, archaeologists also have special insights for the present.

Archaeologists' statements extolling the virtues of linkages of the past with the present have today assumed the characteristics of platitudes. But despite the ease with which the claim can be made, it remains true that the Janus face of removal, a subject rife with pain and despair, is equally charged with hope.

Notes

1. Denis Mahon, "Submit to him names of tenants who propose to surrender or getting crops," 1847 letter, Pakenham Mahon Papers, Strokestown Park House, Strokestown, County Roscommon.

2. Petition of James Killian, North Yard, 1846; James Smyth to Major Denis Mahon, ca. 1846, both in Pakenham Mahon Papers, Strokestown Park House, Strokestown, County Roscommon.

References Cited

Byrne, Gabriel. 1997. Famine Walk. In *Irish Hunger: Personal Reflections on the Legacy of the Famine*, edited by Tom Hayden, 115–116. Boulder, CO: Roberts Rinehart.

Coleman, Anne. 1999. *Riotous Roscommon: Social Unrest in the 1840s*. Dublin: Irish Academic Press.

Doolan, Thomas. 1847. *Practical Suggestions on the Improvement of the Present Condition of the Peasantry of Ireland*. London: George Barclay.

Duffy, Peter. 2007. *The Killing of Major Denis Mahon: A Mystery of Old Ireland*. New York: HarperCollins.

Dunn, Mary Lee. 2008. *Ballykilcline Rising: From Famine Ireland to Immigrant America*. Amherst: University of Massachusetts Press.

Kinealy, Christine. 1995. *This Great Calamity: The Irish Famine, 1845–52*. Boulder, CO: Roberts Rinehart.

Litton, Helen. 1994. *The Irish Famine: An Illustrated History*. Dublin: Wolfhound.

Orser, Charles E., Jr. 2001. Vessels of Honor and Dishonor: The Symbolic Character of Irish Earthenware. *New Hiberia Review* 5:83–100.

———. 2003. *The Beads of Ballykilcline*. In *Lost and Found: Discovering Ireland's Past*, edited by Joe Fenwick, 309–315. Bray: Wordwell.

———. 2006, ed. *Unearthing Hidden Ireland: Historical Archaeology in County Roscommon*. Bray: Wordwell.

Percival, John. 1995. *The Great Famine: Ireland's Potato Famine, 1845–51*. New York: Viewer.

Póirtéir, Cathal. 1995. *Famine Echoes*. Dublin: Gill and Macmillan.

Reilly, Ciarán. 2014. *Strokestown and the Great Irish Famine*. Dublin: Four Courts.

Scally, Robert James. 1996. *The End of Hidden Ireland: Rebellion, Famine, and Emigration*. New York: Oxford University Press.

Tóibín, Colm. 1999. *The Irish Famine*. London: Profile.

Vesey, Padraig. 2008. *The Murder of Major Mahon, Strokestown, County Roscommon, 1847*. Dublin: Four Courts.

Yeats, W. B. (1921) 1989. *The Collected Poems of W. B. Yeats: A New Edition*. New York: Palgrave Macmillan.

Contributors

Bonnie J. Clark is associate professor in the Anthropology Department at the University of Denver and curator for archaeology at the Denver University Museum of Anthropology.

Alex J. Flick is an archaeologist at RGA, Inc.

Adam Fracchia is a postdoctoral associate in the Department of Anthropology at the University of Maryland, College Park.

Audrey Horning is professor of anthropology at the College of William and Mary.

April Kamp-Whittaker is a graduate assistant/associate in the School of Human Evolution and Social Change at Arizona State University.

Julia A. King is professor of anthropology at St. Mary's College of Maryland.

Charles E. Orser is research professor in the Department of Anthropology at Vanderbilt University.

Matthew Reeves is director of archaeology and landscape restoration at James Madison's Montpelier, Montpelier Station, Virginia.

Maria Theresia Starzmann is project manager for the United Nations at the Rosa Luxemburg Stiftung—New York Office.

Terrance Weik is associate professor of anthropology at the University of South Carolina. He is the author of *The Archaeology of Antislavery Resistance.*

Stefan Woehlke is a doctoral candidate in the Department of Anthropology at the University of Maryland, College Park.

Index

Page references in *italics* indicate tables or figures.

Accokeek Creek site, 27
Administrative neighborhoods: definition of, 163; residential blocks as, 167; social neighborhoods compared to, 172
African Americans: economies of scale impacting, 93–94; emancipation for, 86–93; forced migration of, in Orange County, 74, 99–100; incarceration rates of, 190; industrialization of agriculture impacting, 97–98; labor force after Civil War, 88; landownership for, 86, 89–91; at Mount Pleasant tobacco plantation, 80; opportunities of, limited, 74–75; from Orange County, moving away, 83–84; quarry industry work by, 119–20; spatial relationships impacting, 95–96; stereotypes of, 3, 119–20; tenancy in common and, 92
African slaves: for agriculture, 73; escape of, 85–86; hiring of, 82; at Mount Pleasant tobacco plantation, 79–81; in Orange County, arrival of, 78–79; selling of, 85
Agriculture: African slaves for, 73; colonialism influenced by, 23–24; Cotton Belt, 83–84; green revolution impacting, 75; industrialization of, 97–98; mechanization of, 83, 85, 94; in Montpelier, censuses, 78; in Montpelier, changes to, 83; in Montpelier, diversity of, 81–82; plow, 36–37; privatization of, 98–99
Alcohol consumption: in Amache neighborhoods, 174, 176–77; stereotypes, 119–20

Amache neighborhoods: artifacts from, 174–77, *176*; block identities in, 173–74, 183; changes in composition of, 169–71, *170*; cultural features of, distinctive, 172–73; demographic composition of, 168, *169*; landscaping in, 177–83, *178, 179, 181, 182*; layout of residential blocks in, 161–62, *162*; methods for identifying, 164–65; pedestrian surveys of, 165; residential directory of, 168, *169*, 184n2; schematic map of, *166*; social neighborhoods within, 167–74; social organization within, 158–59; social services established in, 171–72; spatial relationships in, 165–66, *166*
Animal husbandry practices, 36
Anthropology: discourses, goal of advancing, 2; of displacement, 22–23; of land competition, 59–65; of materiality, 7–8; Native Americans influencing, 1; salvage, 3–4
Architectural survey, 77, 84
Architecture: at Levi Colbert's Prairie, 53–54, *54*; in Texas (town), *104*, 113–16, *114, 115*, 123n1
Archived maps, 48
Armed conflict, 6
Articles of Peace and Amity (1966), 25
Artifacts: Amache neighborhood, 174–77, *176*; Boggy Depot, 67; Corbin Hollow, 130, *130*, 149–51, *150*; Ireland, 221, *222*; Levi Colbert's Prairie, 52; Monocan, 79; Montpelier, 76; Novotny site, 56–59, *57, 58*; Piscataway, 30–33, *31*; Texas (town), 116–18, *117*. *See also specific artifacts*
Attica Series Desk, 196, *196*

Ballykilcline, Ireland, 218, 221, 222
The Ballykilcline Society, 218
Baltimore, Lord, 24, 25
Bead Hill, 19
Black, Jason Edward, 50
Blacksmithing operation, 80
Block identities, 173–74, 183
Blue Ridge Mountain residents: character-
    istics of, 130–31; lifestyle evaluations of,
    135–41; mountain folk image of, capitalizing
    on, 141–42; public opinion on removal,
    128; voices of displaced, 142–46. *See also*
    Shenandoah National Park
Boggy Depot, 67
Buttons, 117, *117*
Byrd, Harry, 132, 133

Cammerer, Arno, 132
Capital accumulation: dispossession in relation
    to, 103–4, 121–22; exploitation from, 105
Capitalism: cultural landscape shaped by,
    73; green revolution in relation to, 75; for
    maximization of profit, 105–6; preservation
    as threat to, 107; prison system linked to,
    191, 195–96, *196*; racism in relation to, 104;
    role of, in Orange County removal, 74; rural
    removal impacted by, 93
Carceral landscapes: concealment of, 191;
    history of, 206–9; invisibility/visibility of,
    203–6, *204*, *205*; isolation of, 200–201; Na-
    tive American dispossession and, 208
Caribbean, 48
Cass, Lewis, *60*, 61, 63, 65
Cellulose card calendar, 130, *130*
Cemeteries: Conoy Town site, 34; exploitation
    of, 37; St. Joseph's Church, 110, 111, *111*
Ceramics: destruction of, 68; from Novotny
    site, 56–57, *57*; from Piscataway sites, 30–32,
    31; from Texas (town), 116–17
Cession maps, 52–53, *53*
Cherokees, 6–7
Chickasaw removal maps: creation of, 46;
    post-removal, 56–59, *58*; pre-removal,
    51–56, *53*, *54*
Chickasaws: award winning map of, 45–46;
    cession maps, 52–53, *53*; Choctaws in rela-
    tion to, 5, 56–57; Colbert, L., relations with,
    51, 56; cultural history synopsis of, 46–47;

deerskin maps of, 50; Geospatial division
    of, 45, 59; at Novotny, 56–59, *57*, *58*; pre-
    removal land competition regarding, 59–65;
    removal of, future research on, 65–67;
    removal routes of, *66*, 67; rhetoric of, 68–69;
    skills of, revitalizing, 68; Treaty of Pontotoc
    Creek and, 60, 62–63; US-Chickasaw treaty,
    61–62
Choctaws: Chickasaws in relation to, 5, 56–57;
    displacement of, consequences from, 5;
    donations from, 223; Novotny site in rela-
    tion to, 58–59
Choptico, 35
Civilian Conservation Corps, 127
Civil War: African American labor force fol-
    lowing, 88; African slaves escaping during,
    85–86; encampments, surveys locating, 77;
    labor force migration following, 93
Class consciousness, 96–97
Colbert, James, 62–63
Colbert, Levi: Chickasaw relations with, 51, 56;
    relocation land exploration by, 68; treaty
    benefits of, 55. *See also* Levi Colbert's Prairie
Colonialism: agriculture influencing, 23–24;
    debt used by, 63; erasure from, 20; land
    titling from, 50–51; maps as important tools
    of, 48; prison system in relation to, 191, 208;
    scientific, 8–9
Colonists: cemetery exploitation by, 37; Pisca-
    taway relations with, 24–25, 26; reservation
    land disputes with, 35–36
Colony farm, 208
Commercial development, 103, 121–22
Commonwealth of Virginia: land tracts pur-
    chased by, 127; lawsuit against, 145; Virginia
    State Commission on Conservation and
    Development and, 131
Community: destruction of Texas (town), 103,
    121–22; group identity defining, 163; *Hollow
    Folk* ranking Shenandoah area, 128, 137;
    internment camps dividing, 157; Irish immi-
    grant, alienation of, 112; Japanese Ameri-
    cans reestablishing, within camps, 167–68,
    183–84; landscape features, 179–83, *181*, *182*;
    neighborhoods as nexuses of, 158; prison
    system deteriorating, 191–92; resilience of,
    74; social identity of, 38; social interaction
    for, 165, 172; urban renewal maps impacting,

105–6; warehousing of prisoners for controlling, 190
Confederate army, 85, 86
Confinement: Executive Order 9066 for Japanese American, 159; of non-citizen populations, 192–93; West Coast impacted by, 157. *See also* Amache neighborhoods; Internment camps; Prison system
Conoy Town site: cemetery of, 34; excavation of, 30
Cooper, William, 62
Corbin, George, 144
Corbin Hollow: artifacts, 130, *130*, 149–51, *150*; cellulose card calendar from, 130, *130*; Pollock relations with, 133–34, 149; on Sizer, 141–42; Sizer on, 150–51; Skyland resort and, 134, 139, 144–45; Weakley Hollow on, 148–49
Cotton Belt, 83–84
County Mayo, Ireland, 220, 223
Craft production: decline in Piscataway, 33–34, 39; in Weakley Hollow, 141
Crowbar brigades, 222
Cultural displacement, 10–11
Cultural landscape, 73
Cuomo, Andrew, 210–11

Dam building, 10
Davis, James, 62
Dawes Act, 59
Debitage, 32
Deerskin maps, 50
Denver University (DU) Amache Project, 184
Despair: of prison, 189; of removal, 216, 218
Devaluation, labor force, 106
Directionality of power, 193–94
Directory, residential, 168, *169*, 184n2
Discipline and Punish: The Birth of the Prison (Foucault), 193
Discrimination rhetoric, 119–20
Displacement: anthropology of, 22–23; of Choctaws, consequences from, 5; cultural, 10–11; factors contributing to forced, 1; internal, 11–12; material culture's role in, 4; memory and, 20–23; Piscataway effects from, of those who left, 27–34; Piscataway effects from, of those who stayed, 34–39; of prisoners, 197; in Shenandoah National

Park, justification of, 128–29, 135–41; Shenandoah National Park legacies of, 146–51; under-theorization of, 3; unity from, 152; violent, 1–2; from volcanism, 8; after World War II, 3
Dispossession: armed conflict causing, 6; capital accumulation in relation to, 103–4, 121–22; carceral landscapes and Native American, 208; kindred concepts of, 2–5; removal and, defining terms of, 5–8
Dole, Joseph, 189, 199
DU Amache Project. *See* Denver University Amache Project
Dudley, Sandra, 22–23
DuPont, William, 91–92
Dyer, Herbert, 142

Economic exploitation, 10
Economic inequality, 92–93
Economies of scale, 93–94
Economy: diversification of, in Orange County, 82; globalization of, 99; political, 10, 51–52, 195–96, *196*, 198
Emancipation: for African Americans, 86–93; baby boom following, 86; historical trajectory following, 75
Epistemology, 49
Erasure: from colonialism, 20; crowbar brigades contributing to, 222; regarding Levi Colbert's Prairie, 53–54; of Piscataway homeland, 36–37, 39–40; of Texas (town) history, 104
Erosion: prevention of, 79; shoreline, 37
Eviction: benefits from, 219; of Blue Ridge Mountain residents, 145; in Ireland, 110–11, 217–18, 219–20; landscapes impacted by, 219–20; resistance to, 12; violence of, 220
Executive Order 9066, 159
Exile: idealization of, 4; internal, 190
Exploitation: archaeologists fight against, 122–23; from capital accumulation, 105; of cemeteries, 37; economic, 10; of prison labor, 208

Farms: colony, 208; economies of scale impacting, 94; Great Famine/Hunger impacting Ireland, 110–11, 216–17; production for, removing means of, 98–99; in

Farms—*continued*
  Shenandoah National Park area, conditions
    of, 138–40; spatial relationships impacting,
    95–96; wealth gap regarding, 89. *See also*
    Agriculture
FCF. *See* Fishkill Correctional Facility
Federal government, 134–35
Federal Prison Industries, 195–96
Fishkill Correctional Facility (FCF): Google
    Earth view of, 204, *205*; Google Maps view
    of, *207*; history of, 207–9; population of,
    203–4; traffic signs warning of, *204*
Forced migration: of African Americans in
    Orange County, 74, 99–100; anthropol-
    ogy of displacement as study of, 22–23;
    comparisons of, 21; to Cotton Belt, 83–84;
    from federal government, 134–35; between
    internment camps, 160–61; from Ireland,
    217–18; of Japanese Americans, 157–58;
    materiality of, 67–68; skills during, per-
    sistence of, 56; trauma of, 67, 145. *See also*
    Displacement
Forgetting. *See* Memory/memory loss
Fort Hampton, Alabama, 65
Foucault, Michel, 193
Fulton, H. R., 141–42

Garden bed, *182*
General Land Office plat maps: grids for, 50;
    of Novotny site, 57–58, *58*; pre-removal
    Chickasaw, 51–56, *53*, *54*; role of, in re-
    moval, 59–60, *60*
Genetic modification, 97, 98–99
Geographic information systems (GIS): con-
    ference, 45; utility of, 48
Gerrymandering, 199
Gilmore family, 87, 90–91, *91*, 92
GIS. *See* Geographic information systems
Glass jugs, 174, 176, *176*
Globalization, 99
Google Earth, 202, 204, *205*
Google Maps: FCF view from, *207*; Guantá-
    namo Bay Detention Center view from,
    201, *201*; *The Nine Eyes of Google Street View*
    series and, 210, *210*
Gordon, Robert, 62–63
GPR. *See* Ground-penetrating radar
Great Famine/Hunger, 110–11, 216–17

Great Smoky Mountains National Park, 133,
    134
Green revolution, 75
Ground-penetrating radar (GPR), 52
Guantánamo Bay Detention Center, 201, *201*

Harvey, David, 93, 95, 96
Heater's Island site: ceramics and tobacco
    pipes recovered from, 30–32, *31*; excavation
    of, 29–30; small pox outbreak at, 26–27
Henry, Thomas, 137; conclusions of, 138;
    Hollow Folk by, 128, 136; on Shenandoah
    National Park, reflecting, 127
Herculaneum, 8
Hierarchy: of labor force, 106; of material cul-
    ture, 104; rebellion fueled by, 218; separation
    and, in Texas (town), 111–19
Historical Archaeology listserv, 2
"Historic Map of the Unconquered and Un-
    conquerable Chickasaw People," 45–46
The History of Sexuality (Foucault), 193
Hollow Folk (Sherman and Henry): influence
    of, 136, 138; on social development theory,
    128, 137
Holocaust map, 7, 15n1
Human rights, 11
Humphries, Richard, 61
Hurricane Katrina, 3
Hybridization, 97, 98–99

Identity: block, in Amache neighborhoods,
    173–74, 183; clothing for expressing, 117;
    community defined by group, 163; Irish im-
    migrant, acceptance of, 120; persistence of,
    7; of Piscataway, 38
Immobility, 192–93, 195
Incarceration. *See* Internment camps; Prison-
    ers; Prison system
Indian Hill, 19
Indigenous people: African slaves in relation
    to, 73; scientific colonialism impacting, 8–9;
    violent displacement of, 1–2. *See also specific
    indigenous groups*
Industrialization: of agriculture, 97–98; labor
    force impacted by, 93
Inequality: economic, 92–93; health care, 118;
    of labor force living conditions, 113–16, *114*,
    115

Internal exile, 190
Internally displaced persons, 11–12
Internment camps: community divided by, 157; Japanese Americans in, history of, 159–61, *160*; layout and function of, 161–62, *162*; WRA establishing, 160, *160*. *See also* Amache neighborhoods
Ireland: artifacts, 221, 222; Choctaws donating to, 223; crowbar brigades of, 222; eviction in, 110–11, 217–18, 219–20; Great Famine/Hunger in, 110, 216–17; Long Kesh Prison in, 193; rebellions in, 218
Irish immigrants: The Ballykilcline Society formed by, 218; as disposable labor force, 110, 112; identity, acceptance of, 120; labor activism by, 118–19; segregation and removal of, 119–22; separation and hierarchy regarding, 111–19; stereotypes of, 112–13, 119; of Texas (town), 105; violence toward, 113–14

Jacksontown, 86
James, Roberson, 61, 63–65
Japanese Americans: community reestablishment within camps, 167–68, 183–84; forced migration of, 157–58; in internment camps, history of, 159–61, *160*; landscapes changed by, 177–83, *178, 179, 181, 182*; loyalty questionnaire for, 160; social arenas for, 173, 180, *181*. *See also* Amache neighborhoods
Jones, Hugh, 23

Kemp, Lulu, 57–58
Killian, James, 216–17
Kindred concepts, 2–5

Labor force: activism, 118–19; after Civil War, migration of, 93; after Civil War, of African Americans, 88; class consciousness of, 96–97; deskilling of, 97–98; devaluation of, 106; industrialization impacting, 93; Irish immigrants as disposable, 110, 112; living conditions, inequality of, 113–16, *114, 115*; prisoners as, 195–96, *196*, 208; profit over safety of, 110; of railroad industry, 95; spatial relationships impacting, 95–96
Land competition, 59–65
Landowners, African American, 86, 89–91
Landragan House, *104*, 123n1

Landscapes: carceral, 191, 200–201, 203–9, *204, 205*; cultural, capitalism shaping, 73; eviction impacting, 219–20; Japanese Americans changing features of, 177–83, *178, 179, 181, 182*; maps for historical content of, 48; mechanization impacting, 99; of Orange County, removal shaping, 78–79; remembrance programs for, 8; as social arenas, 180, *181*; transformation of, 223–24
Landscaping, 177–83, *178, 179, 181, 182*
Land titling, 50–51
Land tracts, 127
Lassiter, James, 141–42, 143
Leakey, Louis, 9
Levi Colbert's Prairie: archaeology of, 51–56; architecture at, 53–54, *54*; artifacts, 52; erasure regarding, 53–54
Li, Tania, 12, 50–51
Life-without-parole sentence, 189, 199
Limestone industry. *See* Quarry industry
Long Kesh Prison, 193
Loyalty questionnaire, 160
Ludlow Tent Colony Site, 107
Lumbee, 38

Madison, Ambrose, 78, 79–80
Madison, Dolley: Montpelier co-managed by, 82–84; Montpelier sold by, 84–85
Madison, Dr. James, 90
Madison, Frances, 78, 79–81
Madison, James: death of, 84; grandparents of, 78; Montpelier co-managed by, 82–84; Montpelier home of, 75
Madison Sr., James: blacksmithing operation of, 80; Montpelier managed by, 81–82
Mahon, Denis: artifacts from estate of, 221; assassination of, 218; assisted immigration plan of, 217; tenant petitions to, 216–17
Maps: Amache neighborhood schematic, *166*; archaeological approaches to, 47–51; for archaeological site relationships, 48; cession, 52–53, *53*; Chickasaw Nation's award winning, 45–46; deerskin, 50; for epistemology, 49; General Land Office plat, 50, 51–56, *53, 54*, 57–58, *58*, 59–60, *60*; Google, 201, *201*, 202, 204, *205, 207*, 210, *210*; Holocaust, 7, 15n1; post-removal Chickasaw, 56–59, *58*; pre-removal Chickasaw, 51–56, *53, 54*;

Maps—*continued*
of Shenandoah National Park, *129*; of Texas
(town), *113*; urban renewal, 105–6; useful-
ness and importance of, 45, 67–68; of WRA
internment camps, 160, *160*
Marbles, 175, *176*, 177
Marginalization: of labor force, 106, 112; material culture reinforcing, 116, 118–19; political,
198–200; stereotypes for justifying, 119;
violence in relation to, 194
Marye, William B., 20
Material culture: in displacement, role of, 4;
hierarchy of, 104; interactions with, 22;
marginalization reinforced by, 116, 118–19;
prison system and, 190; spatial relationships
and, 112
Materiality: anthropology of, 7–8; of forced
migration, 67–68
Matteawan State Hospital, 207–9
Mechanization: of agriculture, 83, 85, 94; land-
scapes impacted by, 99; of quarry industry,
109–10
Medicine bottles, 118
Memory/memory loss: of Amache neighbor-
hoods, 173; displacement and, 20–23; of
Indian and Bead Hill, 19; remembrance
programs for, 7–8; role of, 222–23; of
Shenandoah National Park, 151–52; of
Zekiah Fort, 20
Metadiscourse, 2–3
Metal detector survey, 77, 80–81
Metal objects, modified, 174–75, *176*
Migration. *See* Forced migration
Miner's disease, 110
Moncure, Henry, 84–85
Monocans: artifacts, 79; removal of, 78
Montpelier: African American population
increase near, 87; agricultural censuses in,
78; archaeological sites identified in, 75–76;
architectural survey of, 77, 84; economic
inequality in, 92–93; Madison J., and
Madison, D., co-managing, 82–84; Madison
Sr., managing, 81–82; metal detector survey
of, 77, 80–81; Moncure purchasing, 84–85;
slavery at, end of, 84–86
Mountaintop removal, 7–8
Mount Pleasant tobacco plantation, 78, 79–81

National Park Service: Cammerer of, 132; on
preservation, 107
National Trust for Historic Places, 75, 77, 92
Native Americans: anthropology influenced
by, 1; dispossession and carceral landscapes, 208; Fort Hampton regulating,
65; incarceration rates of, 190; mound-
building myths, 9; place making by, 20–21;
reservations, 24, 34–36, 39; of Shenandoah
National Park area, 146–47. *See also specific
Native American groups*
Neighborhoods: administrative, 163, 167,
172; definitions of, 163–64; social, 163, 164,
167–74; as social units, 158; spatial units
in, determining, 164. *See also* Amache
neighborhoods
New Deal, 132–33
Nicholson, Francis (Governor), 35, 39
Nicholson, John T., 143
Nicholson Hollows, 138–39, 143
The Nine Eyes of Google Street View series, 210,
210
Novotny, Oklahoma, 56–59, *57*, *58*

Orange County, Virginia: African Americans
moving from, 83–84; African slaves arriving
in, 78–79; class consciousness in, 96–97;
Confederate army in, 85, 86; economies of
scale impacting, 93–94; economy diversification in, 82; emancipation impacting,
86–93; forced migration in, 74, 99–100;
industrialization of agriculture in, 97–98;
Mount Pleasant tobacco plantation in,
78, 79–81; project background on, 75–77,
76; removal shaping landscape of, 78–79;
spatial relationships in, command of, 95–96;
wealth gap in, 89. *See also* Montpelier

Pamunkey, 35–36
Parkin, David, 4
Pearl Harbor, 159
Pedestrian surveys: of Amache neighborhoods,
165; artifacts recovered from, *176*; landscap-
ing features identified during, 179, *179*
Piscataway: archaeological sites of, 27, *28*;
Articles of Peace and Amity impacting,
25; artifacts, 30–33, *31*; cemetery of, Conoy

Town, 34; colonists relations with, 24–25, 26; craft production of, decline in, 33–34, 39; displacement effects on, of those who left, 27–34; displacement effects on, of those who stayed, 34–39; erasure of, 36–37, 39–40; historical background on, 23–27; smallpox outbreak among, 26–27; social identity of, 38; Susquehannocks raids on, 25; traditional practices of, 39; youth abandoning, 23; to Zekiah Fort, relocation, 25–26; Zekiah Fort settlement of, 19

Piscataway Creek, 25–26, 27–30

Piscataway tayac, 23, 26–27, 35

Place making, 20–21

Plow agriculture, 36–37

Political death, 199

Political economy: of prison system, 195–96, 196; of slavery, 51–52; social violence and, 10; threat to, 198

Political marginalization, 198–200

Pollock, George Freeman: Corbin Hollow relations with, 133–34, 149; *Hollow Folk* support from, 138; Skyland resort founded by, 131

Pompeii, 8

Porcelain, 175, 176, 176

Posey site: ceramic and tobacco pipes recovered from, 30–32, 31; excavation of, 29

Pottery. *See* Ceramics

Power, directionality of, 193–94

Preservation problems, 105–7

Prison Diary (Dole), 189

Prisoners: on colony farm, 208; criminally insane, 207–9; displacement of, 197; escaped, 210; immobility of, 192–93, 195; internal exile of, 190; as labor force, 195–96, 196, 208; life-without-parole sentence for, 189, 199; political death of, 199; protests by, 193–94; social death of, 199; television shows portrayal of, 202. *See also* Japanese Americans

Prison system: anatomical approach to studying, 192–93; archaeological politics of sight and, 202–3; capitalism linked to, 191, 195–96, 196; colonialism in relation to, 191, 208; community deterioration from, 191–92; culture of punishment and, 194–97; decommissioning of, 210–11; directionality of power in, 193–94; double function of,

198–99; FCF, 203–4, 204, 205, 207, 207–9; gerrymandering, 199; incarceration rates, 189–90, 199–200; invisibility of, producing, 200–201; invisibility/visibility of, 203–6, 204, 205; landscape histories regarding, 206–9; material culture and, 190; objective of, disagreement on, 189; political economy of, 195–96, 196; political marginalization and, 198–200; privatization of, 192; proliferation of, 209; racism within, 189–90, 199–200, 209; socioeconomic transformations regarding, 207

Privatization: of agriculture, 98–99; of prison system, 192

Profit: over labor force safety, 110; maximization of, 105–6

Punishment: culture of, 194–97; techniques of, changing, 206

Pye, Charles, 35–36

Quarry industry: African Americans working in, 119–20; background on, 107–11, 108; exploitation in, 105; health care inequality in, 118; mechanization of, 109–10; miner's disease in, 110; wealth of, 109. *See also* Irish immigrants

Racism: capitalism in relation to, 104; class consciousness in relation to, 96–97; economic inequality and, 92–93; within prison system, 189–90, 199–200, 209

Rafman, Jon, 209–10, 210

Railroad industry: agriculture relations with, 98; labor force of, 95

Rebellions, 218

Reduccione policies, 6

Refugees: as label, 3; multidimensionality of sorrow, 4; spatial relationships regarding, 22–23

Relocation. *See* Displacement

Remembering. *See* Memory/memory loss

Removal: anthropologies of, 1; dispossession and, defining terms of, 5–8; kindred concepts of dispossession and, 2–5; in theory and archaeological practice, 8–12. *See also specific topics*

Research overviews, 12–14

Reservations, Native American: boundaries for, enforcement of, 34–35; creation of first, 24; disputes over, 35–36; usurpation of, 39
Resettlement Administration, 132–33
Residential directory, 168, *169*, 184n2
Reynolds, Benjamin, 60, *60*, 61, 64
Reynolds, Elmer R., 19
Rhetoric: of Chickasaws, 68–69; of discrimination, 119–20; of land claims, 60; on New Deal rehousing efforts, 133; of removal, 50
Roosevelt, Franklin D., 159

Sake, 174, 176–77
Salvage anthropologies, 3–4
Scientific colonialism, 8–9
Section 35, 60–65
Seeds, agriculture, 97, 98–99
Separation/segregation: hierarchy and, in Texas (town), 111–19; patterns of, 104; removal and, in Texas (town), 119–22
Shenandoah National Park: background on establishing, 131–35; Byrd opposing removal for, 132, 133; displacement justification in, 128–29, 135–41; displacement legacies regarding, 146–51; farm conditions in area of, 138–40; Great Smoky Mountains National Park and, 133, 134; *Hollow Folk* ranking communities of, 128, 137; land tracts for, 127; letters regarding, 141–43; map of, *129*; memories of pre-park, 151–52; Native Americans in area of, 146–47; Nicholson Hollow area, 138–39, 143; slavery in area of, 147–48; Superintendent Lassiter of, 141–42, 143; Weakley Hollow area, 141, 142, 148–49. *See also* Corbin Hollow
Sherman, Mandel: conclusions of, 138; *Hollow Folk* by, 128, 136; motivation of, 137
Sizer, Miriam: bias of, 137; on Corbin Hollow, 150–51; Corbin Hollow on, 141–42; *Hollow Folk* influencing, 138; mountain home assessments by, 136; Weakley Hollow on, 142
Skyland resort: Corbin Hollow relying on, 134, 139, 144–45; Pollock founding, 131
Slabtown, 87–88
Slavery: in Caribbean, 48; at Montpelier, end of, 84–86; political economy of, 51–52; in Shenandoah National Park area, 147–48. *See also* African Americans; African slaves

Small pox outbreak, 26–27
Smithsonian Institution, 3–4
Smyth, James, 216–17
Social arenas: communal facilities developing, 173; public landscapes as, 180, *181*
Social death, 199
Social development theory, 128, 137
Social exclusion, 189, 190
Social identity, 38
Social interaction: for community, 165, 172; for identity, 173; peer monitoring and, 164
Sociality, 164
Social memory, 20–21
Social neighborhoods: administrative neighborhoods compared to, 172; within Amache neighborhoods, 167–74; definition of, 163, 164
Social violence, 10
Socioeconomic transformation, 207
Southern Appalachian National Park Committee, 131
Spatial relationships: in Amache neighborhoods, 165–66, *166*; command of, 95–96; material culture and, 112; regarding refugees, 22–23
Spatial units: in neighborhoods, determining, 164; WRA understanding of, 167
Stereotypes: of African Americans, 3, 119–20; of Irish immigrants, 112–13, 119
St. Jean, Wendy, 50
St. Joseph's Church cemetery, 110, 111, *111*
Survey of Rural Mountain Settlement, 128, 138, 140–41
Surveys: architectural, 77, 84; cession maps created from, 52–53, *53*; metal detector, 77, 80–81; pedestrian, 165, *176*, 179, *179*
Susquehannocks: Piscataway raided by, 25; in Shenandoah National Park area, 147

Taylor family, 90–91
Tenancy in common, 92
Tennessee Valley Authority, 134–35
Texas, Maryland (town): architecture in, *104*, 113–16, *114*, *115*, 123n1; artifacts, 116–18, *117*; background on, 107–11, *108*; commercial development destroying, 103, 121–22; erasure of history in, 104; Landragan House in, *104*, 123n1; map of, *113*; preservation problems

in, 105–7; segregation and removal in, 119–22; separation and hierarchy in, 111–19; St. Joseph's Church cemetery in, 110, 111, *111*. *See also* Quarry industry
Three-Fifths Compromise (1878), 199
Tobacco pipes: from Piscataway sites, 30–32, *31*; from Texas (town), 118
Tobacco plantation, Mount Pleasant, 78, 79–81
Tram massacres, 7, 8
Treaties: Articles of Peace and Amity, 25; Colbert L., benefiting from, 55; US-Chickasaw (1834), 61–62
Treaty of Pontotoc Creek (1832): regarding Colbert, J., 62–63; land allotment procedures and, 60

United Nations Commission on Human Rights, 11
The Urban Experience (Harvey), 96
Urbanization process, 93
Urban renewal maps, 105–6
Urgent anthropology projects, 3–4
US-Chickasaw treaty (1834), 61–62

Via, Robert, 145
Violence: toward Choptico, 35; of eviction, 220; toward Irish immigrants, 113–14; marginalization in relation to, 194; social, 10; state-sponsored, 192; theories on, 9

Violent displacement, 1–2
Virginia State Commission on Conservation and Development, 131
Volcanism, 8

Walker family, 90–91
War-based removals, 6
War Department, US: internment camp specifications provided by, 161; Reynolds, B., letter to, 60, *60*, 61, 64
War Relocation Authority (WRA): internment camps established by, 160, *160*; spatial unit understanding of, 167
Weakley Hollow: on Corbin Hollow, 148–49; craft production in, 141; on Sizer, 142
Williams, George, 35–36
Winn, Elizabeth, 141
Workforce. *See* Labor force
World War II, 3
WRA. *See* War Relocation Authority

Zekiah Fort: Bead Hill relation to, 19; ceramics and tobacco pipes recovered from, 30–32, *31*; confirmation of, 38; excavation of, 29; memory loss of, 20; Piscataway relocation to, 25–26

CPSIA information can be obtained
at www.ICGtesting.com
Printed in the USA
LVHW080141310519
619670LV00002B/2/P

9 780813 056395